D1409474

THE EUROPEAN BACKGROUND
OF AMERICAN LINGUISTICS

"THE EUROPEAN BACKGROUND OF AMERICAN LINGUISTICS "

Papers of
The Third Golden Anniversary Symposium
of the Linguistic Society of America

Edited by HENRY M. HOENIGSWALD

1979
FORIS PUBLICATIONS
DORDRECHT-HOLLAND

Photoset in Malta by Interprint (Malta) Ltd

Printed in Holland by Intercontinental Graphics Dordrecht

PREFACE

Fifty years, almost to the day, after its constituent session in New York, the Linguistic Society of America, holding its 1974 Annual Meeting in the same city, observed the anniversary with the third and final of a series of symposia. The European antecedents of American linguistics were to be the topic, and the participants were to be scholars who had given more than casual thought to the way in which things had developed on both sides of the Atlantic. Those invited—among them our distinguished honorary member, E. M. Uhlenbeck—accepted without hesitation. The program went off as planned, in three sessions held in the morning, afternoon, and evening of December 27 in the Grand Ballroom of the Commodore Hotel. There was lively discussion much of which, thanks to the tapes recorded by Susan Thomas, benefited the final editing of the papers.

As so often in the past, we are deeply indebted to the American Council of Learned Societies which, under the presidency of Frederick Burkhardt, made the Society the award needed to arrange the symposium.

H. M. H.

CONTENTS

INTRODUCTION

EINAR HAUGEN

In the preceding symposia of this Golden Anniversary we have considered first, at Amherst, Massachusetts, the present state of American linguistics, then, at Berkeley, California, the fundamental contributions which Indian languages have made to American thinking on linguistics, and now we turn to the third side of our triangular organon, the European background. In doing so, we go back well beyond the founding of the Linguistic Society, into the period of William Dwight Whitney, who was contemporary with the Neo-Grammarians, and who both learned from them and was critical of them. He established once and for all the importance of historical linguistics in America, and the value of the study of Sanskrit and Indo-European, lessons that have been followed by other early American linguists from Boas to Bloomfield. It would not be hard to list European linguists who have deeply influenced American linguistics: in plain fact, it would be impossible to consider American linguistics historically without taking into account the thinking of their European predecessors and contemporaries.

There are clearly two distinct paths by which European thinking has been diffused to America: by books and by persons. Books are primary, of course, since they are the instruments of our teaching and have been crossing the Atlantic from the days of Bopp and Brugmann to those of Saussure and Hjelmslev. But ideas have also been carried, and often more effectively, by men, either by those who studied in Europe and' came back to tell what they had learned, like Whitney and Bloomfield, or by those who, born in Europe, came over here to live and teach, from Boas to Yakov Malkiel and Roman Jakobson. In the barbaric Middle Ages scholars wandered from university to university in search of learning. In our barbaric Modern Age scholars have wandered, many times in danger of their lives, from country to country in search of an opportunity to teach. Our dialect geography we owe to the work of the Swiss Jud and the French Gilliéron, brought to us by an Austrian,

Hans Kurath. Our structural linguistics we owe in many of its basic outlines to Slavic scholars of the Prague School and its predecessors, who gave us our tools, from the basic terminology of 'phoneme' and 'morpheme' to the very ideas on which our latest transformations are based. Our contemporary leaders claim to be renewing ideas overlooked by an intervening generation in the writings of Descartes, the School of Port-Royal, Wilhelm von Humboldt, and Otto Jespersen. Whatever we as Americans may or may not have contributed to the linguistics of today and tomorrow, we have done it as an indissoluble part of that western culture which is the heir of Greece and Rome, with an occasional obeisance to the mysterious East of which we know chiefly the work of that Indo-European pioneer named Pāṇini.

During the first quarter century of the LSA, there was a strong drift away from the European moorings. Almost exactly midway in the half century that we are here celebrating I ventured to use my opportunity to give a presidential address in which I scolded my colleagues for their neglect of European linguistics (Haugen 1951). In private, colleagues and friends who had long suffered under the arrogance of European linguists scored me for my unpatriotic stand. I specifically said that I disapproved equally of 'those European linguists who overlook the contributions of Americans.' My plea then was for linguistics as an international science, one that would adopt a linguistic metalanguage and not a set of metadialects that required translation for one linguist to understand another.

It is not my job here today to decide whether things have gone as I then hoped. In some respects they have not; we sometimes seem to have gone from metadialects to metaidiolects, with each scholar speaking in his or her glossolalic tongue. But on the whole I am hopeful. Some consensus on basics seems to have been arrived at, with Europeans learning our novel terms, and Americans referring back to European authorities to legitimize their own claims. What none of us could fully foresee in 1951 was the enormous rise in physical mobility that linguists would enjoy, the influx of foreign scholars, the many exchange programs that have spread Americans over the world and have brought all the best to our shores and our universities for longer or shorter periods, or the rise of new countries and their adoption of linguistics. In short, there has been a globalization of linguistics, the greatest step forward that we can hope for. The dream of having at least one native linguist for every language, all trained in a metalanguage usable by all: this is no longer as remote or as unattainable as it once was.

The present symposium was organized and will be chaired by Henry Hoenigswald, who in many respects represents all of the ideals I have here expressed: born and educated in Europe, teaching nearly his entire career in America, skilled in the expounding and the practice not only of his specialty, historical linguistics, but of general linguistic theory as well. I am happy to present him to this distinguished audience, as the one who will chair all of our sessions here today.

REFERENCE

Haugen, Einar 1951. 'Directions in modern linguistics', *Language* 27:211–22.

THE PAST UP TO THE INTRODUCTION OF NEOGRAMMARIAN THOUGHT: WHITNEY AND EUROPE

ROSANE ROCHER

The chapter of American linguistics which has been allotted to me on this panel is the period going from the farthest past to the introduction of neogrammarian thought. Since Amerindian linguistics has been the subject of another panel, and since we are supposed here to consider European scholarship as a backdrop for the American scene, I thought that the most promising line for me might be to examine Whitney's ties with Europe. When Whitney died, he was acknowledged (notably by Ascoli, Hillebrandt, Müller) as THE person who had planted an offshoot of European linguistics on American soil. That his ties were particularly strong with Germany (as noted by Bradke, Delbrück, Jolly, Oldenberg, and Roth 1894), to the point that German scholars (Garbe, Jolly, Oldenberg) claimed him as one of their own, is not only a result of his personal history, but also a reflection of Germany's leadership at that time in linguistics and Sanskrit philology, the twin aspects of Whitney's scholarly activity.

Whitney's ties with Europe are too many to be fruitfully reviewed in the brief compass which I have been granted. I will therefore confine my remarks to three aspects only: first, the European setting which accounts for Whitney's rejection of Indian linguistics; second, his relation to Bopp and his place in the Boppian tradition; third, his reception of the neogrammarian views of language.

The single most important influence on Whitney's development came from Rudolf Roth. Of all the teachers he had in Germany – Weber, Bopp, Heyse, Lepsius –, and indeed of all European scholars, Roth is the only one with whom he collaborated for a lifetime,[1] and about

---

[1] Besides the Vedic concordance written by Whitney (1852) as a student under Roth's direction, and published in Weber's journal, they published a joint edition of the Atharvaveda (Roth-Whitney). Whitney left for Roth's use an index to the verses of the Atharvaveda (1857), also published in Weber's journal, and became a valued collaborator to Böhtlingk and Roth's Sanskrit dictionary, known as the Petersburg Lexicon. Because of Roth's preoccupation with the lexicon, continued work on the Atharvaveda fell mostly to Whitney, but the two scholars continued to confer (see Whitney 1875d).

whose work he never uttered anything but praise. Roth imparted to Whitney his distrust of native oriental traditions. Whitney's first publications after his period of study in Germany[2] echo Roth's view that Western scholarship must free itself from the fetters of native traditions. This was true for lexicography, both Iranian (Whitney 1854a) and Indian (1854b), as well as for Indian grammatology (1854c). In a survey of Avestan studies Whitney (1855b) strongly endorsed Roth's position against Spiegel's on this issue.[3] He returned forcefully to this subject thirteen years later, in an article on Vedic interpretation (1868a), in which he sided with Roth as the principal apostle of independent Western scholarship, but also with John Muir and Max Müller,[4] against the Hindu orientation of Theodor Goldstücker. It is fitting that Whitney's (1893a) contribution to a felicitation volume offered to Roth should consist of an indictment of Sāyaṇa's commentary on the Atharvaveda. This was written in the last years of Whitney's life, and his correspondence with Roth notes their agreement on this issue.[5] Indeed, whereas the authors of several necrologies (Barth 1894a:181;[6] Macdonell 614) and testimonials sent to the Whitney memorial meeting (Garbe 85–86; Pischel 99; Windisch 104) label excessive his severity with the Indian native tradition, Roth (1894:101) and Roth alone singles it out for praise.

The Indian grammarians, like the Vedic commentators, were part of a native tradition which Whitney distrusted.[7] In one respect, in the matter

---

[2]   While a student in Germany Whitney had already sent as a first communication to the American Oriental Society a paper (1853) which was a direct emanation of his studies under Roth, and had translated an article by Roth (1853) for the Society's journal.

[3]   He was to reiterate these views later: see the abstract of his paper (1871d) on Roth's contributions to the interpretation of the Avesta read before the AOS, and the related paragraph in *The Nation* (1871f).

[4]   Although Whitney and Müller happened to be on the same side at this early date, Whitney could not refrain from pointing out that Müller affected a non-controversial tone in the debate. Later on, in the thick of their increasingly personal controversy, he was to downgrade Müller's work on the Rigveda, denying his claim to the authorship of the editio princeps of the Rigveda, and granting him only the title of 'responsible editor of the *editio princeps* of Sâyana's commentary' (1876a:786).

[5]   See the extract of a letter from Whitney to Roth, dated June 16, 1893, reproduced Silverstein 214. Note that Silverstein is mistaken in describing Whitney's contribution to the Roth Festschrift as a study of Hindu grammar.

[6]   He did not repeat this criticism in his testimonial (1894b) to the Whitney memorial meeting.

[7]   Of Indian science in general he said: 'it is the characteristic of Hindu science generally not to be able to stop when it has done enough' (1884a:290; reprinted Silverstein 298). His lack of sympathy extended to Indian thought, religious and philosophical: see his derogatory comments on the Bhagavadgītā, and his characterization of Hindu philosophies as 'examples of acute and hair-splitting subtlety' (1872).

of the accent, he accepted the correctness of their observations. But this was an isolated case: Pāṇini's teachings in this regard meshed with the data in the Prātiśākhyas, the phonetic treatises attached to each Veda, in which Whitney showed great interest,[8] and proved congruent with the facts recorded in accentuated texts.[9] About Pāṇini and his followers, Roth, a Vedic scholar, had little to say specifically. Whitney, on the contrary, denounced them repeatedly,[10] and fostered an aggressive attitude in his students.[11] With regard to Pāṇinian linguistics, a second

[8] He edited and translated with notes the Atharvavedaprātiśākhya (1862a) and the Taittirīyaprātiśākhya with commentary (1871c), and reported to the AOS on several aspects of these studies (1862b; 1863b; 1871e, with full publication of this last report in 1880a). Note also that Whitney's expressly stated (1861:314; reprinted Silverstein 230) approval of the sonant-surd distinction recognized by the Indian grammarians, as opposed to the soft-hard distinction adopted by Lepsius and others refers specifically to observations of phoneticians, rather than to theories of Pāṇinian grammarians.

[9] A survey of Whitney's writings on the Sanskrit accent reveals how reluctant he was to concede this. In his early critique (1855a) of Bopp's *Accentuationssystem*, written immediately upon returning from his period of study in Germany, Whitney accepted the validity of the Indian grammarians' observations, but dismissed their theories. His acceptance was also provisional, until enough accentuated texts would be published, and scrutinized for this particular purpose. Such a study, published the following year, took the grammarians to task, and reiterated his conviction that 'a rational and exhaustive theory of the principles producing the phenomena of verbal accentuation in Sanskrit, could only be arrived at by a careful study of the phenomena themselves, as laid before us in the various accented Vedic texts' (1856:388). In a later comprehensive study of the Sanskrit accent he was forced to concede the importance of the grammarians' testimony: 'In investigating the nature of the Sanskrit accent, we are not limited to the drawing of inferences from the facts of accentuation laid before us in the texts; our chief sources of knowledge are the Hindu grammarians, who have treated the subject, as they have most other departments of grammatical theory, with great fulness and acuteness. The great grammarian Pāṇini, whose work has become the acknowledged authority for all after time, is clear and intelligible in his statements as to accent; and upon the foundation of his work and its commentators alone, without access to any accented texts, Böhtlingk gave in 1843 an acute, intelligent, and very correct account both of the theory and of the main facts of Sanskrit accent, one that in many respects has not been surpassed or superseded by anything that has since appeared' (1871a:21; reprinted Silverstein 262). This uncharacteristic praise of the grammarians' work was tempered by more grudging comments in his usual style (1871a:22, 38; reprinted Silverstein 263, 279). In the recast of this article published in the second series of *Oriental and linguistic studies* (1874a:318–40), the encomium of Pāṇini was allowed to stand, but the admissions made in the first sentence of the above quotation were dropped (1874a:321), while the negative comments were consolidated (1874a:322–23). See also his criticisms (1871b; 1874d) of Haug's reliance on modern recitation practice of the Veda.

[10] Besides criticisms of the Pāṇinian grammarians and of their modern admirers and followers scattered throughout his writings, he devoted three widely publicized articles to their systematic condemnation (1884a and 1893c, published in the *American Journal of Philology* and simultaneously read before the AOS: 1884c and 1893d; and 1893b, published in Europe).

[11] Edgren's (1882, first read before the AOS in 1878) attack on the Dhātupāṭhas (lists of

influence strengthened the general distrust of native science which he had learned from Roth: that of the Berlin school of Indology.

I will come back in a few moments to Whitney's relation to Bopp. For the time being I shall only say that, in spite of disagreements on other points, as far as his attitude toward Indian linguistics is concerned, Whitney was a direct product of the Berlin school of Indology founded by Bopp. It is interesting to compare him in this respect with Otto Böhtlingk, who was Roth's collaborator on the Petersburg lexicon, but who was a product of the rival Bonn school of Indology. Of the two scholars, Whitney was a linguist, Böhtlingk a philologist at heart. One might therefore have expected Whitney, the linguist, to react favorably to the linguistic methodology developed by Pāṇini and his followers. The opposite is true. It was the philologist, Böhtlingk, who was to found Pāṇinian studies in the West,[12] and who, when faced with the seemingly impossible task of describing the language of the Yakuts (Böhtlingk 1851), applied Pāṇinian methods of linguistic description. But Böhtlingk had been trained differently. After a brief stay in Berlin, where he was disappointed with Bopp, he had gone on to Bonn, to work under Lassen, and devote his Ph.D. dissertation (Böhtlingk 1839–40) to a study of Pāṇinian grammar.

Whereas the leaders of the Bonn school of Indology, Schlegel (1832: 31–37) and Lassen (1830), had taken Bopp to task for ignoring the testimony of the Indian grammarians, Whitney viewed it as Bopp's principal merit. He praised Bopp as 'the first who had knowledge and independence enough to begin effectively the work of subordinating Hindu to western science, using the materials and deductions of the former so far as they accorded with the superior methods of the latter, and turning his attention to the records of the language itself, as fast as they became accessible to him' (1884:295; reprinted Silverstein 303).

Footnote 11 continued

roots) antedates his master's most violent diatribes against the Sanskrit grammarians, yet shares their spirit. It preceded the publication of Whitney's list of Sanskrit roots (1885b, to supplement his Sanskrit grammar of 1879), which was based exclusively on texts, without consideration for the Dhātupāṭhas of the grammarians (see also the chronological list of roots, 1886, derived from this monograph). Edgren (1885) later read a second paper in the same vein.

[12] See Salemann and Oldenburg for a bibliographical list, complete up to 1891, of Böhtlingk's works. Note particularly his editions of Pāṇini's grammar (items 1 and 74) and of other grammatical treatises (items 7 and 17), his studies of grammatical texts (items 58, 59, 69, 75, 78, 92), and his attempts to use the works of the grammarians to analyze Sanskrit (items 4 and 5).

Even at the end of his life Whitney[13] rose to Bopp's defense when younger scholars repeated Lassen's judgment that Bopp's neglect of Pāṇini was due to ignorance. Bopp knew Pāṇinian grammar well enough, and even used it too much, Whitney claimed. His merit was to have subjected Sanskrit for the first time to European grammatical science, and the new method of comparative grammar. And on this basis Whitney declared Bopp to have been 'the real Sanskrit teacher to Europe, in a manner and degree far beyond the reach of Lassen' (1893c:196). In this way he gave new expression to the claims of the Berlin school against its archrival Bonn. Characteristically the Bonn alumnus, Böhtlingk (1893), who was not generally fond of polemics, felt compelled to answer Whitney's attacks.[14] In this dispute of the 1890's, the lines between the Berlin and Bonn schools of Indology were still clearly drawn, long after the original protagonists had disappeared.

Of course it would be easy to turn things around, and point out instead what exactly in Pāṇinian grammar offended Whitney. With regard to linguistic categories, Pāṇini ignores the dichotomy which, from Aristotle to modern times, is at the center of Western linguistic analysis, that of subject and predicate. Pāṇini's grammar is neither historical nor comparative, and was at odds with the thrust of nineteenth century linguistics. Pāṇini's rules, which are couched in the most general terms possible, shocked the scholar who made statistics and specificity the basis of his statements. All this is understandable enough. My point is that it offended other contemporary scholars less than it did Whitney.

Whitney was prepared to view Indian linguistics in two ways. Being Indian, it represented an attempt at scientific enquiry by an infant people, an attempt which had some interest, but only in the same way and to

[13]   In a stern critique (1893c) of several publications by two newcomers to the field: Bruno Liebich and R. Otto Franke. He was particularly harsh on Liebich, who had ventured (51–61) to refute his censures of the Sanskrit grammarians, and even accuse him of referring to them superficially and inaccurately in his Sanskrit grammar.

[14]   Although Böhtlingk and Whitney disagreed on this issue, they appreciated each other's scholarship. Whitney (1854b) had lauded Böhtlingk and Roth's Petersburg lexicon right from the start; Böhtlingk (1885) had written a favorable review of Whitney 1885b. Whitney's (1890) review of Böhtlingk's editions of two Upaniṣads was laudatory, with minor criticisms of Böhtlingk's respect for Pāṇinian teachings. Whitney was a much appreciated collaborator to Böhtlingk and Roth's lexicon, and he joined in the defense when Max Müller attacked the lexicon and derided its contributors as a mutual-admiration society (see Whitney's reactions in The Nation, 1876b, c, d, which testify to their rapidly worsening quarrel). Böhtlingk's decision to direct an article against Whitney in defense of Pāṇini is all the more remarkable for their previous close association.

the same extent that Indian astronomy[15] could arouse curiosity. As
linguistics, however, he could measure it only by the standard of his own
nineteenth century Western linguistic principles.[16] As such he found it
wanting, and to be discarded altogether. It was left to his more philo-
logically minded colleagues, like Böhtlingk, to accept Indian grammatical
texts on their own terms. We thus have in the 1890's a replay of the
discussion which, in the first half of the century, had opposed the two
schools of Indology, that of Berlin, led by Bopp, which emphasized
historical and comparative linguistics, and that of Bonn, led by Schlegel
and Lassen, which stressed the study of Indian culture.

The position which Whitney took was to have important consequences. It reduced considerably the influence which Indian linguistics might
have had in the West. In Sanskrit studies, Whitney's grammar was a
landmark, and remains a classic. The fact that it turned its back on
Pāṇinian grammar, has steered generations of Sanskritists away from
Indian linguistic methods. In general linguistics, even though one can
point to some Indian influence in phonetics, on the concept of zero, and
the analysis of compounds (Robins 134–49), the Indian input has been
fairly limited. Certainly it is almost absent in matters of syntax and
semantics, where the Indian tradition can boast remarkable insights.

I now come to the second point which I mean to take up: Whitney's
relation to Bopp, and his place within the Boppian tradition of comparative grammar.

Whitney's feelings toward Bopp were lukewarm at best. He was

[15]   A topic in which Whitney showed not a little interest. It originated in his extensive
work (1860) on the notes given to the AOS by the missionary Burgess, which prompted
him to read papers at meetings of the Society (1859a, b). He felt strongly enough about
the subject to engage in controversy (1863a; 1866) with the French astronomer Biot, Max
Müller, and his former teacher Albrecht Weber, and even to send an article (1865a) opposing
H. T. Colebrooke to a society of which Colebrooke's son was the president. He summarized
his views in the second series of *Oriental and linguistic studies* (1874a:341–421), but was
drawn to return to the subject by the new edition of Colebrooke's *Miscellaneous essays*
(Whitney 1874c), and by the use which some scholars made of astronomical evidence to
date the Rigveda (Whitney 1885c; 1894b).
[16]   Whitney put his faith in logic and reason; he did not seem to entertain self-doubts, or
to contemplate that his reasoning might be culturally or temporally bound. When he dis-
cerned 'monstrosities, unfounded in phonetic reason', he claimed that 'we not only may,
but ought to, refuse to admit them, Pāṇini or no Pāṇini' (1890:410). He swept aside the
grammarians' testimony when it conflicted with patterns recognized by comparative
philology, branding them as 'no matter who authorizes them, . . . horrible barbarisms,
offenses against the proprieties of universal Indo-European speech' (1893c:192). As for
Pāṇini's syntactical categories, they were dismissed as 'crude' and 'unphilosophical'
(1893c:171–72).

clearly disappointed with Bopp as a teacher, and with Bopp's last years as a scholar. Before he became Bopp's student in Berlin, Whitney had already been subjected indirectly to his influence. Both his brother, Josiah Dwight, and his first teacher at Yale, Salisbury, had attended Bopp's classes. He himself studied Sanskrit with the help of a copy of the second edition of Bopp's Sanskrit grammar, brought back by his brother, during the summer of 1849, even before entering Yale (see Lanman 10–13). A paper (1850) published while he was still a student at Yale, and devoted to a comparison of the Greek and Latin verbs, quoted Bopp's *Vergleichende Grammatik* as a primary source. It is then all the more remarkable that his comments on Bopp's scholarship after he returned from his study period in Germany, were less than complimentary. His review (1855a) of Bopp's *Accentuationssytem*, written at that time, is extremely critical. Even his obituary (1868b) of Bopp contains strong negative judgments;[17] that should have been one occasion when praise only might be expected.

And yet Whitney was, over the years, a staunch defender of Boppian orthodoxy in comparative grammar. When new voices protested that too much emphasis was laid on Sanskrit in Indo-European studies, and that too little attention was paid to non-Indo-European families of languages, Whitney continued to stress the special place of Sanskrit within Indo-European, and the special importance of the Indo-European family within the general study of language.[18] He also rejected Oppert's endeavor to drive a wedge between linguistic and genetic relationship.[19] He was later to defend (1873c) the established Stammbaumtheorie against Johannes Schmidt's Wellentheorie.[20] He clung to the last to Bopp's theory that collocation, agglutination, and integration, had been the exclusive means by which Indo-European had

[17]   'Bopp lived long enough to see his science carried further, in many points, by his followers than by himself. At the same time, he was not one who readily assimilated the results won by others. The later years of his life were comparatively unfruitful of valuable additions to science; and when at length he passed away, it was rather the presence of the man than the work of the scholar that was missed by us' (1868b:49).

[18]   Repeating (1867c:522–25; reprinted 1873a:200–3) against T. Hewitt Key the arguments he had put forward in his recent book (1867a:225–37).

[19]   1867c:542–54; reprinted 1873a:224–38, arguing on the basis of his general considerations in 1867a:370–83 (incorporating 1867b).

[20]   A widely circulated article – also in German translation – included the Wellentheorie, without mentioning Schmidt by name, in an enumeration of unacceptable views of language: 'another bold doubter makes a great stir by denying the ordinary family-tree theory of linguistic kinship, and putting in its place a theory of wave-motion, propagated from a centre' (Whitney 1875b:714; German version 1875c:260).

created new forms. He again and again opposed Schleicher's view, which was gaining more and more favor,[21] that vowel gradation was a primary, organic means of expression in Indo-European. He brushed aside the evidence of Semitic languages, and declared himself confident that further study would 'bring it into accordance with the agglutinative methods of all other branches of human speech' (1874b:305). 'All other', in this case, meant the Indo-European family, within an aggregative framework. Whitney realized that no phonetic explanation of vowel gradation was really satisfactory, but he still suggested that it might be due to the influence of the accent (1874b:310). Among contemporary European scholars he considered Georg Curtius 'the soundest and safest' (1874b:315), at the same time recognizing him as the current head of the orthodox school (1875c:259).[22] All in all Whitney held conservative views in the field of comparative linguistics. The most salient example of his antiquated views may well be his explanation (1877) of the middle endings of the Indo-European verb. This explanation, first suggested by Bopp, took them to result from a combination of the active endings with a reflexive pronoun. This was another desperate attempt[23] to find an aggregative explanation for facts that appeared to represent a case of original vowel gradation.

Whitney's conservatism in comparative philology is in sharp contrast with his innovative contributions to general linguistics. Or at least to us they appear to be at variance. For Whitney they were very much of a piece. Whitney's total view of language, including comparative grammar, was a model of consistency. His paramount concern was for logical consistency in views of language, as expressed in his first contribution to the *American Journal of Philology* (1880b). It was in the name of logic, or his perception of it, that he rejected Indian linguistics. Logic, and logical consistency, transcended everything. Explanations of linguistic features, which might otherwise appear satisfactory, were to be subordinated to the desirability of a coherent view of language, and of human history. In Whitney's own words,

---

[21] Whitney (1870:207) took John Peile to task for following Schleicher's lead in this respect. When Peile persisted in the second edition of his work, and attempted to answer (Peile 196–98) Whitney's criticisms, Whitney (1874b) sent an elaborate refutation to the Philological Society in London.
[22] Curtius is not named in the original English version (1875b) of the German article.
[23] He acknowledged: 'It is probable enough, indeed, that no thoroughly acceptable theory will ever be devised', yet refused to reconsider his basic principles: 'Its unattainableness in the case we have been considering need be no cause of want of confidence in our general method of explanation of the genesis of forms' (1877:cxlv).

'our views of the history of language, in order to be defensible and abiding, must be made to fit into our general anthropology, as a consistent part of it; for language is simply one of the various acquisitions by which man has become what he is' (1884b:92). From that point of view it mattered little if Indo-European, or any other language,[24] could be proved to have evolved from original monosyllabic roots. The radicarian theory represented a 'theoretic necessity; since anything devised and created by human beings, as part of their progress upward toward a state of culture, must have begun with what is simplest in its kind' (1884b:90).[25] Whitney's anthropological theory was clear. Since language was one of the institutions which marked man's march on the path to civilization, it must have undergone an evolution from simple to complex, from agglutinative to flectional, from material to form.[26] Languages like Chinese, which had not completed this process, were inferior and rudimentary (1884b:93). He could not accept (1882a:92, 94), against Hübschmann and Delbrück, that case endings might have had an original grammatical value, but stated as an axiom that relational concepts were ultimately derived from immediate physical perceptions.[27] It is noteworthy that the article 'Logical consistency in views of language' (1880b), which represents Whitney's intellectual testament, singles out Bopp for

[24]   He was unshaken by arguments that the history of Chinese offered evidence that monosyllabic root-words had once had a fuller form, and by Lepsius's inference that they were relics of dissyllabic forms: 'there are very fair phonetic reasons for holding the theory that all dissyllabic roots, or roots even with final consonants only, are and must be the result of combination' (Whitney 1885a:155).

[25]   He buttressed his argument with a simile: 'To regard men as using from the start words made up of a radical part and a formative or grammatical part is precisely equivalent to regarding them as having begun to fight and to work with tools that had handles' (1884b:90).

[26]   His programmatic article 'On material and form in language' (1873b), directed against Friedrich Müller's 'Beiträge zur Morphologie und Entwicklungsgeschichte der Sprachen', stated unambiguously: 'the whole history of language seems to prove, not only that elements of material expression can and do become transmuted into formal, but even that formal expression is won in no other way' (1873b:93). He was to repeat these views later on (1884b:90).

[27]   'It may be laid down as a universal truth that all designation, of the relations of objects as well as of objects themselves and their activities, begins with what is most physical, most directly apprehensible by the senses. The whole body of intellectual, moral, ideal, relational expression comes by processes of gradual adaptation from the expression of sensible acts and qualities and relations; such adaptation is all the time going on in the present history of the languages we use, and their past history is in great measure an exhibition of the same movement – the grandest and most pervasive movement which is to be seen in them. We have not succeeded in demonstrating the origin of any bit of expression until we have traced it up to its physical value; if we have to stop short of that, we must not fail to see and acknowledge that our quest has not reached its goal' (1882a:91).

favorable comment. Bopp's aggregative theory is represented as a
triumph of the inductive method: 'This is a true scientific method',
he claimed, 'it is, in fact, the only one' (1880b:337).

If Whitney was ready to give precedence to theoretical considerations,
to a harmonious anthropological theory, if he was willing to consider
only within those limits new comparative theories which, in and by
themselves, better accounted for the facts; if he was even prepared at
times to discount what appeared to be the linguistic facts, he could do so
only because he was not a practicing comparatist. As Saussure (quoted
in Jakobson xxx note 5) noted in his unfinished appreciation of Whitney,
Whitney did not contribute anything new to comparative Indo-European
linguistics. As such he was exactly the opposite of Bopp. If we consider
Whitney's description of Bopp, and turn negative statements into
positive ones, and vice versa, we obtain a fair description of Whitney.
Bopp, said Whitney, 'is a remarkable instance of one who is a great
comparative philologist, without being either a great linguistic scholar
or a profound and philosophical linguist. He knows but few languages, as
compared with many another scholar of the present day, nor are we
aware that he is deeply and thoroughly versed in any, so as to hold a
distinguished place among its students – in the Sanskrit itself, certainly,
he was long ago left behind by the great body of its special votaries.
And of a science of language, as distinct from and developed out of
comparative philology, in its relations to human nature and human
history, he can scarcely be said to have a conception' (1867c:528–29;
reprinted 1873a:207–08). Whitney, on the other hand, knew many
languages, was a superb Sanskritist, and a creative theoretician of
language. But he was not a great comparative philologist; in this field
he fell out of step with the progress of research.

The direction taken by Whitney toward linguistic theory, away from
comparative Indo-European studies, has set the tone for the history of
American linguistics. For a long time America contributed comparatively little to the progress of comparative philology. Although comparative linguistics now appears to enjoy a renaissance in this country, viewed
in the total span of linguistic activity on this side of the Atlantic, comparative studies have flourished less than linguistic theory. Certainly there has not been an American school of comparative linguistics,
to spearhead research, and challenge continued European leadership in the field. Comparative studies have been slower also in
developing a generation of American scholars who were not European-
born or European-trained.

My last point today, Whitney's reaction to neogrammarian thought, has received new attention lately, with the publication of Kurt Jankowsky's book on the neogrammarians. Criticisms have been voiced (Davis 100–1) against Jankowsky's inclusion of Whitney among 'scholars amenable to neogrammarian thought' (Jankowsky 169–72). In this light, and although the general climate of Whitney's relations with the neogrammarians is probably well known to most of you, it may not be out of place to review systematically the comments which neogrammarian tenets elicited from Whitney.

The first encounter focused on a side issue, but one which Whitney had very much at heart. Ever since the early sixties Whitney had accused German scholars[28] of allowing themselves to be swayed by phonetic features peculiar to their own language, and to confuse sonancy with weakness. This was a fault of which he found traces also in Eduard Sievers's *Grundzüge der Lautphysiologie*, and it led him to discuss anew (1878a) the relation of surd and sonant. He returned to it once more four years later (1882b), following the second edition of Sievers's work, the publication of Delbrück's *Einleitung in das Sprachstudium*, and the reading of Osthoff's paper at the Gera meeting of German philologists. To Whitney's dismay the German scholars persisted in their mistaken views on surds and sonants. Worse even, they quoted the conversion of sonants to surds in Germanic as evidence, to deny the importance of the principle of economy in phonetic change. Whitney (1878b) had devoted an earlier article to illustrate the importance of the principle of economy as a phonetic force.

If Whitney's paper thus centered on an issue which had pitted him against other German scholars before the advent of the neogrammarian school, it also gave him an opportunity to react to the new axiom of the exceptionlessness of sound laws. His verdict,[29] that it was 'a dogma

[28] 'This defect is something rather characteristically German' (Whitney 1861:313; reprinted Silverstein 229), against Lepsius. Upon finding the same flaw with the English scholar Peile, Whitney (1870:206) blamed it on the influence of Max Müller, whom he (1865b:573–74; reprinted 1873a:251–52) had already attacked on this score. When Peile persevered in spite of his remarks, Whitney noted that 'Mr. Peile suffers himself here to be unduly swayed by the usage of eminent comparative philologists in Germany, who have not yet worked themselves free from the old German errors on this subject' (1874b:324).
[29] Whitney characterized Osthoff's paper as 'the most striking recent exemplification of the fact that one may be an able and distinguished comparative philologist without being saved from falling into the most palpable errors in matters that concern the life and growth growth of language' (1882b:xviii). This was a rebuke which Whitney had often directed against German scholars. The concluding paragraphs of his *Life and growth of language*, while giving Germany the credit of having developed comparative philology, added:

which is at least premature, and may perhaps be finally found unde-
monstrable' (1882b:xviii), was to become famous, and to be quoted by
Curtius (12) in his censure of the new school. Whitney was to repeat it
in a somewhat more negative form three years later: 'that is not an
induction, nor a deduction; it is simply an assumption, a hypothesis as
yet undemonstrated, and probably never to be demonstrated. Such
a doctrine should be the final goal, not the starting-point, of a new school'
(1885d). These were mild statements, if one remembers that Whitney
had said a few years earlier, before the neogrammarians made it a
controversial issue, that 'every student of phonetic history knows that
the tendencies of phonetic change work most irregularly' (1874b:312).

Whitney appreciated the solid contributions of the neogrammarians
to the study of language,[30] but – and this may be little more than a normal
reaction on the part of a scholar at a late stage of his career, vis-à-vis
a group of Young Turks – he maintained (1885d) that the new school was
less revolutionary than it was made out to be. His opposition to the credo
of the invariability of phonetic change grew with the years. He viewed
it more and more as one of the many mistaken theories which pictured
language as evolving mechanically, and which divested it of its essentially human[31] and social[32] nature: 'to introduce any element of necessity

Footnote 29 continued

'But while Germany is the home of comparative philology, the scholars of that country
have . . . distinguished themselves much less in that which we have called the science of
language. There is among them (not less than elsewhere) such discordance on points of
fundamental importance, such uncertainty of view, such carelessness of consistency, that
a German science of language cannot be said yet to have an existence' (1875a:318–19). The
same judgment was expressed in a contemporaneous article in German (1875c), but there
are indications that Whitney viewed German scholars as particularly poor philosophers
of language; while the German text said only: 'Leider sind sie [die deutschen Gelehrten]
ebenso wie die Gelehrten anderer Länder gleichgültig gegen die Fragen der Sprachphilosophie, oder sie können sich nicht von ungesunden und inconsequenten Auffassungen frei
machen' (1875c:261), the original English article from which this was translated stated
more harshly: 'but the Germans are rather exceptionally careless of what we may call the
questions of linguistic philosophy, or are loose and inconsistent in their views of such
questions' (1875b:715).
[30] He wrote a particularly laudatory review (1892) of Delbrück's *Altindische Syntax*,
which he read from cover to cover, as his 35 pages of detailed criticism indicate.
[31] 'There can be no question here, as among things purely physical, of such a law as "like
causes produce like effects"; because we have not to do with physical causes, but with
causers, human beings, no one of whom is like any other, in any such manner and degree
as should compel accordant action in changing the uttered signs of a language, or their
meanings' (1887:xxxiv).
[32] 'As for those movements of phonetic change by which one sound of an alphabet
undergoes general conversion into another sound, there is nothing to distinguish them in
their causes and methods from the other alterations of speech. They, like the rest, are and
can be only shifts of human habit under due inducement. They too are dialectic; they show

into such processes, like the necessities that connect cause and effect in the physical world, is a regrettable error' (1887:xxxv). Even though Whitney had reacted mildly to the manifesto of the new school, its increasing vogue disturbed him, and prompted him to take a stronger stand. He made 'the method of phonetic change in language' the subject of a communication to the American Philological Association, which concluded that 'to set up the necessity and invariability of phonetic change as a fundamental rule seems equivalent to putting a *dictum*, a *Machtspruch*, in the place of a demonstrated principle' (1887:xxxv). The full text of this communication was never published, but, in the last year of his life, Whitney carried the battle against the neogrammarians to their home ground. His article 'Examples of sporadic and partial phonetic change in English' (1894a)[33] was published in Germany, in the foremost vehicle of neogrammarian thought, the *Indogermanische Forschungen*, in a volume dedicated to none other than August Leskien.

As opposed to the first two sections of this paper, which dealt with real European influences on Whitney's thought, it is clear from the third section that the neogrammarians did not actuate any changes in Whitney's linguistic perception. This is not a question only of Whitney being older than the neogrammarians; the pertinent fact is that his reactions to neogrammarian doctrines took an increasingly negative turn. In this case the pattern of influence was reversed: the American scholar contributed to the emergence of the neogrammarian views. Brugmann's (1894) testimony to that effect is well known.

I cannot stress enough, however, how extraordinary it was at that time for an American scholar to have an impact on a science which had been almost exclusively German so far. In fact, and in spite of Brugmann's eulogy of Whitney, there are signs that German scholars were not used to such foreign influences, and that Whitney's impact was less overt in the early years. I might point here to Franz Misteli's (1880) perceptive article which Jankowsky does not appear to have used. One of the revealing points (Misteli 367) made in this review article of the methodological introduction in Osthoff and Brugmann's *Morphologische Untersuchungen*, is that, although Whitney and Scherer broke ground

---

Footnote 32 continued

themselves within the limits of a community, often of a subdivision of a former more extensive community, being unshared by other subdivisions, often of only a class in a community; they have spread so far as the channels of communication carry them, and no further' (1887:xxxv).

[33] Conceived as an illustration and continuation of the criticisms which his Yale colleague Tarbell (1887) had made of the dogma of the invariability of phonetic change.

for the new school, and Leskien followed in their footsteps, Osthoff and Brugmann refer to Scherer and Leskien, but fail even to mention Whitney. In spite of the fact that Whitney's principal linguistic treatises were translated into German[34] – *The Life and Growth of Language* by Leskien himself –, the neogrammarians did not go out of their way to acknowledge the contributions of the American scholar. This was certainly the case in the 1870's, even though the situation had changed considerably by the time of Whitney's death in 1894. The intermediate period is perhaps the most important one for our purpose; it represents a time when linguistics ceased to be a European, a German science, which happened to be cultivated also in America. Whitney's role in the development of a new linguistic school in Germany marks the internationalization of our discipline. To be sure, it was still possible afterwards – indeed it is still possible today – to distinguish between European and American branches in the field. But never again was linguistics to be the preserve of a single continent. The offshoot of European scholarship which Whitney planted on American soil has flourished under him, and after him. It has flourished to the point that, if we were concerned with the present rather than the past of our discipline, it would make perfect sense today to reverse the proposition which serves as the theme for our panel, and to devote a separate session to the American background of European linguistics.

University of Pennsylvania

REFERENCES

Ascoli, I. Graziadio 1894. [Letter.] In Lanman, 67–68.
Barth, Auguste 1894a. 'Notice sur W. Whitney', *JA* sér. 9.4.177–83.
— 1894b. [Letter.] In Lanman, 68–70.
Böhtlingk, Otto (von) 1839–40. *Pāṇini's acht Bücher grammatischer Regeln*. 2 vols. Bonn, König.
— 1851. *Über die Sprache der Jakuten. Grammatik, Text und Wörterbuch*. Vol. 3 of Alexander Thedorovich von Middendorff: *Reisen in den äussersten Norden und Osten Sibiriens*. St. Petersburg, Imperial Academy. Photoreprint 1964. (Indiana University Uralic and Altaic Series, 35.) The Hague, Mouton.
— 1885. 'Zur indischen Lexicographie', *ZDMG* 39:532–8.
— 1893. 'Whitney's letzte Angriffe auf Pāṇini'. *SbSAW* 45:247–57.
Bradke, Peter von 1894. [Letter.] In Lanman, 72–73.

---

[34] These and other translations are listed in the 'Chronological bibliography of the writings of William Dwight Whitney' (Lanman 121–50).

Brugmann, Karl 1894. 'Zum Gedächtniss W. D. Whitney's', In Lanman, 74–81.
Curtius, Georg 1885. *Zur Kritik der neuesten Sprachforschung*. Leipzig, Hirzel.
Davis, Boyd H. 1974. Review article on Jankowsky 1972, *Historiographia Linguistica* 1:95–110.
Delbrück, Berthold 1894. [Letter.] In Lanman, 83–85.
Edgren, A. Hjalmar 1882. 'On the verbal roots of the Sanskrit language and of the Sanskrit grammarians', *JAOS* 11:1–55. First read before the American Oriental Society in May 1878 (*JAOS* 10:clxv–clxvi).
— 1885. 'On the verbs of the so-called *tan*-class in Sanskrit', *JAOS* 13:xxxix-xl.
Garbe, Richard 1894. [Letter.] In Lanman, 85–87.
Hillebrandt, Alfred 1894. [Letter.] In Lanman, 88–89.
Jakobson, Roman 1971. 'The world response to Whitney's principles of linguistic science', In Silverstein, xxxv–xlv.
Jankowsky, Kurt Robert 1972. *The neogrammarians. A re-evaluation of their place in the development of linguistic science*. (Janua linguarum, series minor, 116.) The Hague, Mouton.
Jolly, Julius 1894. [Letter.] In Lanman, 90–92.
Lanman, Charles Rockwell (ed.) 1897. *The Whitney memorial meeting. A report of that session of the first American congress of philologists, which was devoted to the memory of the late Professor William Dwight Whitney, of Yale University; held at Philadelphia, Dec. 28, 1894*. Boston, Ginn. Also issued as vol. 19 part 1 of *JAOS*.
Lassen, Christian 1830 'Über Herrn Professor Bopps grammatisches System der Sanskrit-Sprache', *Indische Bibliothek* 3:1:1–113.
Liebich, Bruno 1891. *Pāṇini. Ein Beitrag zur Kenntnis der indischen Literatur und Grammatik*. Leipzig, Hessel.
Macdonell, Arthur Anthony 1894. 'Professor William Dwight Whitney', *JRAS* 610–15.
Misteli, Franz 1880. 'Lautgesetz und Analogie. Methodologisch-psychologische Abhandlung', *Zeitschrift für Völkerpsychologie und Sprachwissenschaft* 11:365–475; 12:1–27.
Müller, Friedrich 1894. [Letter.] In Lanman, 96.
Oldenberg, Hermann 1894. [Letter.] In Lanman, 97–98.
Peile, John 1872. *An introduction to Greek and Latin etymology*. 2nd ed. London, Macmillan.
Pischel, Richard 1894. [Letter.] In Lanman, 98–99.
Robins, Robert Henry 1967. *A short history of linguistics*. London, Longmans; Bloomington, Ind., Indiana University Press, 1968.
Roth, Rudolf (von) 1853. 'On the morality of the Veda', *JAOS* 3:329–47.
— 1894. [Letter.] In Lanman, 100–101.
— and William Dwight Whitney (eds.) 1855–56. *Atharva-Veda-Sanhitā*. 2 vols. Berlin, Dümmler.
Salemann, Carl, and Sergei Fedorovich Oldenburg 1892. 'Böhtlingk's Druckschriften', *Mélanges Asiatiques tirés du Bulletin de l'Académie Impériale des Sciences de St.-Pétersbourg* 10:247–56.
Schlegel, August Wilhelm von 1832. *Réflexions sur l'étude des langues asiatiques*. Bonn, Weber.
Silverstein, Michael (ed.) 1971. *Whitney on language. Selected writings of William Dwight Whitney*. Cambridge, Mass., MIT Press.
Tarbell, Frank Bigelow 1887. 'Phonetic law', *TAPA* 17:1–16.
Whitney, William Dwight 1850. 'A comparison of the Greek and Latin verbs', *Bibliotheca Sacra* 7:664–68.
— 1852. 'Tabellarische Darstellung der gegenseitigen Verhältnisse der Sanhitās des Rik, Sāman, weissen Yajus und Atharvan', *Indische Studien* 2:321–68.
— 1853. 'On the main results of the later Vedic researches in Germany', *JAOS* 3:289–328.
— 1854a. Review of J. A. Vuller, *Lexicon Persico-Latinum etymologicum*, *JAOS* 4:462–64.

— 1854b. Review of O. Böhtlingk and R. Roth, *Sanskrit-Wörterbuch, JAOS* 4:464–65.
— 1854c. Review of Th. Benfey, *Handbuch der Sanskritsprache, JAOS* 4:466–71.
— 1855a. 'Bopp's comparative accentuation of the Greek and Sanskrit languages', *JAOS* 5:195–218.
— 1855b. 'On the Avesta or the sacred scriptures of the Zoroastrian religion', *JAOS* 5:337–83. Reprinted 1873a:149–97.
— 1856. 'Contributions from the Atharva-Veda to the theory of Sanskrit verbal accent', *JAOS* 5:385–419.
— 1857. 'Alphabetisches Verzeichniss der Versanfänge der Atharva-Samhitā', *Indische Studien* 4:9–64.
— 1859a. 'On the origin of the Hindu science of astronomy', *PAOS* for May: 8 (not included in *JAOS*).
— 1859b. Comparison of the elements of the lunar eclipse of Feb. 6, 1860, as calculated according to the data and methods of the Sūrya-Siddhānta, and as determined by modern science', *PAOS* for October: 4–5 (not included in *JAOS*).
— 1860. 'Translation of the Sūrya-Siddhānta, a textbook of Hindu astronomy: with notes, and an appendix', *JAOS* 6:141–498.
— 1861. 'On Lepsius's Standard alphabet'. *JAOS* 7:299–332. Reprinted in Silverstein, 215–48.
— 1862a. 'The Atharva-Veda-Prātiçākhya, or Çāunakīyā Caturādhyāyikā. Text, translation, and notes', *JAOS* 7:333–616. Also issued separately.
— 1862b. 'The teachings of the Vedic Prātiçākhyas with respect to the theory of accent and the pronunciation of groups of consonants', *JAOS* 7:lvii.
— 1863a. 'On the views of Biot and Weber respecting the relations of the Hindu and Chinese systems of asterisms; with an addition, on Müller's views respecting the same subject', *JAOS* 8:1–94.
— 1863b. 'The Tāittirīya Prātiçākhya', *JAOS* 8:xii.
— 1865a. 'On the Jyotisha observation of the place of the colures, and the date derivable from it', *JRAS* n.s. 1:316–31.
— 1865b. 'Müller's lectures on the science of language', *North American Review* 100:565–81. Reprinted 1873a:239–62.
— 1866. 'Reply to the strictures of Professor Weber upon an essay respecting the asterismal system of the Hindus, Arabs, and Chinese', *JAOS* 8:382–98.
— 1867a. *Language and the study of language. Twelve lectures on the principles of linguistic science.* New York, Scribner.
— 1867b. 'The value of linguistic science to ethnology', *New Englander* 26:30–52.
— 1867c. 'Key and Oppert on Indo-European philology', *North American Review* 105:521–54. Reprinted as: 'Indo-European philology and ethnology', 1873a:198–238.
— 1868a. 'The translation of the Veda', *North American Review* 106:515–42. Reprinted 1873a:100–82. First read before the American Oriental Society in October 1867 (*JAOS* 9:xxxiv–xxxvi).
— 1868b. [Obituary of Franz Bopp.] *Proceedings of the American Academy of Arts and Sciences* 8:47–49.
— 1870. 'On comparative grammars', *North American Review* 111:199–208.
— 1871a. 'On the nature and designation of the accent in Sanskrit', *TAPA* for 1869–70:20–45. Reprinted in Silverstein, 261–86. Recast in Whitney 1874a:318–40.
— 1871b. 'Examination of Dr. Haug's views respecting Sanskrit accentuation', *JAOS* 10:ix–xi.
— 1871c. 'The Tāittirīya-Prātiçākhya, with its commentary, the Tribhāshyaratna. Text, translation, and notes', *JAOS* 9:1–469.
— 1871d. 'On Prof. R. Roth's recent contributions to the interpretation of the Avesta', *JAOS* 10:xv–xvi.

— 1871e. 'On the collation of a new MS. of the Atharva-Veda Prātiçākhya', *JAOS* 10:xliii–xliv.
— 1871f. [Paragraph on Roth's contributions to the interpretation of the Avesta.] *The Nation* 12:199.
— 1872. 'Johnson's Oriental religions', *The Nation* 15:338.
— 1873a. *Oriental and linguistic studies. The Veda; the Avesta; the science of language.* New York, Scribner Armstrong.
— 1873b. 'On material and form in language'. *TAPA* for 1872:77–96.
— 1873c. 'On Johannes Schmidt's new theory of the relationship of Indo-European languages', *JAOS* 10:lxxvii–lxxviii.
— 1874a. *Oriental and linguistic studies. Second series. The East and West; religion and mythology; orthography and phonology; Hindu astronomy.* New York, Scribner Armstrong.
— 1874b. 'On Peile's Greek and Latin etymology'. *TPhS* for 1873–74:299–327.
— 1874c. 'On the Chinese *sieu* as constellations', *JAOS* 10:lxxxii–lxxxv.
— 1874d. 'On the Sanskrit accent and Dr. Haug', *JAOS* 10:ciii–cv.
— 1875a. *The life and growth of language. An outline of linguistic science.* (International Scientific Series, 16.) New York, Appleton.
— 1875b. 'Are languages institutions?' *Contemporary Review* 25:713–32.
— 1875c. 'Streitfragen der heutigen Sprachphilosophie'. *Deutsche Rundschau* 4:259–79.
— 1875d. 'Report of progress in the edition of the Atharva-Veda', *JAOS* 10:cxviii–cxix.
— 1876a. 'Müller's Rig-Veda and commentary', *New Englander* 35:772–91.
— 1876b. [Paragraph against F. Max Müller.] *The Nation* 22:179.
— 1876c. 'Müller's Chips from a German workshop'. *The Nation* 22:195–97.
— 1876d. [Letter to the editor.) *The Nation* 22:208–9.
— 1877. 'On the current explanation of the middle endings in the Indo-European verb', *JAOS* 10:cxliii–cxlv.
— 1878a. 'On the relation of surd and sonant', *TAPA* for 1877:41–57.
— 1878b. 'The principle of economy as a phonetic force', *TAPA* for 1877:123–34. Reprinted in Silverstein, 249–60.
— 1879. *A Sanskrit grammar, including both the classical language and the older dialects, of Veda and Brāhmaṇa.* Leipzig, Breitkopf und Härtel. — German translation by Heinrich Zimmer 1879, Leipzig: Breitkopf und Härtel.
— 1880a. 'Collation of a second manuscript of the Atharva-Veda Prātiçākhya', *JAOS* 10:156–71.
— 1880b. 'Logical consistency in views of language', *AJPh* 1:327–43.
— 1882a. 'General considerations on the Indo-European case-system', *TAPA* 13:88–100.
— 1882b. 'Further words as to surds and sonants, and the law of economy as a phonetic force', *TAPA* 13:xii–xviii.
— 1884a. 'The study of Hindu grammar and the study of Sanskrit', *AJPh* 5:279–97, Reprinted in Silverstein, 287–305.
— 1884b. Review of Ernst Kuhn. *Über Herkunft und Sprache der transgangetischen Völker*, *AJPh* 5:88–93.
— 1884c. 'The study of Sanskrit and the study of the Hindu grammarians', *JAOS* 11:cxcvii–cc.
— 1885a. 'On combination and adaptation, as illustrated by the exchanges of primary and secondary suffixes', *TAPA* 15:111–23.
— 1885b. *The roots, verb-forms, and primary derivatives of the Sanskrit language. A supplement to his Sanskrit grammar.* Leipzig, Breitkopf und Härtel. – German translation by Heinrich Zimmer 1885. Leipzig, Breitkopf und Härtel.
— 1885c. 'On Professor Ludwig's views respecting total eclipses of the sun as noticed in the Rig-Veda', *JAOS* 13:lxi–lxvi.

— 1885d. [Remarks on F. A. March's paper on the neo-grammarians.] *TAPA* 16:xxi.
— 1886. 'The roots of the Sanskrit language'. *TAPA* 16:5–29.
— 1887. 'The method of phonetic change in language', *TAPA* 17:xxxiii–xxxv.
— 1890. 'Böhtlingk's Upanishads', *AJPh* 11:407–39.
— 1892. 'On Delbrück's Vedic syntax', *AJPh* 13:271–306.
— 1893a. 'The native commentary to the Atharva-Veda', *Festgruss an Rudolf von Roth*, 89–96. Stuttgart, Kohlhammer.
— 1893b. 'The Veda in Pāṇini', *Giornale della Società Asiatica Italiana* 7:243–54.
— 1893c. 'On recent studies in Hindu grammar', *AJPh* 14:171–97.
— 1893d. 'On recent studies in Hindu grammar', *JAOS* 16:xii–xix.
— 1894a. 'Examples of sporadic and partial phonetic change in English', *IF* 4:32–36.
— 1894b. 'On a recent attempt, by Jacobi and Tilak, to determine on astronomical evidence the date of the earliest Vedic period as 4000 B.C.', *JAOS* 16:lxxxii–xciv.
Windisch, Ernst 1894. [Letter.] In Lanman, 103–5.

LINGUISTICS AS A SCIENCE: THE CASE OF THE COMPARATIVE METHOD

RULON WELLS

The topic proposed to me was 'Linguistics as a science in Europe and America'. In the course of considering what I might usefully say on this topic, I made two discoveries. One was that I had more to say about science than about Europe and America; and I am glad to find that my colleagues in this symposium have made up for my neglect. My other discovery was that, in order to discuss the science of language in a unified way, my best policy would be to concentrate on some theme, some strand, that would be less than the whole and yet would represent the whole.

I chose the topic of the comparative method. And I have been able to take advantage of a timely circumstance. The volume on 'traditions and paradigms' heroically edited by Dell Hymes[1] appeared not long ago; it was natural for me to make some comments on its findings. And the frequent mention of Thomas Kuhn served my purposes all the better: Linguistics furnishes, to my mind, excellent examples to show some faults and some limitations in his account of scientific activity.

First thoughts on reading Hymes. The participants in the Hymes symposium of 1964 were supposed to address themselves to Kuhn's paradigm of a paradigm. Some complied, some didn't; those that did came out in the main with negative findings.

One impression that strikes quickly and lingers long is that there were anticipations of this or that idea, e.g. of the comparative method. Of course, to chronicle anticipations is a familiar way of writing history; but some attempts to find anticipations have a heavier yield than others. The Hymes volume has a fairly heavy yield of anticipations, and the

---

[1]   The Hymes volume consists, for the most part, of papers presented to the Newberry Library Conference in February 1968. (Thorkild Jacobsen's paper was added to the volume subsequently, p. 5.) A number of these had been previously presented in August 1964 to the Burg Wartenstein Conference. Some (Gulya; Diderichsen) were presented in 1964 but not in 1968.

reader poses to himself this question: what can these anticipations mean? Several possibilities flash through his mind. (1) Between the date of anticipation and the date when the anticipated event occurred, there was stagnation. This would entail that the anticipated event came to be thought of as a first-time event only through some ignorance on the part of later historians. The thought or the assertion that they labeled as a first-time event was not so regarded by the person who thought or asserted it. (2) There was retrogression. The anticipation occurred, but came to be forgotten; the anticipated thought or assertion was then thought or asserted, independently, a second time. There are many cases, not only in linguistics and not only in science, where we have reason to think that it happened so. Some of these forgettings are plausibly explained by Zeitgeist: 'The time wasn't ripe'. In the Hymes volume I (Wells 1974:435) used the metaphor of sparks that didn't catch fire.

Then, of course, besides genuine anticipations, there are pseudo-anticipations, where the appearance of anticipation is illusory or otherwise misleading; the product, perhaps, of anachronism on the part of the historian who alleged it, or an illusion arising from the neglect of context.

The understanding of linguistic change advanced in a major way in the nineteenth century. This fact is clear, whatever may be the concepts we use to describe it. It is so clear that we ought to use it as a touchstone for our concepts, rather than question it if our concepts cannot provide for it. The concept of historiography that has prevailed in historiographies of linguistics is that history-making events are propositions; for example, that Sir William Jones made history by propounding that Sanskrit and the familiar Western languages have a common ancestor and that this ancestor may now be extinct. But the historiographer needs concepts to provide for advances (and retreats) that do not lend themselves to being expressed in propositions; the advance, for instance, of taking an old idea with new seriousness; of working out a sketchy proposition (e.g.: Latin and Greek are related to Sanskrit) in full detail; of thinking it worth one's while to study this or that (for instance: in the nineteenth century, far more people thought it worth their while to study the relations between Greek and Sanskrit than between Finnish and Hungarian, or between Hebrew and Akkadian).

So the historiographer of linguistics needs to improve his conceptual framework. After beginning with some negative thoughts about Kuhn, I will move on to a positive alternative.

The question arises, 'What is science?'; and also the question 'What constitutes advance (and retreat and digression, etc.) in science?' Linguistics can contribute in a unique way toward answering these questions; the history of linguistics has exhibited some features that no other science has exhibited so well.

Linguistics will never be a science (that is, a natural empirical science) in the highest degree; it has no prospect of achieving the standards of physics. On the other hand it surely differs in some significant way from quackery and from mere opinion. An inductive inquiry lies before us as to whether we can find significant properties that group linguistics with physics and apart from quackery and mere opinion, this grouping to be labeled science. I have found no other way of conducting this inquiry as suggestive as that of studying the history of linguistics. This amounts to saying that the most suggestive way to tackle the question 'What makes linguistics a science?' is by way of the question 'What constitutes advance in linguistic science?'

My own contribution to the Hymes volume was written before Kuhn's book (1962) was published; but now, a dozen years afterward, I am ready to offer some thoughts on his paradigm.[2] There is an initial question whether it is apropos for linguists to discuss his thesis at all, because he specifically limits its application to 'advanced science', which linguistics is not, and secondly because it is specifically a thesis about revolutions, without any definite commitment as to when or how often revolutions will occur. If his thesis applies only to physics, and only to two or three episodes in the last four hundred years, then linguistics can hardly have any bearing on it. However, neither of these reasons is weighty. As for the first reason, it is true that he expressly limits his scope to advanced science, but no sufficient reason for doing so has appeared, so that his restriction appears arbitrary. (A MOTIVE has appeared, but not a sufficient reason.) As for the second reason, the less often revolutions occur, the less his thesis provides a general account of the history of science, and also, the more acute becomes the question whether his concept of revolution is trivial: If a number of changes take place simultaneously and suddenly, they are collectively called a revolution; if not simultaneously or not suddenly, then they are called normal science. In particular, his critics have asked whether there may not be mini-revolutions, and indeed a continuum between non-revolutionary normal science and revolution.

---

[2] I have profited from discussion over the years with Frederick S. Oscanyan (Department of Philosophy, Yale University) and with Bruce Paternoster. A discussion in February 1975 of my paper by Oscanyan's Philosophy of Science group also proved valuable.

In restricting his thesis to revolutions within advanced science, Kuhn
has in effect asserted two distinctions of kind: first, between advanced
science and the rest of science, and second, between normal and revolutionary science. I don't reject the first distinction outright, but I don't see
that it deserves to be treated as a distinction of kind and I don't see that it
warrants his restricting his thesis to the advanced kind. But if his restriction isn't warranted, so that linguistics (among other sciences) may
supply evidence for or against his theses, then the evidence against his
second distinction rises very considerably in amount and proportion.
In particular, a main conclusion of my review of nineteenth century
advances in the scientific study of language change will be that, in the end,
a difference between its study and that of the eighteenth century (Turgot,
Van Lennep, Condillac, Herder, Horne Tooke, etc.) accumulated
which, if it had happened in a very short time, would have deserved to be
called a revolution.

Of course we cannot speak of Kuhn's treatment of linguistics, since
he hasn't given any. But we may speak of Kuhnian accounts if we mean
by that accounts that people might give of linguistics if against his will
they simply transferred to linguistics what he himself says about advanced
science. I propose the following improvement on Kuhnian accounts
of linguistics (and, for that matter, of advanced science as well): Where
these would speak of but a single factor, the so-called paragidm,[3] I
would discriminate three. When we describe what an investigator does,
I propose that we find it useful to discriminate three factors. An investigator (inquirer, researcher) has purposes; employs methods; and
entertains beliefs. Purposes and methods cannot be true or false, at
least not in the same sense as beliefs can; there is even a disagreement
among philosophers as to whether all beliefs are either true or false.
In a few minutes I shall mention a philosophical reason for thinking
that Kuhn's belief, 'Normal science is different in kind from scientific
revolution', has in it an ingredient of decision which is neither true nor
false. Anyhow, a belief, even if it is not wholly true nor wholly false,
involves a CLAIM to be wholly true, and with this claim in mind, I refer
collectively to an investigator's beliefs as his alethic. I refer collectively
to his purposes as his telic, and to his methods as his methodic. I am not
so proud of these names that I would not listen to suggestions for their
improvement. The justification for discriminating these three factors is

---

[3] Kuhn's second-edition replacement (1970.182, 186–87) of 'paradigm' by 'disciplinary
matrix' on the one hand and by 'exemplar' on the other is an improvement, but not a
radical, thoroughgoing one.

that they are to some extent independent, like dimensions of space; the utility of discriminating them is that they let us locate agreements and disagreements. An example that pertains to the history of the comparative method is this one: In the later nineteenth century, comparativists came to distinguish between Ursprache and Grundsprache. Stated in terms of this distinction, the disagreement between Bopp and Brugmann is best described as primarily a disagreement in telic: Bopp aimed to recover the Ursprache, Brugmann only aimed to recover the Grundsprache. It is obvious that a three-factor account can locate difficulties and disagreements more finely – can 'pinpoint' them better – than a one-factor account, provided that the three factors can be discriminated in some objective way; there is also the question whether the refinement is worth the trouble.

To find a difference of kind between normal science and revolution is to treat the differences between the two as collectively more important than the resemblances. Now this question of which is more important, the resemblances or the differences – is it a question of scientific fact, testable by some difference between the empirical consequences of the two answers? The English philosopher John Wisdom (1938) has proposed the opinion that the question is not a factual question; that neither answer is true, and neither is false; that both answers are stipulations, decisions, not findings. I agree with that opinion, and applying it to Kuhn, I reach the conclusion that he, in describing scientists' perception of the facts as colored by their paradigms, has his perception of the fact colored by his paradigm. I don't purport to be superior to him in having a perception uncolored by any paradigm; rather, I propose to get at the pure facts not by perceiving them untinctured by any paradigm, any framework, but rather by cultivating our ability to shift from paradigm to paradigm while retaining the belief that it is the same facts we are perceiving, now colored by this paradigm and now by that one. Kuhn's analogy with Gestalt can be turned against him here, for though some Gestalten are not subject to voluntary switch, others ARE subject.

Independently of John Wisdom, the taxonomist Ernst Mayr has made a similar point, dividing taxonomists into splitters and lumpers. (The same division is made by Francis Bacon, and by Kant.)[4] Now by a

---

[4] David H. French in a paper presented April 1962 cited E. Mayr, E. G. Linsley, and R. L. Usinger, *Methods and principles of systematic zoology* (1953), pp. 308, 314 on splitters and lumpers; cp. (a decade earlier) French in C. Lévi-Strauss, R. Jakobson, C. F. Voegelin, and T. A. Sebeok (editors), *Results of the conference* [July 1952, Bloomington, Indiana] ... (IUPAL No. 8 = IJAL 19(2) Supplement, April 1953), p. 35 bottom. Bacon, *Novum organum* 1.55; Kant, *Critique of pure reason*, p. 666 (first edition) = 694 (second edition). Ernst Cassirer, *The problem of knowledge* (1950) pp. 133–34 quotes Kant.

formally similar dichotomy we can divide students of change into those
who emphasize continuity and those who emphasize discontinuity.
(Note, by the way, that all of these dichotomous divisions may be
reconceived as gradient; e.g. one may admit a gradual, gradient transition from extreme splitters to extreme lumpers.) A Kuhn-minded student
of the history of linguistics would use a framework, or paradigm,
emphasizing discontinuities, but if some other student, myself for
example, were to use a framework emphasizing continuities, neither
framework would be right in any sense that would make the other wrong,
and so if one said that the two frameworks disagreed, it would at least
not be a disagreement about facts.

Linguists learned to describe languages synchronically and idio-
glottically, that is, to describe each stage without regard to what it had
been and what it would be, and to describe each language and each
language-stage in its own terms. Historiographers of linguistics should
learn to do the same thing with linguists. In practice, the chief sins
against these precepts have been three, namely, anachronism, disregard
of telic, and disregard of context.

The idea that languages change was not new to the nineteenth century.[5]
We have to acknowledge this right off, and many historians of linguistics
do so. But then we have to look for some other way of characterizing
what was new to and distinctive of the nineteenth century, for something
was.

One suggestion, made by historians of the nineteenth century in
general though perhaps not by historians of linguistics, has been that the
nineteenth century took time and change MORE SERIOUSLY. Any educated
Frenchman, from the time of Clovis on, would see that his language had
changed from Latin, and would have a roughly accurate idea of how long
this had taken, but the nineteenth century somehow grasped the change
from Latin to French better than that. Well, for one thing, it applied
the idea more widely. For another, it applied the idea to new data, most
notably to Sanskrit. For a third thing, the nineteenth century's account
of the mechanism and the processes of language change was quite different
in detail.

These are all of them good points, but they are not enough. More
important, and more elusive, is the question of the time-span (time-
depth) over which linguistic change was at work. I will partly recapitulate
and partly elaborate things I have said in my essay on 'Uniformitarianism

[5] Cf. Malkiel 1974:318.

in linguistics' in the *Dictionary of the History of Ideas* (Wells 1973). What we must try to do is to recreate the climate of opinion within which language change was discussed.

Now in linguistics, taking time seriously did not mean dealing in vast lengths of time, as it did in astronomy and geology. Rather, it meant two other things, both involving conflict with the Babel story, namely, (1) dealing in LONGER periods than the Biblical chronology allowed, and (2) reinterpreting the 'confusion of tongues' along uniformitarian lines.[6] And under the secularized, uniformitarian interpretation, any 'confusion of tongues' must have come to pass not by any miracle or extraordinary intervention but in one or more of whatever ordinary, nowadays familiar ways language change does take place.

There is an aspect of the Babel story that the historian of linguistics must be prepared to deal with; if he cannot do justice to it, his methodology is inadequate. This is that the influence of the Babel story on linguistics, in the eighteenth and nineteenth centuries, was largely implicit. It was present in the background, tacitly, not outspokenly in the foreground. The most readily available evidence for this is what happened in geology and biology in those centuries. These sciences bore the brunt of overt confrontation with the Bible. It was less clear that Babel would cripple linguistics than that the Hexaemeron and the Flood would cripple physical science. Sapir's remark on Babel as an influence on Herder, quoted by Jespersen (1922:28) and mentioned by Hans Aarsleff (1967:148), may be cited.

Although the comparative method is the topic on which the present paper concentrates, there isn't space to review the beginnings, and after a terminological clarification I plunge *in medias res* with a remark on Bopp.

A clarification of the word 'comparative' cannot be dispensed with. Without attempting a systematic and structurally accurate survey of its senses, I must, for present purposes, take note of four of them: (1) the literal, etymological sense, (2) the sense current in biology, (3) the sense current in anthropology, and (4) the sense current in linguistics. (Logically the senses are not coordinate; the last three all fall under the first, as species, or subspecies, in a 'tree of Porphyry'.)

Hoenigswald says (1963:2) that the sense in which we speak of

---

[6] Northrop Frye, 1947:173–74, speaking of Jacob Bryant (1774) and Edward Davies (1804), says: 'Both wasted great pains and immense erudition in trying to construct the roots of a pre-Babel language out of guesswork, without understanding the phonetic principles on which the Lord had confounded it.'

'comparative anatomy and comparative linguistics (along with old-fashioned 'comparative mythology')' is a 'special, archaic meaning'. It is not his concern there, but it must be ours here, to answer the question 'whether Schlegel's and Bopp's understanding of the work of Cuvier and Oken was genuine'. I turn, then, first to (2), the sense current in biology. Friedrich Schlegel,[7] envisioning a comparative grammar, explicitly envisions it after the model of comparative anatomy; and Hegel, in §117 of his *Encyclopedia*, brackets the two comparative sciences together. '. . . This method has undoubtedly led to some important results; we may particularly mention the great advance of modern times in the provinces of comparative anatomy and comparative linguistics.'[8] But one very considerable difference between Cuvier's comparative anatomy and comparative linguistics is the following: for Cuvier, his comparative anatomy was explicitly static, not evolutionary. We may fairly say that to be static is not part of the very sense of the phrase 'comparative anatomy', but is externally conjoined to it by Cuvier. Nevertheless, even if we take that view of it, so far as Cuvier's work functioned as a model (Kuhn: 'exemplar'), so far as a linguist tried to be like Cuvier, his work would differ alethically in this notable respect from the alethic actually held by comparative linguists. Linguistics was evolutionary before biology was.

(3) As the term is understood in anthropology, the various types envisioned are all of them arrayed in a single linear sequence, so that one may speak of stages, whereas, (cf. Nordenskiöld, 1928:339–40) Cuvier (1817) expressly rejects a linear series of animal types. Boas's critique (1896) is largely directed against the postulation of stages. Marvin Harris's account is wrong (1968:152–53) in thinking that the sense of the expression is the same in biology and in linguistics and in ascribing to biology a commitment to 'the great chain of being', i.e. to a linear series.

(4) In the sense current in linguistics, 'comparison' and 'the comparative method' invariably, unless the contrary is expressly indicated, mean comparative RECONSTRUCTION, in which two or more daughter-languages

---

[7]   1808:28; beginning of Chapter 3; Lehmann (1967:25), and quoted by Pedersen (1962:19), and by Hoenigswald (1963:1).
[8]   This passage is in one of the 'Zusätze' supplied in 1840, nine years after Hegel's death, by the editor Leopold von Henning, and so we have no way of telling whether it was written by Hegel or was said in his lectures, or even of telling whether it is accurately reported. The modern results he alludes to are, no doubt, or include, the works in progress of his Berlin colleagues Humboldt – who brought Hegel to Berlin –, Grimm, and Bopp. Henning with the hindsight of 1840 may well have given the remark more emphasis than Hegel himself did.

are the input and a 'reconstructed', i.e. inferred, mother-language is the output. When linguists wish to speak of comparing languages (in sense 1) without reconstruction, they use such phrases as 'cross-genetic comparison' and 'contrastive linguistics'.

Consequently, the statement[9] that 'every historical grammar is, by definition, comparative' is true of the etymological sense but false of the sense current among linguists; and the equivocation between the two senses diverts attention from the fact that whereas historical linguistics was nothing new, comparative linguistics called for a method that was not even anticipated until the nineteenth century. And to go on and say that 'conventionally one speaks of 'comparative historical grammar' only where more than one daughter-language is contrasted with the ... ancestral tongue' positively encourages misunderstanding; for no mention is made of the crucial fact that when the comparative method is applied, one of the languages involved – the one called the ancestral tongue, or mother-language – is an output of the method, not an input. On the relation between historical and comparative linguistics, see below, p. 56.

My remark about Bopp makes reference to Pieter Verburg's survey of Bopp, reprinted in Sebeok (1966). Verburg contends that the intellectual formation, the *Bildung* of Bopp lies not in the Romantics, not in the turn-of-the-century figures De Sacy, Bernhardi, Adelung, Fulda, not even in the 'Dutch Graecists' of nearly a century before his productive years, but in the seventeenth century rationalism of which Leibniz was (Sebeok 1966:1.246) 'the last great representative'. In the present discussion I shall simply assume that Verburg's contention is correct, because the historiographical remark I want to make is this: EVEN if Verburg is correct, even if in one respect (or one aspect) Bopp is an epigone, yet in another respect he is a shining example of the nineteenth century. It is a challenge to our historiographical adequacy whether we can show how Bopp, even if in one respect a mere echo, is in other respects a new and independent voice.

My three-factor framework of telic, methodic and alethic helps us to

---

[9] Y. Malkiel 1968:73. The formulation in the Hymes volume (Malkiel 1974:318 top) is much improved, but it still characterizes 'comparativism in this context' as 'performed without ever losing sight of the parent tongue as a background'. The crucial difference that is blurred here is the difference between a parent tongue which is present in the background as a datum and one which is present in the background as a quaesitum. The former is the case in historical, the latter in comparative linguistics. The relation is well brought out by Kiparsky's diagram (1974:338). A language which was a quaesitum or output of comparative linguistics may be made to function as a datum in historical linguistics.

do this. The general proposition that language is the simple reflection and representative of thought, taken over by Bopp from rationalism, is part of his alethic, as is the deduction that language expresses thought agglutinatively. (Leibniz's ideal language is agglutinative.) The intention of demonstrating this is part of his telic. The intention of limiting his demonstration – of making it less extensive in order to make it more intensive – in other words, the intention of concentrating and specializing – is also part of his telic. (This part has a national, in particular a German flavor; see below.) As it happens, he specializes in and concentrates on Indo-European. His ventures outside this are unfortunate.[10] His methodic is his version of the comparative method.

Meillet compared Bopp with Columbus; Jespersen (1922:55), wittily and with harmless parti pris elaborating the simile, compared Rask with Leif Ericsson. What is under discussion is Bopp's goals, his telic. He didn't mean to found the comparative method, or to reconstruct Proto-Indo-European; he meant to demonstrate rigorously within a limited scope the correspondence of language to thought.

In what way was Bopp new? In his ability to concentrate and to specialize. He was not a Renaissance man and he was not an Encyclopédiste; he was a Fachmann. He exhibited that Geist der Gründlichkeit of which Kant proudly spoke[11], and that 'Beharrlichkeit und anhaltender Fleiss' which at the end of his *Prolegomena* he attributed especially to Germans, a quality fully shared by Grimm and in which the at least equally brilliant Rask was sadly lacking. Early in life Bopp conceived a vast project, of which he had an Ahnung des Ganzen (to borrow Schleiermacher's phrase about Plato); he stuck to his project, and carried it out to the finish.

Y. Malkiel in his contribution to this symposium has called attention to the passage at the end of *The life and growth of language* where Whitney (1875) contrasts German leadership in 'comparative philology' with its far lesser standing in 'the science of language'. Although I

[10] I may not have chosen the right word to describe them; cf. Whitney 1867:245n. It is the method itself, not good luck or bad luck in choosing instances to apply it to, that is at fault. The attempt to establish cognation between Austronesian (Malayo-Polynesian) and Indoeuropean yielded a valuable lesson: The comparative method, or at least Bopp's version of it, could not distinguish between sound and unsound applications.

[11] 1781:Bxlii. It is noteworthy that in another passage (1790:§29) where Kant esteems the trait of Gründlichkeit, he ascribes it to a Saussure, Horace Benedict de Saussure (1709–90). – Another memorable German phrase, 'In der Beschränkung zeigt sich erst der Meister', should be recalled here; both Grimm and Bopp had, with trifling exceptions, a gift for restricting themselves.

agree with both-parts of Whitney's judgment, I don't here undertake to discuss the second part. As for the first part, while I don't want to be quantitative as Edison was ('Genius is one percent inspiration and ninety-nine percent perspiration'), I do maintain that Ausführlichkeit and Vollständigkeit were a sine qua non to the successes of the nineteenth century.

The nineteenth century was zealous not only in reworking old materials, but in gathering new ones. This zeal I would categorize partly under telic and partly under methodic. To make my meaning clearer, let me illustrate with the collection of manuscripts and inscriptions. In part, special difficulties and risks were required, for example in expeditions to the Near and Middle East. In part, expense was required, for example in certain excavations in Greece and Italy. But in considerable part, only interest and time were required. So far as the project of gathering new materials was conceived as a means to an end, I place it under methodic; so far as an investigator actually held or accepted this end, so far as it actually functioned as his motive, I place it under his telic. It is possible, and was in fact common, that one investigator might choose as his end some task which would serve another investigator as a means to another end; one of the main achievements of the nineteenth century was in the execution of various Hilfsmittel – corpora, concordances, catalogues. Even more importantly for our topic, historical linguistics was used as a means by comparative linguistics.

The question arises how far new materials were the cause of discoveries and progress. I can illustrate the question by the stock example of Sanskrit. What was the role of Sanskrit in the discovery of the comparative method and in the reconstruction of Proto-Indoeuropean?

Whitney was very articulate on this question. After the passage (1867:3) which Mounin has signalized, on 'the recognition . . . of the Indo-European family of languages' as 'the turning-point in this history, the true beginning of linguistic science', he considers on p. 4 and in more detail on pp. 227–29 the contribution of Sanskrit. 'What Indo-European philology might have become without the help of Sanskrit, it were idle to speculate'[12]; but 'in all researches into the beginnings of Indo-

---

[12] P. 4. If Whitney means that counterfactual propositions in general are idle speculation, he goes too far (cf. 15 on the continuum from controlled to uncontrolled use of them); if he means that use of them is idle for the historian, he implies that history does nothing but describe, i.e. that in no degree does it explain.

Jespersen remarks (p. 55, already cited) that Rask 'had discovered Comparative Grammar before Bopp, without needing to take the circuitous route through Sanskrit.' But (1)

European speech . . . , its assistance is indispensable.' This is so particularly because of the transparency of its structure. Whitney virtually
distinguishes between the contribution made by the language itself and
the contribution made by the texts written in it. As regards the latter,
he distinguishes between Vedic and Classical Sanskrit. The value for
linguistics of the Vedas is that they 'appear rather like an Indo-European
than an Indian record; they are the property rather of the whole family
than of a single branch' (227). He accepts the dating of the oldest
Rig-Veda at or near 2,000 B.C. As for Classical Sanskrit, 'nor . . . can
its literature sustain a moment's comparison with those of the classical
languages' (228). The larger context makes it probable, though not
certain, that he means literature in the narrower sense of belles-lettres,
rather than all the texts. In any case, he refers to the linguistic literature
when he speaks of the structure of Sanskrit as 'presented by the native
grammatical science in an analyzed condition, with roots, themes, and
affixes carefully separated, distinctly catalogued, and defined in meaning
and office' (228). Note that this only mentions their morphology and
syntax, though he himself edited two native phonetic treatises and
wrote repeatedly on accent and other phonetic matters. His history needs
to be supplemented by a point that J. R. Firth makes (1957:110–1) in
connection with Sir William Jones, namely that Jones, in his "excellent
account and transcription of the Devanagari syllabary", introduced the
West to 'an eastern source of phonetics, far more competent than
anything hitherto produced in the West'. Pedersen, pp. 21–23, makes a
similar point about Hindu grammar. The Eastern, more precisely

Footnote 12 continued

he did not, at least in his 1814 work, envision the ideal of reconstructing a LOST language.
(2) Jespersen's remark doesn't prove that Sanskrit wasn't necessary. For the cultivation
of IE studies, that Whitney spoke of, required not only a formulation of the method (a
methodical component, to restate the point in my framework), but also an interest in the
method, a stimulus, an incentive, an impetus, a challenge to pursue it – in brief, a telical
component. Sanskrit offered just such a challenge. One thing that it did, among many
others, was to give people a fresh appreciation of an old insight. It had never been supposed
that language is static. The changes were variously regarded as corruptive or as progressive,
but it had always been supposed that there were changes. Still, the doctrine of change had
become stale; it didn't stimulate research, because people thought that the detail of the
changes was in part known to them already, and for the rest lost beyond recovery. What we
have here, then, is a case where the effect of a new challenge is not merely to contribute
new facts but to change attitude, outlook.

In reply to Jespersen, then, we may quote the judicious reflection of Pedersen (1962:256):
'Without Sanskrit it was possible to advance a long step forward, as Rask showed. But it
may be questioned whether it was possible to go appreciably further than Rask.' Cf.
Metcalf (1974), on Jones's (1786) advantage over Andreas Jäger (1686) in knowing of
Sanskrit.

Hindu Indian, morphology, whether or not more competent, was in any case appreciably different from what the West had been used to, and also was better adapted to Proto-Indo-European – because better adapted to Sanskrit – than the Greco-Latin model. Whitney on the whole disdained the Hindu-Indian linguistic work, and I conjecture that this disdain clouded his vision of the fact that, whether it was good or bad, it had a great impact on Western linguistics in the first half of the nineteenth century. Paul Diderichsen (1974:285) reminds us that earlier a similar impact had been made by the model used by grammarians of Semitic languages, which starts its morphology from the root.

The question immediately before us is, what was the role of Sanskrit in the discovery of the comparative method and in the reconstruction of Proto-Indoeuropean? The data of the preceding paragraph show a certain complication that we must reckon with. Just as, in the sixteenth and following centuries the West was simultaneously presented with a new family of languages – the Semitic – and with a new model for describing language, so at the end of the eighteenth century it was simultaneously presented with the Sanskrit language and with the phonetic and the morphological model of the Hindu Indian linguists, and the task of the historian of linguistics is to distinguish between the respective effects of these two novelties. This is not the place to attempt the task, but I would like to offer two helpful thoughts. The first is that the two novelties supported each other, rather than undermining each other, in their effect upon telic. Both the new data, which I categorize as alethical, and the new model, which is methodical, stimulated interest, and interest, a kind of motivation, falls under the telical category. And Whitney incisively describes (1867:3) the nineteenth century telic of gathering facts. The second thought which I offer is that Whitney himself had a strong conviction that the grammarian and the lexicographer should discover facts, not invent them. His distrust of the Hindu Indian grammar and lexicography was due in large part to his belief that they would invent sounds (18 §23a:ḹ: §§104d, 242a: ṝ; on the latter see Wells 1949:113 n. 27), roots and other lexical items, and forms if their theories called for them and they did not occur in their texts. Some particular instances of this sceptical belief have been refuted, but enough have not so that his distrust still seems well advised. Whitney's interest in what was actually spoken, to the exclusion of the creations of scholars, belongs with the watchword that took hold of language study in the mid nineteenth century, the watchword of studying the natural rather than the artificial and the spoken rather than the written language. Abundant documentation of this watchword is to be found in Jespersen's various writings on the history of linguistics, such as his *Language* (1922) and *Linguistica* (1933).

Another matter on which Whitney is eloquent is the reasons why it was the Indoeuropean family which served to establish the comparative method and linguistic science. Pedersen (1962:240ff.) gives more or less the same reasons. There is no serious question whether the Malayo-Polynesian family or the Algonquian family might have been the one to serve in this capacity, but two families are in serious question: Finno-Ugric and Semitic. Pedersen discusses both, Whitney only Semitic. The Hymes volume has an extremely valuable paper by Gulya on Finno-Ugric which advances our understanding considerably.[13]

In considering contrary-to-fact possibilities there is the danger that our musings will get out of control. There is the story of the Utah sheepherder who said, 'If we had some ham we could have ham and eggs, if we had some eggs.' We don't want to say that Finno-Ugric would have led the way if its speakers had occupied a political position of world leadership and its written records had gone back further and the family had had more branches than it did; that would be pointless. But if one or several things had been different, each of which is the sort of thing that we see happening in ordinary life, the counterfactual may make sense. Gulya and others consider the possibility that, in Gyarmathi's time, the political climate had not been so hostile to Northern affinities; and we are familiar with sudden drastic changes in political climate. Or consider the lack of old records: Why should not the Hungarians have had their Bishop Ulfilas or their St. Cyril? Or suppose that successful study of Finno-Ugric comparison required a far larger body of scholars than the Finns and Hungarians could provide. Still it is possible that, for political and religious reasons, German and French scholars might have taken up the task as the French in the Maison Française d'Extrême Orient took up Southeast Asian and the Dutch took up Javanese and Indonesian. Gulya (271) notes how Humboldt was single-handedly responsible for the widespread study of Sanskrit in Germany.

Whitney again and again emphasizes that the interest in Sanskrit and in Indo-European is due mainly to its being cognate with the native languages of the interested people. This explanation is confirmed rather

---

[13]   I take this opportunity to record my indebtedness to Robert A. Orosz, who as a student in my class at the 1964 Linguistic Institute (Bloomington, Indiana) in the History of linguistics wrote a valuable paper on 'Finno-Ugric linguistics prior to 1799' which brought to my knowledge many of the facts reported by Gulya, and some others as well. See also Sullivan 1858:1.102–04.

than disconfirmed by such interests as of the French in Indo-China and of the Dutch in Indonesia, for these latter are quite minor as compared with the linguistic interests in general of the French and of the Dutch. It seems to me that weightier counterevidence against Whitney's explanation lies in the fact that the British, politically interested in India somewhat as France in Indo-China and the Netherlands in Indonesia, showed relatively little interest in Indian languages and in Indoeuropean. But the reasons for that have been credibly explained by Aarsleff (1967).

If Whitney's explanation sustains criticism, the implication for Finno-Ugric studies is the following. The bulk of its students could not come from outside, even from countries that were politically, religiously, or intellectually interested, but must come from nations of Finno-Ugric speakers. In the first half of the nineteenth century, this means, concretely speaking, the Hungarian and Finnish areas. The number would, at the most, have been small compared with the number who did historical and/or comparative work on Indoeuropean languages, so our question becomes, was the latter number larger than it needed to have been? The answer may well be yes in certain densely cultivated areas, and yet if we get into this question further we will find ourselves asking whether the working staff, besides being suFFicient in numbers, was also EFficient in deployment. It seems to me that efficient deployment was one of the reasons for German leadership in Indoeuropean studies; if so, the implication is that a small research force for Finno-Ugristics might have been sufficient for notable accomplishments if it had been deployed with German efficiency.

If we keep our counterfactual reasonings under control, by confining our suppositions to realistically credible ones, we will have no reason to suppose that Indoeuropean studies would have languished if Finno-Ugric studies had flourished. They would, then, have gone on side by side. I don't see any reason for saying that Comparative Finno-Ugristics could have expedited Comparative Indoeuropeanistics by saving it some missteps, or the like. It seems to me that at this point we might as well stop thinking about it, because the role of chance becomes too large, the chance, for example, that produced just two people, Bopp and Pott, who carried on the work of reconstructing Proto-Indoeuropean between (roughly) 1815 and 1845.

The case of Semitic is appreciably different. One main fact here is handled with needless vagueness by the histories, though it can be handled with precision; the fact, namely, that Semitic languages written in cuneiform simply could not be read until 1857, which is the year when the Royal Asiatic Society's assignment of the same text to Hincks, Oppert, Rawlinson, and Fox-Talbot for independent translations produced satisfyingly concordant results.[14] Thus new materials, of the sort that Sanskrit and then a century later Hittite and the two Tocharians brought to Indoeuropean, were late in coming, so there could be no question of Comparative Semitics 'scooping' or 'edging out' Comparative Indoeuropeanistics; but one would have thought that after a late start, it would make up for lost time. Nothing of the sort happened; the question Why not? is one that I am not prepared by training to tackle, and so I pass on to something else.

Let us take a brief look at applications of the comparative method to other language families. In the nineteenth century, there were very few, although the number of recognized families was rather large. Bishop Caldwell's to Dravidian (1856) was the first that I know of. The mention of Dravidian recalls to us the collaborative work a century later (1961, 1968) of Burrow and Emeneau on a *Dravidian etymological dictionary*. It was a forward step in the comparative method when reconstructers were no longer content to judge that a word or other form in language A and a form in language B were cognate, i.e. were daughters of a common parent-form, but required themselves to specify what that parent-form was. The new requirement seems to be credited (Pedersen 267) to Benfey's 1837 review of Pott. What is interesting for the student of the comparative method is that Burrow and Emeneau renounce this requirement. I suppose the implication is this. It is not that the comparative method, once it has been fully developed on one family, is to be applied to other families forthwith in its fully developed version, but that rather a different sort of recapitulation is to take place and a young application may do well to emulate a young stage instead of a more sophisticated stage of the method in its original application.

And I notice something of the same sort within Indoeuropeanistics itself. It is prominent in the papers of the three Indo-European Conferences (Winter 1965, Birnbaum and Puhvel 1966, Cardona et al. 1970). I mean the conspicuous effort to abstract from some problems and

---

[14]   See, for example, Davidson (1933:211ff.); Doblhofer, (1961:131–34); Pallis (1954:58). The Report of the Royal Asiatic Society was published separately in 1857, and was reprinted as *JRAS* 18 (1861) 150–219.

But in addition, the newly available Semitic language was given anything but a warm reception by Semitists. Ernest Renan, author of an *Histoire générale des langues sémitiques*, whose second edition came out the year after the breakthrough, chose to ignore Akkadian because it was not alphabetically written. See Meillet, 1923.

concentrate on others, this abstraction entailing that one remain silent and uncommitted on the matters abstracted from. But reconstructing protoforms means NOT abstracting; for example, at the phonological level a reconstructed form makes a commitment about the roster of vowels and the roster of consonants, and one may want to discuss the vowels and some of the consonants without making commitments concerning unsettled questions about the rest of the consonants. (Even in Indoeuropean, it was customary to reconstruct the vowels and consonants of a protoform but to leave the accent unspecified, even though it was known that there was some accent or other.)

In the 1920's Ogburn's concept of 'culture lag' was much talked about, and has by now become partly commonplace and partly forgotten. We might well employ it in describing the relation between comparative work in other language families and comparative work in Indoeuropean.

I come now to a topic that demands unusually full discussion. This is the place of phonology in the comparative method. I will group my remarks around (i) Grimm, (ii) Bopp, (iii) Pott, (iv) Verner, and (v) the difference between regularity and exceptionlessness.

(i) Grimm spoke, in the second edition (1822) of the first volume of his *Deutsche Grammatik*, of letters, rather than of sounds, though we should note that he spoke of 'Lautverschiebung', not of 'Buchstaben-verschiebung', and Pedersen (p. 303) says that his finding eight sounds in *Schrift* shows 'a minimum of phonetic sense'. Jespersen (*Linguistica* 58–61; more briefly *Language* 68–70) tells us how Grimm's neglect of phonetics provoked Rapp and Raumer into their minute investigations.

But it does not appear that the more accurate phonetics introduced by Rapp and by Raumer had any appreciable bearing on comparative work, and this may be part of the reason why their work was ignored by comparativists. On the contrary, as Bloomfield noted (1927:217, quoted in Wells 1974:437): 'No wonder that the earlier linguists spoke in terms of "letters"; the actual continuum of speech sound (la parole) was not what they meant, and they had no term for the abstraction of the socially determined features of this sound continuum.' We may say that the distinction between letters and sounds served to distinguish, in a very crude way, between emics and etics; and that it therefore functioned, so far as a crude means can function, to take advantage of the fact that (Bloomfield 1933:309) 'the comparative method tell us, in principle, nothing about the acoustic shape [i.e. the etics] of reconstructed forms.' Hindsight shows us, and it was already plain to Sweet (1913:398) in

1878, that Grimm, whether insightfully or unwittingly, achieved a fruitful abstraction.[15]

But as the example *Schrift* shows us, the contrast of letter from sound has several other functions in Grimm. Besides serving to contrast phonemics from phonetics, it also serves to introduce diachronic considerations. Grimm is in effect exploiting the fact that written language is conservative, relative to spoken language. The *sch* of German orthography reflects in the spoken German of Grimm's time an emically and etically indivisible sound (š) – though as late as 1876 the eminent phonetician Brücke was able to analyze this sound as consisting, synchronically and phonetically, of *s* plus *kh* (see Sweet, 1913:87); but it reflects in sufficiently earlier times an articulatorily and auditorily distinguishable sequence of *s* plus *k*. And if the Lautverschiebung be assumed to have been unconditioned (standard recent theory, e.g. Bloomfield 1933:350, 353, holds that it was conditioned, not taking place after *s*; and there is also the accent-condition noted by Verner), then between the original pronunciation and the pronunciation as an indivisible sibilant spirant š there must have been a stage of *s* plus aspirate *kh*. And if, moreover, not only does every aspirate become the homorganic spirant but conversely every spirant came from the homorganic aspirate, then the letter *f* and the synchronic-phonetically indivisible sound that it reflects in the German of Grimm's day must have come from earlier *ph*. And so, granted all these assumptions, preceding the stage [š rift] of Grimm's day there must, just as he says, have been a stage [skhripht]. But these are considerable assumptions; what Grimm says about *Schrift* presupposes a good deal of theory: (a) phonemics versus phonetics, (b) the diachronic interest in dealing with as early a stage of the language as possible, (c) Grimm's detailed version of

[15]   There is nothing to stop the word *letter* from coming, by metonymy, to mean 'sound correlated with a letter'; in Aristotle (*Historia animalium* 2. 12:504b1, the process has gone a step further, and *gramma* means 'articulate sound [whether or not correlated with a letter]': "Certain species of birds above all other animals, and next after man, possess the faculty of uttering articulate sounds . . ." I don't mean to say that all talk of letters rather than of sounds is harmless; for example, Guichard, in the passage cited in footnote 17, thinks that the right-to-left order of Hebrew writing can cause metatheses, and other reversals of the normal order, in the speech of languages other than Hebrew, and Brosses, cited in the same footnote, suggests that the Romans got their word *quinque* 'five' from the 'Etruscan' [Umbrian] and Celtic word *pempe* in this way: the Celts and Etruscans wrote from right to left; and their letters were mirror-images of Roman letters; the Romans, encountering that word, rewrote it from left to right, and reversed the two *e*'s, but left the two *p*'s in mirror-image form (the *m* is the same as its mirror-image); this made the Celtic-Etruscan *p*'s look like Roman *q*'s, and so they began pronouncing their rewritten *pempe* as *qemqe*. (How they got from *qemqe* to *quinque*, de Brosses does not say.)

Lautverschiebung according to which every tenuis becomes an aspirate and every aspirate a spirant, and correspondingly in reverse.

This lengthy analysis gives us a vantage point from which we can see that it was poor analysis to charge Grimm with poor phonetics. Unless 'phonetics' is used so widely as to merge with phonology, whatever mistakes Grimm may have made here are not aptly labeled phonetic.[16]

(ii) Although we find the concept of regular sound-change in Grimm – he appreciated, publicized, and developed Rask's discovery, and called it die Lautverschiebung –, it proves convenient to break the discussion of phonological regularity into two parts, one part focused on Bopp and the other part not focused on any one person. This two-part discussion will bring the history of the comparative method up to, but not including, the Neogrammarians.

Except for two or three defects which we can specify precisely, Pedersen's account seem to me substantially correct and, as far as it goes, adequate. The gist of it is as follows. Bopp did comparative work and did it in Indoeuropean, but did it without a phonological component. Grimm, in his second edition (coming out only three years after the first, and enormously modified under the influence of Rask), had a phonological component, but his treatment was historical, not (with notable exceptions, especially the Lautverschiebung) comparative work, and also (again with notable exceptions, including again the Lautverschiebung) he worked not in general Indoeuropean but only in the Germanic branch of it. Applying the comparative method to Indoeuropean, Pott, concentrating on the lexical component (etymology), and Schleicher, concentrating on the grammatical component, introduced and made basic a phonological component. (And Diez, doing historical work in the Italic (Romance) branch, likewise introduced a phonological component.) Grimm, Pott, Diez, and Schleicher all taught the doctrine of the regularity of sound-change; but not until the next stage, the Neogrammarian, was regularity taken to mean exceptionlessness.

One of the precisely specifiable defects in Pedersen's account is his proposition that Bopp had no phonology. Besides being an exaggeration – taken literally, it is false –, this proposition is seriously misleading. The proposition might be taken to mean that Bopp has no *ex professo* phonology; that he didn't, as Schleicher did, put together in one set of consecutive pages the things he said about sounds. As I said, this is an exaggeration, though his section on 'Schrift- und Lautsystem' is shorter than its counterparts in Grimm and (cf. Delbrück 1880:46) in Schleicher.

But this might be a mere matter of organization; Pott, so loosely organized, didn't have an *ex professo* phonology either. No, what is wrong with Pedersen's proposition is that it is misleading. As with his criticism of Grimm, he has a good insight but gives a bad formulation of it. Instead of saying that Bopp had no phonology, Pedersen should have said that Bopp's phonology was (a) traditional and (b) wrong.

That it was traditional explains why he gave almost no *ex professo* treatment of it. There was no need to do so. He had hardly any phonological *theses* to contend for; he took phonological commonplaces and applied them in new ways to new materials with new results. Verburg's essay (1966) very ably points up Bopp's conservative side.

The first and most basic point to make about Bopp's traditional phonology is put very simply by Delbrück (1880:39): Only after Bopp did people come to realize that different languages had different sound laws (in the strictest sense of 'soundlaw'). Bopp, like his predecessors, denied this – implicitly, if not explicitly. In denying it he was from the logician's point of view asserting a language-universal proposition. To formulate it we need something like the notion of a statistical correlation, whose two limiting extremes are zero correlation and 100 percent (invariable, universal, exceptionless) correlation. And for the purpose of this formulation, we will imagine ourselves as restating every putative sound-change as a correlation. Lastly, we will want to speak of heightening a correlation, e.g. from 20 to 40 or from 60 to 80 or from 80 to 100 if it is stated quantitatively, or from sometimes to often or from more often than not to usually of from usually to without exception if it is stated serially. Now, what Bopp implicitly asserted is this: Given a correlation based on all the languages of the world at all times, no heightening of the correlation can be achieved by narrowing the basis of the correlation.

What Bopp implicitly asserted was wrong. There is no decisive turning point in Bopp's thinking, but let us take 1833, the publication-date of the first volume of his *Vergleichende Grammatik*, as a date that is as good as any other to work around. That what Bopp implicitly asserted was wrong had been thoroughly proved by half a century, and pretty clearly by a quarter of a century, after 1833. The proof consisted in giving counterexamples.

In general, when people believe a universal proposition, complete induction is not the basis of their belief. Nor do I, ascribing to Bopp a belief in a certain universal proposition, mean to imply that he had considered every possible correlation, and every possible narrowing of its scope, and concluded that for every pairing of a correlation and a narrowing, no heightening would result. Quite the contrary: As far as I know, he gave no or hardly any thought to the universal proposition which he so firmly believed; he believed it without subjecting it to any critique or test; and this must be one of our main criticisms of his mentality and his work. Not merely did he not question it; when others questioned it, he ignored the questioning. But this doggedness, this inflexibility, this 'going his own way', which everyone who writes about Bopp emphasizes, is the absolute essence of Bopp. I know no better example (although I know an example in my own day just as good) of Kenneth Burke's brilliant aperçu (1935:70) about vision, that a way of seeing is a way of not seeing.

In certain instances, Bopp contends that this or that sound-change is exceptionless – if not for all languages at all times, at least for the transition from PIE (as we now call it) to this or that historically attested language) Delbrück (pp. 22–3) considers one example at length, and says that others could be cited 'ins Unendliche'. We learn from this that the idea of a 100 percent correlation, and the idea that a correlation whose value is less than 100 percent may rise to 100 percent if its scope is narrowed in a certain way, are perfectly familiar to Bopp; I accordingly qualify and complicate what I said a page above. It is not that Bopp admits no exceptions to the universal proposition about heightening correlations; rather, the exceptions don't have on him the effect of calling the proposition in general into question, much less do they lead him to entertaining the bare possibility that the contrary of his proposition might be the truth, in other words, the possibility that EVERY sound-change, formulated as a correlation, might by narrowing its basis be heightened to a 100 percent correlation unless it already is one. The possibility that I have just characterized as contrary to his own is nothing other than Neogrammarian Ausnahmslosigkeit. And because the Neogrammarian thesis and Bopp's virtual, largely implicit thesis about sound-change are contraries, extreme opposites, I believe that Delbrück (essentially followed in this by Pedersen) does right in treating Bopp as the alpha and Neogrammarianism as the omega of a spectrum traversed in 60 years (1816–76) of the Nineteenth Century.

It doesn't hit the nail on the head if we say that Bopp had no phonology. We may say that from a certain point of view he had too powerful a phonology, meaning by this that the rules of diachronic phonology with which he operated were so powerful ('latitudinarian', Delbrück 1880–24; 'flexible', to use the word which Pedersen (1962:270 applies to

Schleicher) that he could get almost any result he wanted. Karl Popper
has signalized refutability as the essence of a scientific hypothesis. If a
proposition has scientific status, there are possible conditions under
which it would be false; it has consequences which might clash with the
facts. Given this general consideration from scientific method, we can
produce a version of it which is specifically adapted to comparative
linguistics. Since language signs have two faces or sides, their semantical
side and their phonological side, we can expect that hypotheses about
them will have two sets of consequences, their semantical consequences
and their phonological consequences. A hypothesis of comparative
linguistics will be refutable on its semantical side insofar as its semantical
consequences can clash with the observed facts, and likewise mutatis
mutandis for its phonological side. (The technical sense of 'refutable'
needs to be kept in mind; it doesn't mean false, nor does it mean dubious;
the proposition 'The sun rose yesterday' is refutable in Popper's sense.)
Refutability is an ideal extreme which hypotheses approach more or less;
some hypotheses are more refutable, others less so. Now I believe that the
point which Pedersen was trying to make against Bopp, but he lacked
the resources in scientific method to do it with finesse, is that Bopp's
hypothesis were insufficiently refutable on their phonological side;
they were too invulnerable, too immune to empirical counterevidence.
Linguistics may not be entitled to demand perfect refutability, but there
is some level of refutability that it is reasonable for linguistics to demand,
and Bopp's hypotheses were, by and large, on their phonological side
below that reasonable level.

Bopp's style is illustrated by the word eleven (Pedersen p. 243).
Satisfied on semantical grounds that it contains the word 'ten', he forced
the phonology into agreement, i.e., he posited such sound-changes as
were necessary to pass from his protoform for 'one-ten' to the historically
attested Germanic words for 'eleven'. Not that he always started from
the semantical 'face' of the linguistic sign. The instance of the augment
signifying past time (Delbrück 1880:13, 31; Verburg 1950:229–30;
Kiparsky 1974:344) shows otherwise. Here, obviously, the heuristic
order is that Bopp was struck by the homonymy (phonological resemblance) and sought to match it with a synonymy (semantical resemblance). Whether the rules by which he proposed to derive a later
semantical difference from an earlier semantical resemblance are
plausible or acceptable (Kiparsky calls his semantics 'homemade') is
no more and no less relevant than the question whether, when starting
from the signifié-face and moving to the signifiant-face, his rules for
deriving phonological difference from phonological resemblance are

plausible or acceptable). Delbrück (1880:23) puts it nicely: In judging cognation, 'für ihn war . . . stets der Gesamteindruck . . . entscheidend, und diesem Gesamteindruck hatten sich die Laute zu fügen. . .'.

The commonplace (though false) statement that Bopp lacked a phonological component sometimes gives birth to the statement that he was deficient in phonetics. Against this, quite properly, Kiparsky (1974:339–40) reacts sharply. Some of the responsibility for the mis-apprehension must lie with Pedersen and with Jespersen. In Pedersen's case, his translator (p. viii) makes matters worse, and as for Jespersen, such claims as that 'the science of language would have made swifter and steadier progress if Grimm and his sucessors had been able to assimilate the main thoughts of Rapp' reflect his failure to appreciate two distinctions – that between phonetics and phonemics, already mentioned, and that between descriptive and explanatory diachronic phonetics, which will be taken up next.

There are two propositions in Bopp's theory which are phonetic in the strictest sense of the term; both are diachronic; one is descriptive, the other explanatory. These propositions comprise his 'mechanical law' (Delbrück 1880:17) governing stems and endings. A finite verb form is made up of a stem and an ending. Stems occur in two forms, which he calls light and heavy; so do endings. The descriptive proposition is that if the stem is light, the ending is heavy, and if the stem is heavy, the ending is light. His labels, being metaphors drawn from mechanics, seem intended to explain as well as to describe: It is as if a certain total weight is always present, equipoise is impossible, and so one pan of the balance must come down and the other go up. Verburg vividly brings out the explanatory intent of Bopp's 'mechanical law'. And Bopp himself reveals the intent of opposing Grimm's 'organic' account of Ablaut by a rival account, compatible with Bopp's fundamental thesis (that morphemically complex words are agglutinative in origin), in which Ablaut is originally meaningless – the difference between light and heavy is not originally a grammatical device, but is extrinsically forced upon the language.

Note that Delbrück (1880:20) in effect accepts Bopp's description and rejects his explanation; writing (1880) in the afterglow of Verner, he thinks of accent rather than of weight as the explanation. The point of present interest is not whether Bopp's description and his explanation are right or not, but just that they are both of them phonological, and that perhaps the description and certainly the explanation deserve to be called phonetic in the strictest sense of the term.

(iii) I turn now to Pott.

The witticism ascribed by Max Müller to Voltaire, that in etymology
the vowels count for nothing at all and the consonants for very little, is
not far from the following sober declaration by Voltaire's contemporary
Charles de Brosses: 'In etymology in the comparison of words, one need
not have any regard for the vowels, nor for the consonants except
insofar as they are of different organs.' The similar statement of Guichard,
a century and a half before Brosses, has become well known.[17] Now
we have only to look at the Indoeuropean situation to realize that
Voltaire's apocryphal *mot*, though a parody, is recognizably close to
the truth until the 1870's. Even Pott and Schleicher still operated
with one vowel, unable to account for its three different reflexes, *a, e,*
and *o*, and with one guttural series instead of the three (Brugmann) or two
(Meillet) nowadays recognized. Pedersen 277–89 gives a good précis.

Voltaire's parody lost its force when two general propositions were
brought into etymology, propositions that are primarily alethical but
with methodical implications. (1) We should and often can distinguish
between inherited and borrowed words. (2) Diachronic linguistics can
confine its attention to soundlaws that are not panglottic and panchronic,
but rather are idiochronic and idioglottic. Delbrück notes that this
second proposition came only after Bopp. Nor did it have to wait until
the Neogrammarians, because, as Delbrück emphasizes again and again
in his *Einleitung* (if never in so many words), we should distinguish
between the proposition that idiochronic and idioglottic soundlaws
are regular and the proposition that they are exceptionless; the latter,
stronger proposition was peculiar to the Neogrammarians, but even
even the former, weaker proposition, admitting exceptions but still
asserting regularity, was a novelty of the Nineteenth Century. More
general propositions had been asserted, especially the ease-theory of
phonological change, but only as ever-present tendencies, not as forces

[16]   This point is developed below, in the subsection on Bopp.
[17]   Müller ascribes this witticism at the beginning of Chapter six of his Second Series of
Lectures on the science of language. Bloomfield (1933:511, note and §1.3) reports that he
failed to trace the *mot*, and I do not know of anyone that has succeeded. However, something
very like what Voltaire said in jest, if he said it at all, is said in earnest by Guichard in 1606
and by de Brosses in 1765. Guichard is quoted by Müller, a page or two later; by Benfey
(1869:232); by Arens[1] (1955:61 §19 end) = Arens[2] (1969:76 §26) end; and by Aarsleff
(1969:27–8 n. 29). (He gives the name as Guichart and the date as 1618.) De Brosses is
quoted by Aarsleff (1967:35 n. 41). The passage is 2.158–9 §190 in the 1765 edition, 2.150
§10.21 in the 1801 edition. A passage three sections later – in the first edition, 2.166 §193,
in the second edition 2.156–57 §10.24 – is quoted by Benfey 1869:289 n. 2, who comments
that it 'fast noch über Guichard . . . hinausgeht'; from Benfey it is taken up by Verburg
1952:375. This passage, and the one by Guichard, are discussed in note 15.

that are sure to act on every language at every time though not necessarily on every word.

The series of discoveries – Grassmann's Law, Verner's Law, the Law of Palatals – which caused the Neogrammarian position to become articulated, plausible, and popular may well be left out of account here, as belonging to the Neogrammarian stage by presaging it. I will content myself with a word about its import for Kuhn's theory of paradigms. The neogrammarianism of Leskien, of Osthoff, of Brugmann (after, though – cf. Pedersen 1962:293 – not including his 1877 paper on nasalis sonans), and others, cannot be regarded as a new paradigm in Kuhn's strictest sense. Delbrück, more or less followed by Bloomfield, emphasizes the gradualness and the continuity of the steps that led to Neogrammarianism; Pedersen, bringing in a nuance which Delbrück is at pains to keep out, signalizes the personal side – imprudence on Brugmann's part, clash between an in-group and an out-group, and so on. The very fact stressed by Kiparsky (1974:340, misreading Bloomfield, as though Bloomfield denied it or didn't duly appreciate it), that the 'score' or 'record' of non-Neogrammarians in discovering soundlaws is about as good as that of the Neogrammarians, shows that the disagreement lay more in theory than in practice. But a Kuhnian paradigm comprises practice as well as theory. Moreover, adherents of different paradigms are supposed not to be able to communicate with each other. But the Neo's and the non-Neo's quarreled, and thus communicated, endlessly with each other. Finally, the respects in which Neogrammarianism is a culmination rather than an initiation make it undeserving of being called a breakthrough. Not every major advance is a breakthrough.

After these propaedeutic paragraphs about phonological regularity, let me make a few comments about the man who first applied the new concept to etymology in a sustained and fruitful way. Pott's many contributions to general linguistics would make him a significant but not a major figure; what makes him major is his contribution to Indoeuropean etymology. Of the four who launched the comparative method, Grimm (born 1785) was the oldest, then Rask (1787), then Bopp (1791), and Pott (1802) was the youngest. Already in the first volume (1833) of his *Etymologische Forschungen* he displayed himself to be in many matters a follower, and in some matters an explicit defender, of Bopp. I don't find anywhere in his book an explicit criticism of Bopp (and one would hardly expect it from a Docent at Bopp's university), but his leading original thought – to separate the wheat of etymology from the chaff by the winnowing-fan of phonological regularity – is wholly at odds with Bopp's ways of proceding, and the paean to Grimm in his opening pages (quoted by Benfey (in Sebeok 1966:1.130), Delbrück 1880:33, Meillet 1937:462) is, in its silence about Bopp, eloquent and pointed. Gabelentz (Sebeok 1966:1.256) speaks of him as 'supplementing' Bopp, Delbrück (1880:23, just after the passage about *Gesamteindruck* quoted above) as 'filling a gap'. It seems to me that it would be apter to speak of correcting Bopp, because it isn't that he did something that Bopp didn't do at all, but rather that he did better something that Bopp did badly.

What Delbrück and Gabelentz have in mind is that Bopp didn't do etymology (or did it only sporadically). But this is only true if etymology be taken in the narrowest sense. It is customary to distinguish between lexical and grammatical elements, and to say that etymology and lexicography deal with the former, grammar (morphology and syntax) deals with the latter. In a finite verb form (for example), the root is a lexical element, and all prefixes, suffixes, and endings are grammatical elements. Now, if the question is posed to us; To which kind of element did Bopp pay more attention – the lexical or the grammatical?, then no doubt the better answer is, The grammatical. But the question itself is ineptly put. Bopp could not compare Sanskrit *duhitar* with German *Tochter*, in order to establish an Indoeuropean suffix *-tar*, without thereby also establishing an Indoeuropean *duhi-* or the like; and if establishing the cognation of the suffixes is grammar, establishing the cognation of the roots is etymology. Moreover, his big idea is that the roots *as* and *bhu* are to be recognized in various suffixal forms. Bopp did a lot of etymology, but (in the main, with many exceptions) he worked with the easy, obvious etymolgies and reserved his efforts for the grammatical elements. Pott, by contrast, worked hard over many difficult, non-obvious etymologies. We may say that Bopp NOTICED many cognations, both 'etymological' (lexical) and grammatical, but (in the main) INVESTIGATED only grammatical cognations.

The same passage (cited above) that extols Grimm says that 'the letter . . . is a surer guide in the dark labyrinth of etymology than . . . the word-meaning.' This exaggeration can only be justified as a corrective, redressing a one-sided error by going too far in the opposite direction. The two faces of the linguistic sign, the signifiant (expression) and the signifié (content), are of equal importance in establishing cognation. What better contrasts Pott with Bopp is that Pott pursued etymology in the wide sense, i.e. including both grammatical and lexical elements, and subjecting them to the same treatment. In the passage (1880:23) from which I quoted earlier, where he says that for Bopp it was always the total impression of cognation that was decisive, Delbrück goes on to say that 'he didn't in sufficient measure introduce control of one assertion by comparison with the otherwise attested outcomes of the same sounds that were in question.' Pott introduced control.

The Neogrammarian historians of linguistics present Pott as a major step on the road from Bopp to Neogrammarianism. Such a presentation is not false, but it is one-sided. It is the easier for us to do justice to the other side, thanks to the work of Hoenigswald, who has with increasing explicitness over the years emphasized that "the core of our present-day understanding of the 'comparative' method" (1974:352) consists in certain propositions of phonology. These propositions employ the concepts of merger, shared innovation, and subgrouping. Two historical remarks immediately strike the historically minded reader. One is that the concepts of merger and of the shared innovation are the achievement of the Neogrammarians. The other is that Exceptionlessness – generally taken to be the essence, as it is the shibboleth, of Neogrammarianism, does not figure in the list.

As for this latter point, the reply is that if exceptionlessness (Hoenigswald calls it regularity, but I will shortly propose to distinguish the two concepts) is not explicitly mentioned, this is only because it has receded into the background, as taken for granted. For instance (Windisch in Sebeok 1966:1.369–70, 372; Delbrück 1880:58–9, 132; Pedersen 1962:278; Saussure, *Mémoire*, in Lehmann 1967:219), Curtius in 1864 proposed to regard as a shared innovation of the European languages, in contrast from Indic and Iranian, the vowel e which is represented in the latter two by a. And from this shared innovation he inferred, as the Neogrammarians would, a subgrouping. Nevertheless, Neogrammarians would not accept European e from PIE a as a shared innovation, because the Lautgesetz 'Proto-Indoeuropean a becomes Proto-European e' has exceptions. A 'Spaltung' (Curtius's own word) of PIE a into PE a and e is posited, i.e. in effect two rules are posited, (1) $a \rightarrow a$ and (2) $a \rightarrow e$, but no conditions are posited to determine when Rule (1) applies and when Rule (2) applies. To restate the same point in the language of logic, Curtius proposed two particular propositions – SOME a remains a, SOME a changes to e, whereas only universal propositions (beginning with 'all', not with 'some') are fit data for comparative reconstruction.

Hoenigswald's account of the comparative method differs considerably from that of, say, Pedersen. In the history of this methodologically very parochial Neogrammarian, there is no thematizing of the concepts of

merger and of shared innovation. Another Neogrammarian concept
is the one which, by a metaphor with mathematics, Hoenigswald calls
the algorithm. This concept too is slighted by Pedersen, who takes note
of it only under the general rubric of method (e.g., p. 243, Bopp had in
phonology no method but a lack of method). The reason why phonology
is basic in the comparative method is that, unlike the other components
of language, it comes close to furnishing an algorithm. The inputs for
the algorithm are (Hoenigswald 1973:26, 42) phonemic mergers, and
the reason why they furnish an algorithm is that they are irreversible
and so let us 'retrieve the lines of descent'. The shared innovation that
is of use to the comparativist is the shared phonemic merger. Just as
with a shared error in manuscript stemmatology, 'its real function is
to give away, by random accident, an otherwise irretrievable state of
affairs' (1966: 6 note 13). We may summarize all this by an epigram:
phonological innovations are significant because they are insignificant;
i.e., they are significant for the comparativist because they are insignificant for the speakers who innovated.

The implication of Hoenigswald's cumulative account is that the
comparative method proper began with the Neogrammarians. Rask,
Grimm, Bopp, Pott, Schleicher, Curtius, Scherer paved the way, but it
is no diminution of what they did to reclassify it as preparing for rather
than founding the method. Hoenigswald has greatly altered our appreciation of what Schleicher did. I have nothing to say in this connection
about Schleicher, but about Pott I repeat what I said two pages ago, that
to present him as a major step on the road from Bopp to Neogrammarianism is one-sided, and I am now ready to present the other side.

Pott had little grasp of those phonological concepts that the Neogrammarians articulated. How was it possible for him, then, to make a
major contribution to phonology? First, he stressed regularity, compiled
exhaustive lists of regularities, and ventured to reject semantically
attractive etymologies that flouted these regularities. Second, he saw
that phonological regularity provides the solution to the problem that
had vexed etymologists, how to distinguish between inherited and
borrowed words (1883:2.349; cited by Oertel, 1901:54–5). And third, he
made it clear that what is required to establish the cognation (etymological identity) of two words is not 'Gleichklang' but correspondence of
regular soundlaws. As Max Müller, with his taste for epigram, put it,
'Sound etymology has nothing to do with sound' (1865:259; this is in
the sixth lecture of the Second Series, two pages after the *mot* ascribed
to Voltaire).

In this connection, Pedersen's account of Pott has a flagrant mistake which I am unable to account for. On p. 304 he quotes a passage where Pott 'defends himself with great emphasis against exaggerated claims for phonetics'. The passage is 1833:1.69, and it has nothing to do with phonetics in any ordinary sense.[18] Pott draws a contrast between etymological agreement and 'Gleichklang'. Most people think that what is required to establish cognation is Gleichklang, whereas in fact it is etymological agreement. As an example of the popular though erroneous notion, Pott cites a recent series of articles by the celebrated Orientalist, Josef von Hammer. The example is well chosen for three reasons: (a) Hammer IS celebrated, (b) his series of articles is very recent, and (c) their point is to show a remarkable amount of agreement between Persian and German by means of a *Leporelloliste* (Pott 1.70 says he borrows the expression from Klaproth) of words alike in sound and in meaning. Pott then proceeds to show in two ways that the popular approach illustrated by Hammer is wrong: He produces (a) pairs of words that are like-sounding but not, as far as we can tell, historically connected, and (b) pairs of words that would not strike anyone as alike in sound, but which we happen to know are historically identical. Among his many examples are, for the first kind, New Persian and New English *bad*, and, for the second kind, New Ossetic *cho* and New English *sister*. These two examples are cited by Pedersen in a different context (1931:263–4).

As there are very few mistakes of sheer fact in Pedersen, I am at a loss to account for this one. I hazard the conjecture that in writing up

[18] Biographical information on Josef von Hammer (1774–1856; in 1835 he legally changed his surname to Hammer-Purgstall) in Wurzbach 267–89, in *Allgemeine Deutsche Biographie* 10 (1879) 482–7, and in the *Enciclopedia Italiana*; a sketch in the anthology edited by Weber (1957). A complete bibliography in the *Almanach der kaiserlichen Akademie der Wissenschaften* [*zu Wien*] 1851.191ff., 1852.141–2, 1858.77ff.

The series of articles to which Pott refers was published in the *Jahrbücher der Literatur*, Anzeige-Blatt section, volumes 49–53 (volumes 49–52 in the year 1830, volume 53 in 1831). Pott and others refer to this journal as the *Wiener Jahrbücher der Literatur*, misleadingly, because although published in Vienna it is catalogued under J and not under W (*National Union Catalogue, Pre-1956 Imprints* 276 (1973) 227A; [*British*] *Union Catalogue of the Periodical Publications* . . . (London, 1937) 284B number 8990; *British Museum Catalogue* 186.760).

Paul Horn, in the *Grundriss der iranischen Philologie* (edited by Wilhelm Geiger and Ernst Kuhn, Strassburg, 1895–1904) 1(2) 12n. cites this series as an antiquated curiosity.

On the supposed close connection between Persian and German, see W. Streitberg 1915:182–86; Jespersen 1922:35, who cites Streitberg; Pedersen 1931:7, who uses Streitberg's findings; Bernhard Dorn (= Boris Andreevich Dorn, 1805–1881), 1827:91–135, cited by Pott 1833:1.69.

Pott's example *bad* is repeated, though in a wholly different place and context, in his second edition 1833:4.865 no. 1865.

his treatment he worked from notes on Pott without checking the original, and was misled by his notes.

In summary of Pott, I would say that it was his main contribution to promote phonology, not in the sense in which a real estate agent promotes a housing development, but in the sense in which authorities promote a student from kindergarten to first grade, or an army officer from captain to major.

(iv) About Verner, I have no new fact to adduce; rather, I want to make just one comment on an old fact. What is involved is the concept of phonetics. In Verner's own entertaining account of his discovery (as told by Jespersen; reprinted in Sebeok 1966:1.539), "... I got a book to send me to sleep. It happened to be Bopp's *Comparative Grammar* ... I turned up a passage and there the two words *pitár* and *bhrátar* stared me in the face, and it struck me that it was strange that the one word had a *t* in the Germanic languages and the other a *th* . . .' Hoenigswald remarks (1974:353) that Verner 'was struck in an almost graphic way ... by the correlation between the Germanic 'exception' and the Sanskrit accent. ... Phonetic considerations seem to have had nothing to do with it . . .' I don't suppose that Hoenigswald means that it was not phonetic but graphic considerations that were at work. His meaning must be that Verner's basic consideration, viz. that the contrast between *t′* and *′t* correlated with the contrast between Proto-Germanic *t* and Proto-Germanic *th*, was not a phonetic consideration. Maybe not, in the narrow sense that it is not a consideration that would find mention in a treatise on phonetics, such as the one (by Brücke) that Verner himself cited. But let us recall that immediately after Verner's publication, phonetic treatises (I have especially Sievers in mind) DID begin mentioning, and indeed making much of, putative correlations between accent-contrasts and other contrasts. The more important reply may be made very briefly, because it merely applies to Verner two distinctions that have already been made in connection with Bopp. If Verner's basic consideration was not phonetic, it was certainly phonological. But it was a phonological description, not a phonological EXPLANATION. Like Bopp's description of the correlation between light stems and heavy endings, it was accompanied by a proposed explanation. But just as later generations accepted Bopp's description while discarding his explanation, so with Verner – 'who throughout his life kept up a lively interest in phonetics' (Pedersen 1962:304) –: 'The phonetic explanation of his famous law which he gives in his principal article is hardly tenable in individual details. At least it has been seriously doubted recently, although belief in the law itself has not been shaken' (305).

In sum, we have to distinguish between phonology (which subsumes technical phonetics) and phonetics; and within each of these we also have to distinguish between description and explanation. Verner's Law is not an explanation; so whether we assign it to (descriptive) phonetics or to (descriptive) non-phonetic phonology, we will in any case not assign it to explanatory phonetics. And if phonetics *tout court* is explanatory phonetics, then indeed as far as the law itself is concerned, phonetic considerations had nothing to do with it.

(v) At the beginning (p. 39) of this section on the place of phonology in the comparative method, I said I would group my remarks around five subheadings. I come now to the fifth and last of these, the difference between regularity and exceptionlessness.

Apropos of Verner, Pedersen writes (1962:282): '. . . I have mentioned the irregularities in the Germanic sound-shift in the case of medial sounds. . . . The irregularities occur abundantly . . ., and prevail . . . throughout the inflection of strong verbs. This last feature is most striking in Old High German. . . . No one had been able to explain it . . . Therefore the effect of Verner's article . . . was immeasurable. Now there were no more exceptions to the Germanic sound-shift, and this absence of exceptions . . . had . . . as strong an effect . . . as the chief laws [formulated by Rask, Bredsdorff, and Grimm] applying to the sound-shifts had exerted in their time. Then, scholars were beginning to understand that there *were* laws of phonology; now, they were awakening to the fact that such laws operate regularly.'

The term 'exception' here is objectionably misleading, inasmuch as one thinks of 'exception' as a statistical notion: exceptions are in the minority, and, except exceptionally, in the small minority. But the exceptions, *alias* irregularities, under discussion here are statistically no small proportion of the whole. Similarly when we were considering Curtius's 1864 proposal, we found that whichever way the rule was stated – whether that PIE *a* became European *a*, or that it became European *e*, or that it became European *o* – the proportion of exceptions was far from insignificant. It is true that Pedersen's usage of the term in this passage is the same as his usage throughout his book and that it is simply the current, standing usage of Neogrammarians; but this merely points up the fact that in Neogrammarian eyes one exception is the same as a thousand. In this respect the Neogrammarians are

adherents of the Stoic philosophy, which denies differences of degree
and among whose 'paradoxes' (cf. Plutarch's treatise 'On the paradoxes
of the Stoics') is that all sins are equal. But I propose to maintain
that this position is both self-defeating for the Neogrammarian and
stultifying for the historian. I abstain in this paper from going into the
import for the Neogrammarians, but speaking as a historian I find the
stultification to lie in the result that it pegs acceptance of the concept
of merger and its congeners, shared innovation and subgrouping, to
acceptance of exceptionlessness, whereas a student might very well
agree that we should set up *e, o,* and *a,* for PIE, unlike all the pre-Neo-
grammarians, and hold that these three distinct phonemes had merged
in Indo-Iranian, without subscribing to the doctrine of exceptionlessness.
Such a student would think of Verner not as explaining exceptions to
Grimm's Lautverschiebung and not even as treating them as merely
apparent exceptions but as virtually treating the Lautverschiebung as a
conditioned, not an unconditioned shift, in which the conditions concern
place of the word-accent.

   Pedersen recognizes two stages: The first stage acknowledges laws, and
the second stage acknowledges that they operate regularly. But what is a
law that doesn't operate regularly? We need a label for it. We could call
it a prevailing, or a tendential law as contrasted with a regular one, but
since the Neogrammarians themselves took up the term 'exceptionlessness', it is wasteful to make the term 'regularity' a mere synonym of it.
I propose, therefore, to take regularity as something more general of
which exceptionlessness is the extreme case, so as to say that if a law is
exceptionless it is a fortiori regular, but it may be regular though not
exceptionless. With this terminology we can conveniently describe the
position of Bopp, for example, that some laws are exceptionless,
such as the law of Greek that every wordfinal prepausal stop consonant is lost, and other laws are merely regular, and the position of
Curtius, that alongside of the sound-changes subject to exceptionless or to regular laws we should also acknowledge merely sporadic
changes.

   Under Pedersen's usage of 'regular', what is a law that is not regular?
He doesn't answer the question in so many words, but I get the impression
that he regards an irregular law as a contradiction in terms. His general
account differs markedly from Delbrück's. Delbrück, as I remarked
earlier, presents the passage from Bopp to the Neogrammarians as the
steady growth of an idea, as it comes to be more and more sweepingly
applied. Pedersen presents the same passage as a change from flashes of

light to steady light, with an added note of exasperation, as though it was by some stubbornness that the earlier students turned away from the light after they had had glimpses of it. His terminology, whereby an irregular law is made to seem a contradiction in terms, encourages his picture, and my alternative terminology encourages the alternative picture given by Delbrück.

This distinction of senses is made even plainer by the next passage that Pedersen quotes, a passage from Brugmann which contrasts the 'history of sounds' with the 'physiology of sounds'. The former gives the phenomena, in particular the sound-laws; the latter gives the explanation. These two contrasts, which Brugmann correlates – history and physiology, phenomena and explanation – correspond respectively to diachronic description and to explanation.

Brugmann's sharp distinction has proved to be well-advised. Today, a hundred years later, next to no progress has been made with explanatory phonetics, whereas the concept of soundlaw, which belongs to descriptive diachronic phonemics, has continued to find fruitful exploitation.

There is a clear sense, then, in which neither Bopp in 1816 nor Brugmann in 1876 made phonetic claims or commitments. But there is another, equally clear sense in which Bopp did not but Brugmann did. Think with Saussure and Hjelmslev of the two faces or planes of the linguistic sign, the plane of expression and the plane of content. All that belongs to the signifiant, to the plane of expression, is phonetic in that broadest sense in which linguistics is divided into phonetics dealing with signifiants, semantics dealing with signifiés, and grammar dealing with the relations between the two. It isn't true that Bopp made no commitments about signifiants, but his claims were far weaker than Brugmann's; to put the point in another way, he was far less ready than Brugmann to recognize facts about signifiants that would militate against this or that diachronic description. The familiar example of his explaining Germanic 'eleven' as 'one-ten' instead of as 'one-left' illustrates this.

The concept of soundlaw (whether with or without exceptions) belongs here, in the plane of expression, and if I pass over it without comment it is not because I regard it as minor – quite the contrary – nor because I have nothing to say about it – again, quite the contrary – but because what I could say about it in brief compass would not appreciably enhance the account that I am in the course of giving, apropos of other topics, of the scientific treatment of language change.

Jespersen says, (1922:66), 'Classicists were no doubt perfectly right when they reproached comparativists for their neglect of syntax, which to them was the most important part of grammar.'[19] I would make two observations here, bearing on the advance of science. First, the closer the comparativists got to Proto-Indoeuropean, the less syntax there was to do, given the lack of hypotaxis, and especially the lack of reconstructible particles. Still, this is not to say that comparativists did all they might have done. But, assuming that their total input of energy, of effort, of time remained constant, if they had given more input to syntax, they would have had less to give to phonology. And I have the impression that, speaking in very broad terms, their preoccupation with phonology was beneficial, was a good thing. If I relabel my impression an hypothesis, and if I raise the question how this hypothesis might be put to rigorous test, I see that the history of linguistics would have to move into a wholly new phase of method to make such a test. All we can say in our present phase is this: that, as judged by the standards of present-day linguistics, the recognition of the phonological component of language was a major insight; that nothing like our present-day recognition came until the period between Bopp (1816) and Brugmann (1876); and that from our present-day vantage-point it does not appear that any major reasonably foreseeable blunder was made, or much time lost, by giving more time (or effort or energy) than it needed. But all these judgments are very much subject to revision.

A distinction was drawn (p. 31) between comparative and historical linguistics. We may reintroduce it in a seemingly backhanded way, by facing a certain terminological question. If historical linguistics considers, say, Latin and French, is it considering one (and the same) languages or two (different) languages? At the bottom of the quandary is a philosophical problem, technically denoted by W. V. Quine's term as the problem of identity-conditions. My article 'What has linguistics done for philosophy?' (Wells 1962) goes into this.

I propose the following as a serviceable though unusual terminology. We will speak of 'language states' and, if A and B would commonly be called different stages or periods of the same language, we will say that A and B are different language-states of the same language. As a language may be diversified over time, so may it be diversified over space, and the terminology of language-states will be applied analogously, so that for example present-day Low German and Swiss-German will be called different language-states of the same language, Present-day German.

---

[19]   Cf. Meillet 463. But note (Schwyzer and Debrunner 1950:2, n. 1) that Philipp Buttmann, no comparatist, also slighted syntax.

It is left open whether finer division into substates is possible, e.g. whether different substates of the language-state Present-day Swiss-German are to be distinguished.

Two different language-states A and B need not belong to the same language (example: Present-day Swiss-German and Present-day Swiss-French), but unless they do, comparative linguists are not ordinarily interested in considering the pair $\{A, B\}$.

This terminology will not solve the problem of identity-conditions, but it will allow us to state it conveniently. Nothing can solve the problem, for it is caused by the discrepancy between two identity-conditions, each very plausible: (1) If A and B are indistinguishable, they are identical; (2) identity is a transitive relation (Wells 1974:437–41). (3) This ineluctable discrepancy leads to such consequences as this: We want to say that French is Latin; we want to say that Italian is Latin; but we don't want to say that French is Italian.

Given the senses in which the two expressions 'historical linguistics' and 'comparative linguistics' are actually used, there are three important differences between historical and comparative linguistics.

Historical linguistics considers, two (or more) at a time, language-states A and B; its data are (1) A, (2) B, and (3) the proposition that A is an ancestor of B (B is a descendant of A). In more ordinary parlance, any two things that historical linguistics considers are assumed to be an earlier and a later state of the same language. Comparative linguistics considers language-states three (or more) at a time, A, B, and C, its data being (1) A, (2) B, distinct from A, and (3) the proposition that A and B have a common ancestor, C, not necessarily distinct from A.[20] (Of course when we allow the possibility that A may be its own ancestor, we must be speaking in the mathematicians' way (Russell 1910–13:1.545, 558; 560 Def. 91.04; Quine 1957:254 top) which says that if x is ancestor or descendant of anything, it is its own ancestor of the zero'th power.) From these data, collectively called its input, it infers output (= quaesitum) C. The data do not include any chronological orderings.

[20] If C is not necessarily distinct from A, the possibility is admitted that C = A. In other words, it is possible to take an ancestor and some descendant as the two inputs of an application of the comparative method. The particular interest of the case is that it can be used as a test of the method, since in it the inferred language-state C should turn out to be identical with one, say A, of the two datum language-states. Hoenigswald has repeatedly drawn attention to this case, (1) Greenberg 1963:25 = 1966:33); (2) in Birnbaum and Puhvel 1966:2–3; (3) in Hymes 1974:352 (middle paragraph); and (4) in his Hoenigswald 1973:4–5 §§1.11–2 and 26 §2.5.

Now the difference between historical and comparative linguistics, as stated above, may be broken up into three parts. (1) Historical linguistics considers language-states two (or more) at a time, comparative linguistics three (or more) at a time. (2) All the language-states that historical linguistics considers are data for it; in each application of comparative linguistics, one of the states it considers is inferred by it, all the others are data for it. (3) It is a datum for historical linguistics, but not for comparative linguistics, that all the language-states it considers are related by ancestry in a single linear chronological series.

The comparative method deals only with the case where one language splits into two. Whether the opposite case occurs, where two languages merge into one, is a question.[21]

Historical and comparative linguistics do not jointly exhaust the possible ways of considering language-states two or more at a time. Besides the obvious possibility of considering A and B without assuming that they are cognate, there is the case, so-called Internal Reconstruction, where one of the two states under consideration functions as datum (input), and the quaesitum (output of the internal-reconstructive inference) B is a state earlier in time than A and ancestral to it. Internal reconstruction resembles comparative linguistics in being inferential, and historical linguistics in considering language-states two at a time.

I am defensive about the fact that my essay has had nothing to say about America, much less about the Linguistic Society of America. In effect its span of attention ends with the advent of Neogrammarianism, half a century before the LSA. It does not even consider every major aspect of linguistic change. What it does do is to to focus on one particular method of dealing with linguistic change and to consider the bearing of this method on the question, In what way is linguistics scientific? And it is able to do something, though much more remains to be done, towards undermining Thomas Kuhn's account of change by revolution in science.

Yale University

---

[21] Whitney maintained, against Renan and Max Müller, that it does not occur; but Rosane Rocher has pointed out (orally) that Lepsius's *Nubische Grammatik* of 1880 caused him to change his mind. Schuchardt's studies came mostly after Whitney's death. Interest in pidgins and creoles has burgeoned in recent years, after decades of almost solitary work by R. Hall, J. E. Reinecke, and D. Taylor, and the hypothesis that many dead languages that had not previously been recognized as creoles actually were creoles (in a very wide sense, to be sure) is giving a new direction to present-day scientific studies of language change.

REFERENCES

Aarsleff, Hans 1967. *The study of language in England*, 1780–1860. Princeton University Press.

— 1969. 'The study and use of etymology in Leibniz,' in Kurt Müller and Wilhelm Totok (eds.), *Studia Leibnitiana. Supplementa* 3:173–89.

Arens, Hans 1955. *Sprachwissenschaft*. Freiburg and Munich, Karl Alber.

— 1969. Second edition of the same; same place and publisher.

Bacon, Francis 1620. *Novum organum*. London, John Bill.

Benfey, Theodor 1869. *Geschichte der Sprachwissenschaft in Deutschland*. Munich, Cotta.

Birnbaum, Henrik and Jaan Puhvel (eds.) 1966. *Ancient Indo-European dialects*. Berkeley and Los Angeles, University of California Press.

Bloomfield, Leonard 1927. 'On recent work in general linguistics,' *Modern Philology* 25:211–30.

— 1933. *Language*. New York, Holt.

Boas, Franz 1896. 'The limitations of the comparative method of anthropology,' *Science* 4:901–8; reprinted in Boas 1940:270–80.

— 1940. *Race, language, and culture*. New York, Macmillan.

Bryant, Jacob 1774. *Ancient mythology*. London, T. Payne.

Burke, Kenneth 1935. *Permanence and change*. New York, New Republic.

Burrow, Thomas, and Murray B. Emeneau 1961. *A Dravidian etymological dictionary*. London, Oxford University Press.

Caldwell, Robert 1856. *A comparative grammar of the Dravidian or South Indian family of languages*. London, Harrison.

Cardona, George; Henry M. Hoenigswald; and Alfred Senn (eds.) 1970. *Indo-European and Indo-Europeans*. Philadelphia, University of Pennsylvania Press.

Cassirer, Ernst 1950. *The problem of knowledge*. New Haven, Yale University Press.

Cuvier, Georges 1817. *Le règne animal*. Paris, Deterville.

Davidson, E. F. 1933. *Edward Hincks*. London, Oxford University Press.

Davies, Edward 1804. *Celtic researches*. London, John Booth.

Delbrück, Berthold 1880. *Einleitung in das Sprachstudium*. Leipzig, Breitkopf und Härtel.

Diderichsen, Paul 1974. 'The foundation of comparative linguistics', in Hymes 1974:277–306.

Doblhofer, Ernst 1961. *Voices in stone*. New York, Viking Press.

Dorn. Bernhard 1827. *Ueber die Verwandtschaft des Persischen* . . . Hamburg, Meissner.

Firth, John Rupert 1957. *Papers in linguistics*. London, Oxford University Press.

Frye, Northrop 1947. *Fearful symmetry*. Boston, Beacon Press.

Gabelentz, Georg von der 1888. 'Pott,' reprinted in Sebeok 1966:1:251–61.

Grimm, Jacob 1822. *Deutsche Grammatik* (First volume, second edition). Göttingen, Dieterich.

Gulya, Janos 1974. 'Some eighteenth century antecedents of nineteenth century linguistics: The discovery of Finno-Ugrian,' in Hymes 1974:258–76.

Harris, Marvin 1968. *The rise of anthropological theory*. New York, Crowell.

Hegel, Georg Wilhelm Friedrich 1840. *Enzyklopädie* . . . *Erster Teil. Die Wissenschaft der Logik*. Herausgegeben von Leopold von Henning. [This was published as Volume 6 in the edition of Hegel's *Werke* put out by the Verein von Freunden des Verewigten. It is reprinted in Volume 8 (1970) of the twenty-volume edition published in Frankfurt am Main by Suhrkamp. Henning's account of the 'Zusätze' that he incorporated into his edition is conveniently summarized in Volume 10 pp. 424–25 of the Suhrkamp edition. The three editions (1817, 1827, 1830) that Hegel published do not contain the Zusätze.]

Hoenigswald, Henry M. 1963. 'On the history of the comparative method,' *Anthropological Linguistics* 5:1:1–11.

— 1966. 'Are there universals of linguistic change?,' in Joseph Greenberg (ed.) *Universals of language* (Second edition) 30–52. Cambridge, Mass. and London, M.I.T. Press.

— 1966a. 'Criteria for the subgrouping of languages,' in Birnbaum and Puhvel 1966:1–12.

— 1973. *Studies in formal historical linguistics*. Dordrecht, Reidel.

— 1974. 'Fallacies in the history of linguistics,' in Hymes 1974:346–58.

Hymes, Dell (ed.) 1974. *Studies in the history of linguistics*. Bloomington and London, Indiana University Press.

Jespersen, Otto 1922. *Language*. London, Allen and Unwin.

— 1933 *Linguistica*. Copenhagen, Levin and Munksgaard.

Kant, Immanuel 1781. *ritik der reinen Vernunft*. Riga, Hartknoch. (Second edition, 1787, same place and publisher.)

— 1790. *Kritik der Urteilskraft*. Berlin and Libau, Lagarde und Friederich.

Kiparsky, Paul 1974. 'From paleogrammarians to neogrammarians,' in Hymes 1974:331–45.

Kuhn, Thomas S. 1962. *The structure of scientific revolutions*. University of Chicago Press. (Second edition, 1970, same place and publisher).

Lehmann, Winfrid P. (ed.) 1967. *A reader in nineteenth-century historical Indo-European linguistics*. Bloomington and London, Indiana University Press.

Lévi-Strauss, C.; R. Jakobson; C. F. Voegelin; and T. A. Sebeok (eds.) 1953. *Results of the conference*. (Supplement to *International Journal of American Linguistics*, Volume 19, Number 2, April 1953; also issued as *Indiana University Publications in Anthropology and Linguistics*, Memoir 8.) Baltimore, Waverly Press.

Maher, John P. 1966. 'More on the history of the comparative method: The tradition of Darwinism in August Schleicher's work,' *Anthropological linguistics* 8:3:2:1–12.

Malkiel, Yakov 1968. *Essays on linguistic themes*. Berkeley and Los Angeles, University of California Press.

— 1974. 'Friedrich Diez's debt to pre-1800 linguistics,' in Hymes 1974:315–30.

Mayr, Ernst; E. G. Linsley; and R. L. Usinger 1953. *Methods and principles of systematic zoology*. New York, McGraw, Hill.

Meillet, Antoine 1923. 'Renan linguiste', *Journal de psychologie* 20:331–34; reprinted in Meillet 1936:169–73.

— 1936. *Linguistique historique et linguistique générale*, Volume 2 Paris, Champion.

— 1937. *Introduction a l'étude comparative des langues indo-européennes*. (Eighth, posthumous edition.) Paris, Hachette.

Metcalf, George J. 1974. 'The Indo-European hypothesis in the sixteenth and seventeenth centuries,' in Hymes 1974:233–57.

Müller, F. Max 1864. *Lectures on the science of language. Second Series*. London, Longmans. [Subsequent British editions differ a good deal from the first in pagination; moreover, each British edition was soon matched by an American edition (New York, Appleton), again with different pagination.]

Nordenskiöld, Erik 1936. *The history of biology*. New York, Tudor.

Oertel, Hanns 1901. *Lectures on the study of language*. New York, Scribner.

Pallis, S. A. 1954. *Early exploration in Mesopotamia*. Copenhagen, Munksgaard.

Pedersen, Holger 1931. *Linguistic science in the nineteenth century*. (Translated by John W. Spargo.) Cambridge, Mass., Harvard University Press. [Reprinted 1962 as *The discovery of language*, Bloomington and London, Indiana University Press.]

Pisani, Vittore 1951. 'Studi sulla fonetica dell'armeno. III. . .,' *Ricerche linguistiche* 2:52–62.

Popper, Karl 1959. *The logic of scientific discovery*. London, Hutchinson.

Pott, August Friedrich 1833. *Etymologische Forschungen* . . . Lemgo, Meyersche Hofbuchhandlung. 2 volumes, 1833 and 1836. Second edition, 6 volumes, 1859–76.

Quine, Willard V. 1940. *Mathematical logic*. Cambridge, Mass., Harvard University Press.

Schleicher, August 1869. *Die deutsche Sprache.* (Second edition, edited by Johannes Schmidt.) Stuttgart, Cotta.

Schlegel, Friedrich 1808. *Über Die Sprache und Weisheit der Indier.* Heidelberg, Mohr and Zimmer.

Schwyzer, Eduard, and Albert Debrunner 1950. *Griechische Grammatik,* Volume 2. Munich, C. H. Beck.

Sebeok, Thomas A. (ed.) 1966. *Portraits of linguists.* (Two volumes.) Bloomington and London, Indiana University Press.

Streitberg, Wilhelm 1915. 'Persisch und Deutsch,' *Indogermanische Forschungen* 35:182–86.

Sullivan, William Kirby 1858. 'On the influence which the physical geography . . . etc. . . . exert upon the languages . . . of mankind . . .,' *The Atlantis. A register of literature and science. Conducted by members of the Catholic University of Ireland* (London, Longmans, Dublin: Fowler) 1:1:50–128 (January 1858) and 2:3:125–200 (January 1859).

Sweet, Henry 1913. *Collected papers.* Oxford, Clarendon.

Verburg, Pieter A. 1950. 'The background to the linguistic conceptions of Franz Bopp,' reprinted in Sebeok 1966:1:221–50.

Wells, Rulon S. 1949. 'Automatic alternation,' *Language* 25:99–116.

— 1962. 'What has linguistics done for philosophy?,' *Journal of Philosophy* 59:697–708.

— 1973. 'Uniformitarianism in linguistics,' in Wiener 1973:4:423–31.

— 1974. 'Phonemics in the nineteenth century,' in Hymes 1974:434–53.

Whitehead, Alfred North, and Bertrand Russell 1910. *Principia mathematica.* Volume I. Cambridge University Press.

Whitney, William D. 1867. *Language and the study of language.* New York, Scribner.

— 1889. *A Sanskrit grammar.* Second edition. Leipzig, Breitkopf and Härtel.

Wiener, Philip P. (editor) 1973). *Dictionary of the history of ideas.* (Five volumes.) New York, Scribner.

Windisch, Ernst 1886. 'Georg Curtius,' reprinted in Sebeok 1966:1:311–73.

Winter, Werner (editor) 1965. *Evidence for laryngeals.* The Hague, Mouton.

Wisdom, John 1938. 'Metaphysics and verification'; *Mind* 47:452–98, reprinted in Wisdom 1953:51–101.

— 1953. *Philosophy and psycho-analysis.* Oxford, Blackwell.

BRÉAL vs. SCHLEICHER: LINGUISTICS AND PHILOLOGY DURING THE LATTER HALF OF THE NINETEENTH CENTURY

HANS AARSLEFF

The papers of Professors Wells and Rocher deal with two major figures in the study of language. Bopp laid the foundations of comparative and historical philology and thus of the discipline that was one of the great scholarly creations of the nineteenth century. It has been called the first scientific model for the study of language and seen as the origin and archetype of all later linguistic study. Whitney worked within that tradition, but he also became its critic. Professor Wells has given a perspicacious conceptual analysis of some crucial features that reveal Bopp's accomplishment. To borrow a term from recent work in the history of science, this paper is a good example of the 'internal' history of a subject; it shows how the sharpening of method and technique advances the objectivity of knowledge, its 'timelessness', so to speak. Professor Rocher explores Whitney's debt to his German teachers, including Bopp and Weber with whom Michel Bréal a few years later also studied at Berlin during the 1850's. Her study examines biography, personal relationships, and influence to show how German scholarship was brought to this country and given a place in academic teaching and research. With their different approaches, the two papers illustrate the fruitful work that can be done by concentrating on particular aspects of the German philological tradition that was launched by Bopp in 1816. Whitney often observed that Germany was the home of language study. Owing to its great prestige, philology gained a prominent place in the universities, during the early decades until about 1840 at the expense of natural science which had to make its way against the prestige of Naturphilosophie. This philosophy was the close relative of philology, both being expressions of Romantic thought and aspirations. Thanks largely to Wilhelm von Humboldt's philosophy and educational reforms both in secondary and higher education, philology gained recognition and regular academic chairs in at least a dozen universities. This institutionalization insured advances, but ultimately also caused rigidity, insensitivity, and even hostility to innovation. The radical innovation that occurred during the later decades of the nineteenth century did not occur in Germany, where the new developments, though important, stayed closer to accepted institutional forms.

THE PROBLEM

It is this innovative reaction that I wish to examine. Where and when did it first appear? Who spoke for it? Who were the targets of the critique? What were its sources? What principles did it adopt? Needless to say, given the limitations of space and time, this can only be a sketch, but it seems worth doing in order to question what would appear to be the widely held though unexamined assumption that all later study of language has been spun out of the Bopp tradition. I propose in other words to deal with the subject suggested by Whitney's critique of the tradition.

The problem is obvious. If it is argued that with Bopp the study of language was somehow transformed and codified, then we are left with the consequence that the domain of language study has been severely diminished. But if we take history seriously, this is not a satisfactory solution. Both before and after the dominance of the Bopp tradition, the study of language has covered a much wider territory, a fact that cannot be ignored except by making a number of ad-hoc decisions, e.g., that only with Bopp did the study of language become 'scientific,' a claim that has been repeated in the 1930's with exclusive reference to Bloom-field's *Language*; or that Bopp was the first to study language for its own sake, as if motivation (whether imputed or real, if determinable at all) were sufficient to establish legitimacy – on that principle many figures have no place in the history of science, e.g., Copernicus, Brahe, Kepler, Mersenne, Boyle, Newton, and Linnaeus.[1] Among the sources of this self-serving distortion, the most prominent is respect for a historio-graphical tradition that was ideologically designed to celebrate the Bopp tradition and its institutional status; this respect is sustained by a

---

[1]   Koerner 1972a:216 says: 'Bopp's work is surely the first important step towards the positivistic attitude which attempts to study language for language's sake (and not in order to gain insight into the culture, philosophy and literature of earlier periods of mankind), a trend which became very powerful during the last decades of the nineteenth century.' This statement is typical of the sort of ad-hoc myth by which the conventional history is maintained.

positivist view of natural science that was cogently criticized even in the nineteenth century. The matter reached absurdity in the 1860's when it was dogmatically claimed that language was a natural organism with its own life and laws independent of speakers, and that as a consequence the study of language was – or ought to be – a natural science.

It was at this point that the reaction set in. In 'Schleicher and the physical theory of language' (1871), Whitney wrote that Schleicher's 'deserved reputation as a philologist . . . gives a dangerous importance to his opinions as a . . . student of the theory and philosophy of language. There is, unfortunately, no necessary connection between eminence in one of these characters and in the other' (299). Whitney was making the now familiar distinction between philology and linguistics.[2] The occasion for the reaction was chiefly Schleicher's two pieces (1863, 1865) on what he took to be the implications of Darwin's recently published *Origin of species* for the study of language. It is surely to put our own intelligence and judgment on a very low level not to recognize the embarrassing, inconsistent, and even offensive nonsense stated in these pieces. Take, for instance, this passage, with its obvious racist implications: 'So wie wir nun wahrnehmen können, dass gewisse Völker, so die Indianerstämme Nordamerikas, schon ihrer unendlich complicierten und in Formen wahrhaft wuchernden Sprachen wegen für das geschichtliche Leben ungeeignet sind und deshalb nunmehr einer Rückbildung, ja dem Untergange verfallen, so dürften sich auch höchst wahrscheinlich nicht alle auf dem Wege zur Menschwerdung begriffenen Organismen bis zur Sprachbildung hinauf entwickelt haben.' This is on the level of the most vulgar journalistic readings of Darwin. The previous page has this remarkable statement: 'Die Sprachen, welche wir jetzt sprechen, sind, wie alle Sprachen geschichtlich bedeutender Völker, senile Sprachexemplare' (1865:27).[3]

---

[2] In Whitney 1867, this distinction was intimated but not made explicit, e.g. p. 241, and in the subtitle 'Twelve lectures on the principles of linguistic science,' though the substance of the book went beyond mere philology. Whitney 1875a:315 stated the distinction; the comparative method 'is insufficient as applied to the whole study – the science of language.' On the distinction, cp. Hjelmslev 1937:10.

[3] Maher 1966 argues that the 'tale' of Schleicher's Darwinism is 'wholly apocryphal,' but this goes against the plain dictionary meaning of Darwinism and Darwinian, the latter meaning a follower of Darwin as the term was used soon after 1859 of dozens of figures by themselves or others, even though what they claimed had little or no basis in an understanding of the *Origin of species*. Schleicher's two pieces protest emphatic adherence to what he took to be Darwinism, though he had of course earlier, like others, treated language study as a natural science. Even on the criteria for Darwinism that Maher accepts (p. 2 in quotation from Wellek), Schleicher fits, e.g., by his commitment (1863:4–5) to 'Kampf ums

THE 1890's

By the 1890's the reaction was evident; it will therefore be useful to look at a few examples that point both forward and backward. They show that the reaction and the innovation were designed to overcome Schleicher and the tradition he stood for. During this decade, Saussure wrote some well-known notes that spoke critically of the German tradition and its final embodiment in 'Schleicher's laughable attempt that collapses under its own ridiculousness'; Schleicher was a 'complete mediocrity, which does not exclude pretensions.' By contrast Saussure wrote, citing Whitney's words, '"language is a human institution." That changed the axis of linguistics.' The linguistic sign is arbitrary: *cow, vacca*, and *vache* can all mean the same thing.[4] The credit and the criticism are clearly assigned to Whitney and Schleicher, neither of them French and both then dead. It is useful to bear in mind that credit and blame that is fixed on distant and dead figures, may have their aim closer to home. Thus in the 1890's the *Revue de linguistique* held closely to the Schleicher line, consistently criticizing the men who, like Bréal and Meillet, were associated with the Société de linguistique de Paris and its publications. A good example of such strategic displacement, as it may perhaps be called, is the nineteenth-century critique of Locke and the eighteenth century which was in fact aimed at the contemporary utilitarian philosophy.[5]

During the same decade Bréal published his *Essai de sémantique*

Dasein,' that is 'the struggle for existence,' which is the title of the chapter in which Darwin, with mention of Malthus, introduces the concept of natural selection. As will be seen below, the reaction against the F. Schlegel-Schleicher doctrines was also a reaction against its racism. There is relevant material in Poliakov 1971.

[4] Some of Saussure's notes will be found in Jakobson 1971. For the original, see Godel 1954, esp. pp. 59–60.

[5] See, e.g., the opening words of Hovelacque 1877: what marks modern linguistics is that it has recognized and proclaimed 'qu'il existait une *vie du langage*; que chaque langue passait inévitablement par telles ou telles périodes biologiques; en autres termes, qu'elle partageait le sort commun à tous les organismes, à toutes les fonctions naturelles. La vérité de ce fait éclate aux yeux de tout observateur.' Cf. Whitney's review of Hovelacque 1876: 'It has far too much of fact and too little of inference and reasoning for a manual of science . . . His main authority is Schleicher, than whom a more untrustworthy guide in these matters could not well be found; and he adopts and puts nakedly forward, without any attempt to establish or to refute the reasoning by which they have been repeatedly overthrown, such dogmas as that the study of language is a natural and not a historical science; that languages are born, grow, decay, and die, like all living creatures' (Whitney, 1876). On a widely held view of Locke during the nineteenth century, see Aarsleff 1971, which also has information about Victor Cousin and his critique of the eighteenth century.

(1897), which, as he and others made clear, dealt with a subject that had occupied him for thirty years, e.g., his early essays (1866b, 1868b).[6] Bréal studied, he said, 'les causes intellectuelles qui ont présidé à la transformation de nos langues' (5); he wished his study to say something about the language now spoken and to have general utility – like Jespersen, Bréal was deeply involved in problems of language teaching and generally in educational reform. Bréal argued against Schleicher's doctrines of organicism and the decay of language, against these habits of thought, 'qu'on aurait plutôt attendues chez quelque disciple de l'école mystique,' by which he meant Herder and German romanticism. He rejected anthropomorphism and the abuse of metaphor that gave literal sense to such locutions as the birth, struggle, propagation, and death of words and languages (4). He studied language in its social dimension, as a means of communication, constantly being shaped by its speakers. Near the end of the *Essai* he revealed where his own sympathies lay; speaking against organicism once more and the philologists who declared that man counts for nothing in the development of language, he wished to be done with this phantasmagoria: 'Nos pères de l'école de Condillac, ces idéologues qui ont servi de cible, pendant cinquante ans, à une certaine critique, étaient plus près de la vérité quand ils disaient, selon leur manière simple et honnête, que les mots sont des signes . . . ils n'ont pas plus d'existence que les gestes du télégraphe aérien' (277). In a favorable review, Meillet observed that Bréal's book was 'l'un des rares livres de linguistique qui présentent un intérêt immédiat pour la sociologie' (Meillet 1903–04:640; cf. Meillet 1898). In his obituary of Bréal, Meillet said that everything in the *Essai* 'est raisonnable et intelligible; l'éspèce de mysticisme latent qui subsiste du fait que la linguistique historique s'est developpé au milieu de l'époque romantique en est entièrement banni' (1916a:17). Meillet also said on at least two occassions that 'M. Bréal et Ferdinand de Saussure ont été les deux maîtres qui ont donné à l'école française de grammaire comparée un caractère propre' (1915:120). Finally, again with references to the *Essai*

---

[6] See Bréal's own remarks 1897:6–7. The word 'sémantique' was introduced by Bréal in 1883 '. . . comme cette étude . . . mérite d'avoir son nom, nous l'appelerons la SÉMANTIQUE . . . c'est-à-dire la science des significations' (1883:133). The term was already in common use, that is without explication, in the late 1880's, e.g., by Gaston Paris and Victor Henry. The *Revue de linguistique et de philologie comparée* carried a very unfavorable review by Paul Renaud, saying that Bréal's *Essai* 'fait penser à la *Pluralité des mondes* mise au point, quant à forme, par une émule de Renan, et c'est tout dire.' The same review also argued against Bréal's critique of organicism and 'the life of language' (Renaud 1898). Renan referred to Bréal as 'my friend and colleague,' but Bréal criticized Renan's linguistic philosophy, as will be seen below.

and Bréal's semantic studies, Meillet stressed Bréal's rationalism (1930: 227).[7]

Among the representative works of the 1890's is also Jespersen's *Progress in language* (1894) which by its very title announced its opposition to Schleicher's doctrine of linguistic decay.[8] Jespersen concluded: 'On every point our investigation has led us to scepticism with regard to the system of the old school of philology' (126). Exposing the comic inconsistencies of Schleicher's discourse, Jespersen rejected the dogma that linguistics is a natural science, by contrast taking for his guide 'an idea expressed long ago and with considerable emphasis by Wilhelm von Humboldt, that language means speaking, and that speaking means action on the part of a human being to make himself understood by somebody else.' The virtue of a language is measured by its efficiency, that is, its ability to accomplish 'much with little means, or, in other words . . . to express the greatest amount of meaning with the simplest mechanism' (12–13). Schleicher had contrasted the Gothic *habaidêdeima* with English *had* to show how 'our words, as contrasted with Gothic words, are like a statue that has been rolling for a long time in the bed of a river till its beautiful limbs have been worn off, so that now scarcely anything remains but a polished stone cylinder with faint indications of what once it was' (11).[9] Jespersen drew the opposite conclusion, citing all fifteen forms of the Gothic for 'had' against the single English form – and in so doing he not only opposed Schleicher but repeated both example and argument from Bréal's "De la forme et de la fonction des mots" (1866).

---

[7]   The first two editions of the *Essai* (1897, 1899) contained two supplementary essays, to which two more were added in the 3rd ed. (1904), one of which is entitled 'La linguistique est-elle une science naturelle?' Here (pp. 312–314) Bréal again criticized 'la théorie mystique,' which he had already identified in 1866a:viii, xxiiif. In this context he made one of his not infrequent remarks about the racist implications: 'On imaginait un passé lointain qu'on décorait de toutes sortes de qualités dont les temps nouveaux étaient devenus incapables . . . Ce qui se trouvait au fond de toutes ces spéculations, c'était le dédain et le mépris de la raison. Un certain orgueil de caste s'y mêlait aussi: l'idée de races privilégées, parmi lesquelles on n'oubliait pas de se placer, ne pouvait déplaire. Ce côté personnel se montre dans l'expression *indo-germanique*, créée pour désigner l'une des grandes familles d'idiomes.' Bréal was born in 1832 of French-Jewish parents at Landau in what was then the Bavarian Rhineland; during the reaction following the coup d'état in 1852, he was one of several Jewish students excluded from the École normale. See Gerbod 1965:333.
[8]   Jespersen 1894 is, as the author says (*ibid.*, p. v), 'to a certain extent an English translation of' Jespersen 1891, which also makes reference to Bréal.
[9]   This passage is cited from the beginning of the second chapter in Schleicher 1869:34. Jespersen also cited 'Schleicher's opinion that English shows "how rapidly the language of a nation important both in history and literature can sink"' (15).

Bréal's early essay reads like a blueprint for Jespersen's *Progress*. Reading Bopp and Schleicher, said Bréal, 'on pourrait croire qu'en vérité on lit un traité de géologie du monde ou qu'on assiste à une série de cristallisations de la parole.' He respected 'cette méthode purement expérimentale qui a donné les résultats dont s'engorgueillit la linguistique moderne.' He immediately proceeded, however, to state the qualification that reveals his own orientation: "Mais faut-il croire que la science que nous étudions consiste uniquement dans cette observation extérieure des formes du language?. ... Nous ne le supposons point. Il ne faut pas que la description du langage humain nous fasse oublier l'homme, qui en est à la fois le principe et la fin, puisque tout, dans le langage, procède de lui et s'adresse à lui" (249). The science of language must study both the forms and functions of words. It must include what he later called 'sémantique,' i.e., "la signification des mots" (243). The mere empirical observation of forms is insufficient, for "elle nous laisserait ignorer la cause première de la transformation des langues, qui n'est pas fournie par l'analyse des mots, mais qu'il faut chercher en nous-mêmes" (257). The principle that the history of language follows is not its own, "elle marche toujours d'un pas égal, sinon avec l'histoire politique, du moins avec l'histoire intellectuelle et sociale du peuple" (264).

Bréal's concentration on the social and communicative dimension of language is already prominent in his earliest writings before he could have read Whitney. Citing Humboldt, he agreed with Jespersen that, 'il n'y a pas de langage en dehors de nous: mêmes gravées sur la pierre ou sur l'airain, a dit Guillaume de Humboldt, les langues n'ont qu'une existence idéale. Les mots n'existent qu'au moment où nous les pensons et les comprenons' (265). Consequently he did not admit any necessary connection between the decadence of words and that of thought; words may retain their function in spite of 'mutilations,' as illustrated by the forms *habere* and *avoir*. They can also cut themselves loose from their etymological meanings, which thus are not the final criterion if we wish to understand the language we speak now – and that was Bréal's chief interest. He was therefore also committed to the uniformitarian doctrine that the creation of idioms, i.e. languages, did not occur merely at the point of origin (as, e.g., Max Müller felt compelled to argue by his postulate of an initial, never-repeated linguistic miracle): 'Nous les créons à tout moment, car tous les changements qui les affectent sont notre oeuvre' (265). Bréal shared Whitney's and Jespersen's interest in the problem of the origin of language as a legitimate question for linguistic scholars; he was committed to the characteristic eighteenth-century doctrine of the continuing creation of language. It is not surprising that Bréal and Jespersen cited each other, and that both Bréal and Victor Henry in reviews gave high praise to Jespersen's book.[10] Bréal referred to Jespersen on the unnecessary luxury of a redundant multiplicity of endings. Jespersen credited this observation to J. N. Madvig who as early as 1836, in one of his first critiques of German philology, had written: "Diese ganze Entfaltung von Formen am Prädikat und Attribut ist (– ich wage es kaum die ketzerische Wahrheit zu sagen –) eine luxuriöse Verzierung, enstanden aus der Unbehülflich-keit der jungen Sprache, aus ihrem Streben nach Deutlichkeit bei noch nicht festen und klaren Normen oder aus ihrer kindlichen wieder-holenden Umständlichkeit" (1971:66 [28]).[11] Jespersen's book is one long illustration of Madvig's admiration for the "praise-worthy simplicity of English," a point Madvig first made in the context of rejecting F. Schlegel's and K. F. Becker's organicism; caught in this prejudice, said Madvig, these linguists 'werden inconsequent, wenn ihnen die englische, in ihren Formen so überaus einfache Sprache begegnet; weder dass das Volk, welches sie benutzt, eine reiche und lebendige Anschauung hat, lässt sich läugnen, noch dass sie Kraft und klare Fülle entwickeln und die tiefsinnigsten Gedanken auszudrücken vermag' (1971:50, 65–66 [6, 26–28]; 1836; Jespersen 1894:32–35). It is striking evidence of the tradition linking Schlegel and Schleicher that Madvig so early fixed the same critique on the former that a generation later was aimed at the latter. Madvig, Bréal, and Jespersen all saw this link. It is brought out by the example of Chinese; to Schlegel it was a language governed by purely exterior and mechanical rules as opposed to the mysterious organic perfection of early Indo-European; Jespersen reversed these relations.[12]

Citing a few prominent examples, I have tried to show that during the 1890's it became evident on all sides that the study of language was being transformed. Saussure, Jespersen, and Meillet stated the principles

---

[10]   Bréal 1896; Henry 1894, 1896:15. Jespersen referred to Bréal 1876 as a 'sober critical article' (1894:114).
[11]   The figure in square brackets is the page reference to Madvig 1875. The date is that of the year of the Danish text. I have not had access to the Danish text of Madvig's essays. Bréal 1897:25 refers to Jespersen 1894:33–36. It is curious that Bréal echoes Madvig on a point that I don't see in Jespersen: 'Le langage s'est dépouillé de ce luxe un peu enfantin.'
[12]   See esp. Jespersen 1894:80–111. In various ways, Chinese has been a sort of linguistic test case since at least the seventeenth century, e.g., in Leibniz.

which they continued to argue and develop; Saussure in the *Cours*, Jespersen in subsequent writings (for instance in *Language* (1922) which verbatim includes whole passages of *Progress*), and Meillet by his well-known commitment to the sociological aspects of language and its study. Bréal's *Essai de sémantique* was often re-issued. The reaction against the German tradition was triggered by Schleicher and continued to be aimed at his French devotees. The central principle of this innovation held that language does not have independent existence as a product of nature, but is the expression of human activity. It is an institution, its function is communication, its being is social, and the linguistic sign is arbitrary. Since historical study cannot take account of these factors, it provides an insufficient basis for the understanding of the system or structure of language at any given moment. Disengagement from history means interest in the present state of language. Owing to Saussure's teaching during the Paris years, the distinction between diachronic and synchronic study was taking shape. 'Les linguistes, on le sait,' said Meillet, 'étudient le langage à deux points de vues; tantôt ils observent et décrivent l'état d'une langue à un moment donné; et tantôt ils suivent les transformations d'une langue aux diverses périodes successives de son histoire' (1900–01:597).[13] Bréal, Whitney, and Jespersen took a

---

[13]   In the same review, Meillet stated his sociological view: 'Le langage est une institution sociale dont les conditions d'existence et de développement ne sauraient être conçues qu'à un point de vue sociologique' (598), already advanced in one of his earlier publications: 'De tous les faits sociaux, le langage est sans doute le premier qui est été étudié scientifique-ment' (opening words of Meillet 1893). Meillet took credit for this view; Bréal, he said, 'voyait nettement qu'une langue était l'organe d'une société . . . Mais il n'aurait pas dit volontiers, comme je l'ai fait le jour où je lui ai succédé, et comme l'a dit à Genève, dans son cours de linguistique générale, F. de Saussure, que le langage est un fait social' (1930: 226). Meillet credited the synchronic, diachronic distinction to Saussure, who 'voulait surtout bien marquer le contraste entre deux manières de considérer les faits linguistiques: l'étude de la langue à un moment donné, et l'étude du développement linguistique à travers le temps' (1913–14:183). Meillet saw the *Cours* as representing Saussure's teaching in Paris: 'Je n'ai jamais entendu le cours de F. de Saussure sur la linguistique générale. Mais la pensée de F. de Saussure s'était fixée très tôt, on le sait. Les doctrines qu'il a enseignées explicitement dans ces cours de linguistique générale sont celles dont s'inspirait déjà l'enseignement de grammaire comparée qu'il a donné vingt ans plus tôt à l'École des Hautes Études, et que j'ai reçu. Je les retrouve telles qu'il était souvent possible de les deviner' (1916b:33). Cf. Mauss 1900: 'La langue d'une société n'est autre chose qu'un phénomène social' (141). The interest in the social aspect of language had political implica-tions; see, e.g., this passage in Worms 1894 about James Darmesteter: 'Il fut de ceux qui encouragèrent les étudiants à "se tourner vers le peuple," à fraterniser avec les ouvriers, à se consacrer aux oeuvres d'éducation populaire et de sagace bienfaisance sociale.' Cp. Mauss 1937.

genuine interest in the problem of the origin of language. Here as in
other respects, the reaction against the romantic tradition meant a
revival of the classical eighteenth-century philosophy of language.

MADVIG

The reaction and the new orientation that showed so clearly in the
1890's were not new. The first articulate and consistent critic was
J. N. Madvig, who between 1832 and 1881 published a number of essays
in Danish devoted to general linguistics or to what Charles Thurot in a
review called 'grammaire générale' (Thurot 1875:16).[14] In 1842
Madvig gave this summary of his linguistic theory: language is 'in ihrem
Ursprunge ein Produkt der durch den Trieb der Darstellung und
Mittheilung hervorgerufenen Thätigkeit in Verbindung lebender
Menschen ... [Sie ist] ein in artikulirtem Laute ausgeprägtes, in allen
Theilen zusammenhängendes und gegenseitig bedingtes System von
Zeichen für Vorstellungen und ihrer Verbindungsverhältnisse, die durch
die Anerkennung und Sanktion der an der Sprache Theilnehmenden
gelten und nur in dieser Anerkennung und durch sie Bedeutung haben.'
To this he joined the uniformitarian principle, 'dass der Akt der
Sprachbildung kein anderer war als derjenige, wodurch die wirkliche,
jetzt existierende Sprache als verständliches und freies Mittel der
Mittheilung hervorgebracht ward; der Ursprung der Sprache kann
nicht dem Dasein und Leben der Sprache, ihrer Existenzform wider-
sprechen' (1971:86 [55–56]).[15] Madvig therefore ridiculed the notion of
the decadence and decline of language (e.g., 1971:240 [267–68]; 1856–57).
The linguistic sign is arbitrary, 'der Laut der Wörter steht also in keinem
natürlichen und nothwendigen Verhältniss zur Vorstellung und ihrem
Gegenstand' (1971:89 [59]; 1842). Language is the work of man, created
to serve the social needs of communication. As early as 1841, he had
blamed 'à Bopp et à son école d'oublier que le langage tout formé est
l'essentiel et que la véritable valeur d'un mot n'est pas dans son origine,
mais dans ce qu'il est devenu pour ceux qui parlaient et écrivaient la

---

[14]   Before Madvig 1875, only Madvig 1843 (from a Danish text 1841) had appeared in
German.
[15]   It is generally believed that the uniformitarian principle, when it makes its appearance
in the study of language, had been suggested by Lyell's writings on geology. But Madvig's
use of this principle in 1842 was almost certainly independent of Lyell. I say more about
uniformitarianism below.

langue,' a point he often stressed, thus coming close to making the distinction between diachronic and synchronic study (Thurot 1870: 381).[16]

Madvig saw comparative philology as an auxiliary discipline to history. He rejected the notion of organicism as mere metaphor, both generally and with references to F. Schlegel: 'Die Verkehrtheit der anderen Richtung zeigt sich in der unklaren und nebelhaften Vorstellung und Rede von der Sprache als einem selbstständigen, ich weiss nicht wie erschaffenen, sich selbst fortbildenden Organismus, indem man vergisst, dass auch die kleinste Modifikation des Gebrauchs eines einzigen Worts einer besonderen Sprache durch ein menschliches Individ angefangen, durch andere fortgesetzt und festgestellt ward' (1971:88 [58–59]; 1842).[17] Consistent with the doctrine of institution and the arbitrariness of the sign, he sarcastically rejected the notion of sound symbolism as a piece of mysticism (1971:89–92 [59–63]). He maintained that words take their origin in concrete, sensible things: 'Dass alle Sprachbildung von der Bezeichnung sinnlicher Vorstellungen ausgeht, ist . . . ein Satz, der schlechthin aus der Natur der Sprache und der nothwendigen Weise ihres

---

[16] Thurot is quoting from Madvig 1843:17; Madvig 1971:327–36 has only excerpts from this essay. Cp. Madvig. 'Keine historisch-etymologische Forschung kann die systematische, verstandesmässige Darstellung des Gebrauchs der Formen ersetzen, die, wenn sie einen wahren Inhalt geben soll, tüchtiges Abstraktionsvermögen und logische Klarheit erheischt' (1971:203[216]; 1856–57). Cp. also this passage from M. Cl. Gertz's detailed lecture notes (1866): 'Die Bedeutung der komparativen Sprachforschung ist also von wesentlicher Art; aber man darf nicht vergessen, dass alles rechte Sprachstudium einer einzelnen Sprache auf eine Erkenntnis dessen ausgeht, was in dieser einzelnen und völlig fertig dastehenden Sprache Geltung hat und gebraucht wird, auf die Einsicht in die Phänomene der Sprache; denn nur dies, was gilt und gebraucht wird, ist das Wahre; alles übrige, was die vergleichende Sprachforschung leisten kann, sind nur Nebendinge, die die Erkenntnis der Phänomene der einzelnen Sprache nichts angehen oder deren Vollständigkeit befördern' (1971:391).
[17] Cp. 'Aber mit nüchterner Besonnenheit wird keiner etwas auf einem so bildhaften Sprachgebrauch aufbauen, wie es derjenige des Wortes Organismus, gebraucht von der Sprache, ist' (1971:322; 1832). On F. Schlegel see 1971:50, 169 [5, 169]; 1836, 1856–57. Madvig ridiculed the talk of 'das Tiefe und Geheimnisvolle,' e.g.: 'Sollte es nun jemandem scheinen, dass ich "das Tiefe und Geheimnissvolle" im Sprachbau verwischt habe, kann ich nur antworten, dass ich mich selbst bestrebt und andere aufgefordert habe, nach Kräften scharf und schwindellos in die Tiefe hinabzuschauen, um wirkliche Gestalten zu entdecken und eine wahre Vorstellung von dem, was dort vorgehe, zu erhalten. Vielleicht wird auch der eine und andere meinen, meine Betrachtungsweise setze die Bedeutung der Sprachwissenschaft herab . . . Die vergleichende Sprachforschung soll uns zeigen, was sie zeigen kann, die Verwandtschaft der Sprachen und den Zusammenhang ihrer Entwickelung . . . aber sie soll nicht Aufklärungen über Seiten des Geisteslebens versprechen, die ausserhalb ihres Gebietes liegen' (1971:252 [283–284]; 1856–57). Cf. 1971:173 [175]; 1856–57.

Werdens und Entstehens folgt' (1971:98 [72]; 1842; cf. 51 [6]).[18] Madvig often criticized 'eine in der neueren empirischen Sprachforschung häufig hervortretende verkehrte Würdigung der Bedeutung des Physischen und Phonetischen in der Sprache im Verhältniss zum wahren geistigen Inhalt. Man spricht, als ob man in den Lautgesetzen das Leben und Wesen der Sprache zu fangen hoffe . . . aber das Wissenschaftliche in dem Studium der einzelnen Sprachen liegt ganz anderswo, in dem vollen Ueberblicke des faktisch daseienden (dagewesenen) Sprachvorraths und Systems, in der sichern Erkenntniss und Verfolgung der Bedeutungen und Anwendungen nach allen Richtungen, in der scharfen Erfassung der syntaktischen Gesetze in aller ihrer Biegsamkeit und des Zusammenwirkens aller Glieder zum Aufbau der klaren und bestimmten Rede' (1971:192 [200]; 1856–57).[19] Thus like Bréal, Madvig found the omission of syntax and semantics a serious error, citing Jacob Grimm's statement that syntax lies half outside grammar (1971:203 [215]; 1856–57).

Since languages are the work of man, Madvig places much emphasis on the principle that the grammatical categories are universal and thus do not reveal intellectual or cultural aspects of particular languages and their speakers; the presence or absence of gender, for instance, does not indicate spiritual superiority or inferiority.[20] By contrast he found,

[18]   The doctrine of the 'sensible' origin of all words is important in the seventeenth century, best known perhaps from Locke's famous statement that became one of the most frequently cited texts in the linguistic philosophy of the eighteenth century (See, e.g., Aarsleff 1967:31). It is also in Bréal, e.g., 1866b:251.

[19]   In this passage Madvig uses the word 'phonetic' in a sense that is strange to us, but common before the word late in the century took the meaning we now are accustomed to. See, e.g., this passage in Renan; referring to Bopp and his followers, Renan wrote: 'Ce qui fait surtout la solidité de cette méthode, c'est la phonétique. La théorie de la transformation des sons est la véritable base de la méthode comparative' (1878:1215). It was in opposition to this sense of the term that Bréal created his term 'sémantique': '. . . la science que j'ai proposé d'appeler la *Sémantique* . . . par opposition à la *Phonétique*, la science des sons' (1897:9; it was during the 1890's that Rousselot became director of the first phonetic laboratory thanks to Bréal's support and influence). Cp. Madvig: 'Erstens will ich sehr stark das Geistige und Innere der Sprache (aber wie es wirklich erfasst und erkannt wird, nicht als ein unbegreifliches Mysterium) als dasjenige hervorheben, das der Sprachforschung die wesentlichste und wichtigste Aufgabe stellt im Gegensatz zu einem übertriebenen Hervorheben des Aeussern und Lautenden' (1971:276 [315]; 1871).

[20]   See, e.g.,: 'Die grammatischen Bezeichnungen [i.e. categories] haben also (im Ganzen) einen allen Völkern gemeinschaftlichen, in der Natur der Anschauungsform gegebenen und darauf beschränkten Inhalt' (1971:122 [105]; 1856–57). Cp. 'Wir müssen hervorheben, wie die Wirklichkeit uns gar keine Veranlassung giebt unsere Sprachbetrachtung mit der Voraussetzung eines gewissen grammatischen Normalbaues oder eines direkten Verhältnisses zwischen dem in der Sprache und im Sprachgeschlechte zu Stande gebrachten

like the eighteenth century, that the linguistic relativity principle operates in the lexicon, in 'was oft als die materiellere, mit der Eigentümlichkeit des Geisteslebens weniger zusammenhängende Seite der Sprache bezeichnet wird, nämlich in ihrem Wortschatz und, was davon nicht abgetrennt werden kann, ihrem Bedeutungsvorrat. Hierin zeigt sich der bis zur Bezeichnung gelangte Vorstellungsreichtum des Volkes' (1971:338; 1842).[21]

This survey shows that Madvig's philosophy of language was, as Jespersen said, 'on the whole rationalistic' (1894:59); it was anti-romantic.[22] There is no major and hardly any minor aspect of the critique of the German tradition that set in after Schleicher that had not in the previous generation been advanced by Madvig.[23] As some of the cited passages show, Madvig knew that his views were unorthodox. Though a classicist, he did not find antiquity superior to modern times, not even classical literature; and he wondered how Goethe and Schiller could reconcile their admiration for Greece and Rome with slavery and the position of women in those societies. He supported educational reforms that reduced the classical curriculum to make room for modern languages and natural science.

In the preceding pages I have deliberately avoided citation of statements that Madvig made after 1866. The reason is this: By 1871 it had

---

Footnote 20 continued

besondern Bau und der geistigen Disposition der Völker anzufangen' (1971:126 [111]). Much of Madvig's argument is directed against Wilhelm von Humboldt whom he found the most interesting exponent of the views he opposed. Madvig especially criticized Humboldt's efforts to identify Kantian categories in grammar; these categories were designed to refer to real relations, while Madvig held that grammar and language express only the work of the mind, its 'Vorstellungsart.' His critique therefore is not aimed at the classical eighteenth-century doctrine.

[21] The entire essay (1842) on 'Verhältnis und Stellung der Sprachen in der Kulturentwicklung' (1971:337–344) is devoted to this subject.

[22] On Madvig's philosophy of language, see also Friis Johansen 1971. Siesbye 1887–88:124–38. Jensen 1963:44–87. DeMauro 1969 (esp. 76–77, 173) has pointed to the importance of Madvig and his similarity with Bréal. I have earlier indicated my general agreement with DeMauro, suggested by the fact that we have both independently cited the same passage in Thomsen 1902:38, for the same purpose (DeMauro 58–59; Aarsleff 1967:8).

[23] Madvig also briefly stated some of the same views in his writings on Latin and Greek grammar and syntax; in their German and French translations, these works were widely reviewed in the *Revue critique*, chiefly by Charles Thurot (who called Madvig 'le premier latiniste de l'Europe' (1870:380)), during the years when Bréal was one of its editors. Thurot began teaching at the École normale in 1861; in 1868 he published his well-known *Notices et extraits de divers manuscrits latins pour servir à l'histoire des doctrines grammaticales au Moyen Age.*

come to his attention that Whitney's *Language* (1867, based on lectures given during 1864 and January 1865) came uncomfortably close to presenting principles and ideas already argued in Madvig's Danish publications (1971:258). Ten years later, Madvig was more explicit in a lecture 'Was ist Sprachwissenschaft?' given at Oslo and the same year (1881) published in Sweden (where a translation of Whitney 1875a had just appeared in 1880). Referring to Whitney 1867 and 1875a, Madvig found 'eine merkwürdige Ähnlichkeit zwischen der darin entwickelten Betrachtung des Wesens und Lebens der Sprache und derjenigen, die ich in sehr kurzen Züge im ersten Abschnitt dieses Vortrages angedeutet habe.' He concluded: 'Ich muss also mit aller Bestimmtheit aussprechen, dass die leitenden und wesentlichen Grund-gedanken der Schriften von Whitney – über das Verhältnis von Laut und Bedeutung, vom Ursprung der Sprache, von ihrem Ausgang von der Bezeichnung des Sinnlichen her, vom Entstehen der Flexionsformen und von dem vollen Recht der neueren Sprachen, sich den alten flexions-reicheren an die Seite zu stellen usw., usw. – von mir teils 25 Jahre vor dem Erscheinen der ersten Schrift von Whitney ausgesprochen worden sind . . . teils vor mehr als 10 Jahren . . . und zwar teilweise schärfer und stringenter.' Madvig still rejected the suggestion of any dependence on Whitney's part, though not without adding, 'aber die Uebereinstimmung in den Gedanken und in deren Ausdruck erscheinen mir weiterhin merkwürdig und auffallend' (1971:356–57).[24]

Whatever the truth – and it would be well worth knowing, though that is hardly possible today – the similarities are indeed striking, even in minor details that emerge in a consecutive reading of Madvig and Whitney. In any event, the near unanimity of Madvig, Whitney, and Bréal on so much can be read as an example of what in the history and sociology of science is called 'multiples' (the term is Robert K. Merton's (1973)), that is, the simultaneous but independent appearance of the

---

[24] Madvig first mentioned the Whitney matter in a footnote to the Danish text of his essay of 1871 (1971:468); in Madvig 1875 this was placed in the "Vorrede" (1971:394–96). He returned to this matter in his *Memoirs* (1881; (1971:401–402)). It is also dealt with in the editor's Introduction and notes (1971:37 and 468–69). In the Memoirs, Madvig said: 'Gegen diese Vermutung hat Whitney, der ein Mann von sehr umfassenden und selbst-ständigen Studien ist, Einspruch erhoben [see note, p. 493], und ich lasse sie gern fallen, um nur die Bestätigung der Wahrheit der in den betreffenden Arbeiten ausgedrückten Betrachtung beizubehalten und hervorzuheben, die in dem unabhängigen Auftreten samt Durchführung der Grundgedanken an zwei so weit voneinander entfernten Orten liegt.' In this Madvig saw the consequence of publishing in a language of a small nation; it surely seems likely that Madvig's decision to bring out the German version of his essays in 1875 was caused by these events.

same discoveries, a phenomenon that has received a good deal of attention lately as an especially fruitful means of historical insight, though it has not penetrated the history of linguistics. We see, for instance, that the social nature of language that later emerged as the linkage between linguistics and sociology was neither new nor forgotten; stressed by Locke, it was central in the classical eighteenth-century tradition and was throughout the nineteenth century recognized in England, e.g., by the Utilitarians and John Stuart Mill. It is only when the German tradition is considered the norm that the social dimension appears to require special explanation. This fact, along with many others, suggests that it is rather German philology, no matter how prominent it was for some fifty years, that must be seen as a special phase, not the norm, if we are to gain both coherence and order, that is to say understanding in the history of linguistics. As Madvig, Whitney, Bréal, and others insisted, comparative historical grammar and philology do not encompass all of the study of language.

WHITNEY

Since the principles that are often credited to Whitney are already in Madvig, there is no need to detail them. A couple of points deserve mention, however. In *Language* (1867), Whitney did not make any critical comment on Schleicher, quite the contrary, perhaps because Schleicher was then still living. But Whitney does remark that to speak of language 'as having independent and objective existence, as being an organism or possessing organic structure, as having laws of growth . . . all these are figurative expressions, the language of trope and metaphor' (35). Still, he never quite abandoned this conception, as the title of his second book (1875a) shows.[25] This aspect of Whitney would seem to be

---

[25] See also 1867:46 which takes back part of what he said on p. 35. Henry 1887 opened with the observation that 'avant et surtout depuis le grand ouvrage de M. Whitney [1875a] on a beaucoup parlé de la vie du langage; mais je ne sais si l'on est toujours tombé parfaitement d'accord sur la valeur et la portée de ce terme.' The publication of A. Darmesteter 1887 caused much discussion of this issue. Inconsistencies on fundamental principle are not uncommon in Whitney; thus 1867:373–74 argues that 'language is no infallible sign of race,' though 'it still remains true that, upon the whole, language is a tolerably sure indication of race.' Whitney doesn't hesitate to speak of a 'superior race,' of 'barbarism,' and the like. Later in the same book, he contradicts himself: 'The extent to which the different races of men have availed themselves of language, to secure the advantages placed within their reach by it, is, naturally and necessarily, as various as are the endowments of the races . . . Language makes each community, each race, a unit' (446–47). Such thinking was rejected both by Madvig and by Bréal.

related to another that is more important: the pervasive historical positivism that marks all his work, as, for instance, in the opening pages of *Language*. For Whitney there was no valid study and explanation of linguistic phenomena that is not historical. In this respect he differs greatly from Madvig and Bréal; the latter was well aware of this trait in Whitney, contrasting Max Müller's adherence to Herder with Whitney as a 'positiviste convaincu' (Bréal 1900). Even in its context, Whitney's positivism was a bit old, and by the 1890's it was out of fashion.

BRÉAL

The reaction against Schleicher first occurred in France during the 1860's. The first unmistakable sign was Bréal's decision to translate not Schleicher's *Compendium* (1861–62) but Bopp's *Vergleichende Grammatik*.[26] The first volume of this translation (1866) opened with a long Introduction (dated 1 November 1865) which clearly staked out the views that Bréal was soon to develop. The comparative method could best be learned, Bréal observed, from Bopp's work, the source and example of German linguistic scholarship, which, Bréal said, was characterized by the accumulation of detailed observations while general questions were put aside or only lightly touched as being the last rather than the first a science should solve (iv). Thus Bréal very early introduced the theme that was to play such a prominent role in the reaction, the German indifference to theory. Bréal admired Bopp precisely because his sober scholarship had overcome the linguistic mysticism which Bopp's teacher Windischmann, drawing on Herder, shared with the Schlegels, with Creuzer and Görres. 'Bopp contribua,' said Bréal, 'plus que personne à dissiper le mystère dont ces intelligences élevées, mais amis du demi-jour, se plaisaient à envelopper les premières productions de la pensée humaine' (viii–x).[27] Throughout the Introduction, Bréal was

[26] The significance of this decision was noticed, e.g., by Egger 1873; it was also pointed out by Meillet 1916a:12. It was Egger who advised Bréal to undertake the translation (Bréal 1866a:lvii). Bréal 1866a has only few mentions of Schleicher, none of them critical; Schleicher was then still living, and Bréal may not yet have known Schleicher 1863, 1865. Bréal 1866a is dated 1 November 1865. On p. liv, Bréal gives mildly qualified praise to the *Compendium*. Bréal was never on any subject so outspokenly and impatiently critical as Whitney. For an interesting discussion of events and figures (including Bréal and Gaston Paris) in the 1870's, see Dionisotti 1972.

[27] One of the notable facts about Bréal is his close knowledge of German life, intellectual history and literature; he published extensively on the history and organization of German education (see, e.g., 1884) and he also wrote on German literature. In France he was throughout his career, though chiefly during the early years, deeply involved in the reform

sharply critical of F. Schlegel on the same points that were soon brought against Schleicher: the organicist doctrine, the abuse of metaphor, the belief in the original mysterious perfection of language and its later decadence, the romantic notion of 'une éducation mystérieuse que le génie humain ou du moins une portion priviligée de la famille humaine, aurait reçue dans son enfance' (xxiv). He knew that Schlegel's book *Über die Sprache und Weisheitder Indier* (1808) after the initial chapters (which as I have shown elsewhere depend heavily on Sir William Jones's *Anniversary Discourses* [9] Aarsleff 1967:115–161) got lost in 'a thick fog of hypotheses, which Wilhelm von Humboldt and Bopp also found troublesome (see, e.g., Bopp, *Vergleichende Grammatik* §108). Bréal also knew that Schlegel, 'comme les autres, puisait sa science dans les Mémoires de la Société de Calcutta,' whose facts he adapted 'à une chronologie de son invention et à une philosophie de l'histoire arrangée d'avance' (x–xiii).[28] After citing Jones's famous passage on the affinity of Sanskrit and other Indo-European languages, Bréal underscored that at the beginning of Sanskrit studies, 'le sanscrit est présenté comme la langue soeur et non comme la langue mère des idiomes de l'Europe' (xviii–xix), a signific-

Footnote 27 continued
and administration of education (see, e.g., 1886). He was one of the chief organizers of the École pratique des Hautes Études (established in 1868 largely on the German model). a close adviser to Victor Duruy and Jules Simon, and for a period of ten years inspector general of public instruction for higher education (from 1879 to 1888 when the post was discontinued for budgetary reasons). His writings on these subjects show that his interest in the social dimension of language was not merely scholarly; it was also a practical concern. He was opposed to the ruling elitist education which divided the people in two nations that linguistically did not understand each other: 'Nous avons deux nations en France: l'une pense, lit, écrit, discute et contribue au mouvement de la culture euopéenne; l'autre ignore cet échange d'idées qui se fait à côté d'elle, ou si elle essaye d'en prendre connaissance, elle ressemble à un homme jeté au milieu d'une conversation depuis longtemps engagée avant qu'il vienne, et où il entend prononcer des noms et débattre des intérêts qui lui sont également inconnus' (1886:76). It is curious that Bréal uses the observation about the two nations that is generally associated with Disraeli's *Coningsby* (1844); Bréal often shows good knowledge of English and English affairs. In the same book (1886:398–99), Bréal also made one of his critical remarks about assigning national differences to inherent racial features. He constantly tried to join public and academic interests; he regularly contributed to at least half a dozen journals of general circulation. He was one of the founders of the Société de linguistique de Paris, for long one of its secretaries (during the Paris years choosing Saussure as joint secretary, whom Bréal had also proposed for membership), and its most active member. There is a close link between Bréal's linguistic and public stature during the last four decades of the century; no attempt to understand his importance can ignore this link, well known in the history of education on all levels. In this respect, he resembles Madvig who played a prominent role in similar reforms, for a while as minister of education.
[28]   Madvig made the same point 1971:50, 169 [5, 169]; 1836, 1856–57. Whitney (1871:311) talked of F. Schleggel as representing the 'antediluvian period of linguistic science.'

ant historical fact that seems to have been widely forgotten in the later historiographical tradition, which is marked by ignorance of Jones's *Discourses* except for isolated quotation of the statement of affinity repeated by Schlegel, like so much else he read in Jones. In the concluding pages of the Introduction (xxxviii ff), Bréal pointed out, as had Madvig, that Bopp had concentrated on 'la phonétique et la théorie des formes' at the expense of syntax. Bréal's Introduction states virtually all the criticisms that he and others were to bring against the German tradition.

A few years later, in December 1867, Bréal delivered an inaugural lecture at the Collège de France on 'Les progrès de la grammaire comparée' (printed 1868) in which he set forth his critique of comparative grammar in more detail. In the same year he also appeared as editor of a French translation of Schleicher's two pieces (1863, 1865) on linguistic Darwinism. These pieces were noted as the reaction took shape. Whitney wrote a review of the first volume of the *Bulletin* of the Linguistic Society of Paris, in which Bréal (1868a) was published, observing that one of the two pieces that held high interest was 'by Bréal, one of the soundest and most esteemed of the younger philologists of France,' treating, Whitney said, 'of the "Progress of Comparative Grammar,"' and it is a careful and suggestive exposition of the errors into which students in this branch are liable to fall' (Whitney 1868).[29] Reviewing the same publication, Gaston Paris also called attention to Bréal's essay, a piece that was replete, as one would expect, he said, 'de fines et péné-trantes remarques d'autant plus intéressantes cette fois qu'elles roulent surtout sur un sujet tout-à-fait à l'ordre du jour, l'état actuel et les divisions (on pourrait presque dire les schismes) de la science allemande' (Paris 1868a:248).

The same year Paris also reviewed the French translation of Schleicher. He commented critically on Schleicher's statement that languages are natural organisms: 'Tous ces mots ne sont applicables qu'à la vie animale individuelle et si on emploie légitimement en linguistique de pareilles métaphores, il faut se garder d'en être dupe. Le développement du langage n'a pas sa cause en lui-même, mais bien dans l'homme, dans les lois physiologiques et psychologiques de la nature humaine; par là

---

[29]   The next year Whitney voiced his first critique of Schleicher in the obituary devoted to him (a practice, incidentally, quite foreign to Bréal's urbane temper): Schleicher was 'a vehement champion of the paradox that a language is a "natural organism," growing and developing by internal forces and necessary laws; and his statement and defence of his doctrine are so bald and extreme as to be self-refuting; he was not unskilled as a naturalist, and his studies in natural history, by some defect in his logical constitution, seems to have harmed his linguistics' (1869:70).

il diffère essentiellement du développement des espèces, qui est le résultat exclusif de la rencontre des conditions essentielles de l'espèce avec les conditions extérieures du milieu. Faute d'avoir présenté à l'esprit cette distinction capitale, on tombe dans des confusions évidentes.' In conclusion he cited Bréal's very brief preface to the effect that even those who did not share Schleicher's ideas would find them stimulating (Paris 1868b).[30]

It is abundantly clear the Bréal initiated the reaction against Schleicher and the German school. In 1866, in 'De la forme et de la fonction des mots,' he argued that comparative grammar offered a purely exterior study of words which needs to be illuminated and checked by the study of meaning (243), that there is no necessary link between the decay of words and that of thought, that language study must not forget that man is both its ruling principle and its end, and that the history of language goes hand in hand with the intellectual and social history of its speakers. His social orientation and semantic aim were already firmly stated by 1868.[31]

Without questioning Bréal's originality, we may ask: What sources

---

[30] In this review, Gaston Paris referred to his own inaugural lecture at the Sorbonne in 1867, in which he had also opposed the abuse of metaphor, and to Bréal 1866b on the same question. Paris repeated the passage on metaphor in his review of A. Darmesteter 1887 (Paris 1887:66). For a cogent critique of organicism and the organic metaphor, see Tarde 1896. The occasion for Whitney 1871 would also seem to be the same French translation of Schleicher, cited near the end of that essay with the remark that 'even so sound and careful a philologist as M. Bréal has been misled into giving the inauspicious beginning [of the series] an implied sanction by letting his name appear alone upon the title-page, as author of the Introduction . . . and in it he indicates – though, in my opinion, in a manner much less distinct and decided than the case demanded – his at least partial non-acceptance of Schleicher's views.' As Paris's review shows, there were no grounds for this petulant observation; Bréal never used Whitney's sledgehammer methods, and his views on Schleicher were already clear enough. In 1869, Bréal published a review of Benfey 1869, remarking that Benfey was too indulgent on F. Schlegel's theory of flexions and that the history was distorted by rather strong patriotic sentiments, 'on croirait qu'entre la civilisation antique et l'activité scientifique dont l'Allemagne est aujourd'hui le principal foyer, il n'y ait eu place pour aucune haute culture de l'esprit, et que ces deux périodes soient séparées par un désert intellectuel . . . Nous citons seulement ces passages pour montrer que le patriotisme germanique n'est pas toujours exempt de ces accès de jactance qu'il relève avec raison quand il les trouve chez d'autres peuples.' This critique was well founded, raised often both then and later, by men of different nationalities. It is worth noting that this, like other statements to the same effect, was written before the Franco-Prussian war.

[31] E. F. K. Koerner writes: 'Bréal's sociologism can, as we believe, be traced to Whitney's *Vie du langage* (Paris 1875), and thus it is conceivable that the sociological tradition in linguistics was initiated by the American linguist who was the first to incorporate sociological notions (probably under the influence of Spencerian ideas) into the study of language' (1973:227). As already shown, Bréal's view of linguistic 'sociologism' was independent of Whitney, argued by Bréal prior to any possibility of dependence on Whitney. The

did he draw on, what mode of language study did he admire as an answer to the shortcomings of comparative philology? Owing to his frequent historical references, the answer is simple: the classical eighteenth-century tradition. I have already cited the well-known passage in the *Essai de sémantique* expressing admiration for Condillac and *les idéologues*, but to it much evidence can be added, in addition to the manifest similarity, also seen in Madvig and Whitney. The most striking piece of evidence is 'Les idées latentes du langage' (1868b) which is a companion piece to 'La forme et la fonctions des mots.' It is the thesis of this essay that the mere exterior mode of comparative grammar must be supplemented by 'cet assemblage de principes et d'observations dont Port-Royal a donné le premier modèle, et qui est connu sous le nom de grammaire générale ou philosophique'. Since it is the aim of universal grammar to show the interrelations of the operations of mind and linguistic expression, it is not opposed to the analysis of forms. On the contrary, 'il est bien plus vrai de dire qu'elle [la grammaire générale] trouvera dans les observations de la linguistique un surcroît d'intérêt et de solidité' (299). The essay is devoted to the well-known concept of sub-audition or ellipsis, so central in universal grammar; Bréal proposes to examine what one could call "ellipse intérieure, s'il ne valait pas mieux désigner cet ordre de phénomène sous le nom plus général *d'idées latentes du langage*' (301).

Footnote 31 continued

indebtedness, if any, is rather the other way round. I have also pointed out the quite obvious fact that the social nature of language is the common view, from Mersenne and Locke to Madvig, Mill, and the Utilitarians; it is its absence in the German school that is remarkable, not its presence elsewhere. Whitney is not at all 'the first to incorporate sociological notions . . . into the study of language,' a contention that is typical of the sort of historical distortion that is the consequence of fixation on the German tradition as the norm. Further, if Bréal were to have found this view in Whitney, there is no reason to think it would be from Whitney 1875a. In his Introduction (dated 27 August 1872) to vol. IV of the translation of Bopp, Bréal referred to Whitney 1867 (in the 2nd ed., London 1868) as 'un ouvrage trop peu connu en France.' He repeated this reference in Bréal 1873. Collin 1914:28 intimates that Whitney 1875a was translated into French by Bréal; that of course is possible, but Collin gives no reason for the attribution, his work is so sloppy as not to inspire confidence, and the very carefully catalogued Whitney Papers in the Yale Library do not indicate any communication between Bréal and Whitney such as one might expect if Bréal were the translator. Koerner 1973 is not about the subject; it is almost wholly about the mass of secondary literature, most of it unusually trivial. There is little knowledge of the primary literature, no grasp whatever of the intellectual history of France and Europe during the latter half of the nineteenth century, and no acquaintance with the rich periodical literature (both special and general) that must always be the first aid to intellectual history. Since there is no secondary literature on Bréal (except for the now old pieces by Meillet), Koerner seeks refuge in one of his frequent protestations of trust in the authority of communal belief ('as we believe'). See also Aarsleff 1976b.

Bréal argues that there is no exact correspondence between meaning and form; the outward forms of language only incompletely express thought and would not be able to express even the simplest and most elementary thought unless the mind did not constantly come 'au secours de la parole, et ne remédiait, par les lumières qu'elle tire de son propre fonds, à l'insuffisance de son interprète. Nous avons une telle habitude de remplir les lacunes et d'éclaircir les équivoques du langage, qu'à peine nous sentons ses imperfections' (300). This is not a deficiency; on the contrary, a language that at any given moment represented what is in the understanding and which gave expression to what went on in the mind, would become a nuisance, 'car il faudrait qu'à chaque notion nouvelle la langue se modifiât, ou que les opérations de notre esprit restassent toujours semblables à elles-mêmes, pour ne pas briser le mécanisme du langage' (301). In other words, 'notre entendement achève ce qui est seulement indiqué par le langage' (303). The source of these currently familiar ideas is well known, as we are reminded by this statement: 'Toute la syntaxe a d'abord résidé dans notre intelligence, et si plus tard des différences de forme ont plus ou moins séparé les parties du discours, c'est que le langage a fini par porter l'empreinte du travail intellectuel qu'il représente. C'est notre esprit qui anime le verbe d'une force transitive, enchaîne et subordonne les propositions, et dépouille certains mots de leur signification propre, pour les faire servir comme les articulations et comme les jointures du discours. L'unité de la proposition et de la phrase, non moins que celle du mot, est le fait de l'intelligence' (320).

As in Madvig, the consequence is the rejection of the doctrine that expressed forms – such as genders, cases, etc. – measure the cultural or spiritual quality of languages and their speakers. Languages use different means to achieve similar ends, thus all are equally good: "Il ne faudrait point aujourd'hui . . . nier *a priori* chez les hommes d'autre race que la nôtre l'existence de toute notion qui ne serait point marquée d'un signe spécial dans leur idiome. L'esprit pénètre la matière du langage et en remplit jusqu'aux vides et aux interstices. En n'admettant chez un peuple d'autres idées que celles qui sont formellement représentées, nous nous exposerons à négliger peut-être ce que son intelligence a de plus vivant et de plus original' (322). To illustrate what he had in mind, Bréal used an image already well-known in the seventeenth century: that of a painting which the mind observes differently at a distance and close-up. Standing back, it is easy to tell the background from the foreground and note light and shadow though the canvass is bathed in the same light. Close-up it all becomes unconnected details, but again standing back 'notre vue, cédant à une longue habitude, fonde les tons, distribue le jour, relie les traits et recompose l'oeuvre de l'artiste' (321).[32] It is the mind that interprets and creates what is there on the canvas.

Bréal's two essays 'De la forme et de la fonction des mots' and 'Les idées latentes du langage' present a reaffirmation of the principles of universal grammar, which must, he argues, complement comparative philology if we are to achieve a fuller understanding of language; this understanding must include syntax and what he then called the significations of words. Historical knowledge of forms may contribute to, but does not itself create or constitute, this understanding. Universal grammar relates the phenomena of language to mind, and it is in these terms that syntax must be studied. In this reaction against the insufficiency of historical study, he is advocating synchronic study. When Saussure in the *Cours* wished to explain the terms diachronic and synchronic, he referred the former to the Bopp tradition and the latter to 'les "grammairiens" inspirés par les méthodes traditionelles,' of which he gave the Port-Royal grammar as an example: 'Il est curieux de constater que leur point de vue, sur la question qui nous occupe, est absolument irréprochable. . . . Leur programme est strictement synchronique' (118).[33] Further, for Bréal universal grammar does away with the romantic

[32]   In a note to 1868b:322, Bréal wrote: 'En écrivant ces lignes, je songeais au livre de Schleicher: *Die Unterscheidung von Nomen und Verbum in der lautlichen Form.*' Since Schleicher had recently died, Bréal added: 'J'étais loin de me douter que la science allait perdre cet éminent savant.' In 1871, Whitney conducted a somewhat similar argument, which he illustrated with an image so similar to Bréal's that one is tempted to see a connection. Whitney said: 'Now it is easy to throw a group of objects, by distance and perspective, into such apparent shape as shall obscure or conceal their true character and mutual relations. Look at a village only a little way off . . . so in language: if you insist on standing aloof from the items of linguistic change and massing them together, if you will not estimate the remoter facts by the nearer, you will never attain a true comprehension of them' (1871:313–14). Whitney 1875 (48–49), in discussion of form and meaning, also resembles Bréal's discussion of form and function. There are striking similarities between Bréal 1866b, 1868b and Madvig. Thus in 1836, Madvig wrote: 'Es ist ein grosser Irrthum anzunehmen, dass das allgemeine in der Anschauung liegende Verhältniss nicht ebensowohl da für den Sprechenden da sei, wo es kein besonderes Zeichen hat, weil ein solches nicht nothwendig war und keinen Anlass fand sich zu bilden oder verschwunden ist, als wo das Zeichen sich findet' (1971:52 [8]). In a note to the German text 1875, Madvig said that the entire passage had been shortened in the German version, because he had since, in 1856–57, dealt with the subject at greater length. The longer passage in the Danish text of 1836 is given in German translation pp. 410–12. It seems to me clear that Bréal's argument is very similar to Madvig's, except that Madvig does not refer to the Port-Royal and universal grammar. I find this puzzling and see no easy way to account for it. Is it a 'multiple'?

[33]   Cf. *ibid.*: 'On a reproché à la grammaire classique de n'être pas scientifique; pourtant sa base est moins critiquable et son objet mieux défini que ce n'est le cas pour la linguistique

doctrine, also combatted by Madvig, that the richness or poverty of existing forms can be used to assess the spiritual or cultural 'merit' of languages and their speakers; it does away with the very real racist elements that are inherent in much nineteenth-century philological doctrine. Finally, Bréal is, again with Madvig and the classical eighteenth-century philosophy of language, committed to uniformitarianism: 'Ce n'est donc pas seulement à l'origine des races qu'il faut placer la création des idiomes: nous les créons à tout moment, car tous les changements qui les affectent sont notre oeuvre' (1866b:265).[34]

Bréal's knowledge of eighteenth-century doctrine also shows in several of his other essays, e.g., in 1879 when he discussed a theme that is central in Condillac, 'le génie de la langue.' Recalling Quintilian's metaphor of words as counters or coins with conventionally accepted values (used by Bacon, Hobbes, Locke, Leibniz and many others, with the implication that words are arbitrary signs), Bréal repeated Locke's observation that our thinking and speaking routinely runs on words rather than on concepts and things: 'Nous ne pensons qu'à l'aide des mots, ou plutôt nous pensons les mots, car cet instrument du langage est encore plus nécessaire que nous ne le croyons . . . nous imitons les banquiers qui ont des valeurs entre les mains et qui les traitent comme si elles étaient le numéraire lui-même, parce qu'ils savent qu'à un moment donné ils pourront les changer contre le numéraire.' This is a way of saying that what matters to the speakers is the current value system; its history or origin is at that point irrelevant, though the study of it may yield another kind of knowledge.[35] The subject of the influence of language on mind,

---

Footnote 33 continued
inaugurée par Bopp.' Cf. also: 'C'est à la synchronie qu'appartient tout ce qu'on appelle la "grammaire générale"' (141).
[34] Wells 1973 credits linguistic uniformitarianism to Max Müller, without mention of Madvig and Bréal. That the classical eighteenth-century doctrine was uniformitarian must be evident to any reader of its chief exponent, Condillac; as in Bréal, it is a consequence of the mind's constant activity in the use of language, manifest also textually in Condillac's frequent use of the word 'generate' and its derivatives to describe this linguistic activity. Müller's critics would not have granted that he was uniformitarian, precisely because he did not apply this principle at what was for them the crucial point: the origin of language. See quotations on uniformitarianism above, esp. from Madvig.
[35] On this metaphor and a characteristic nineteenth-century version of it, see Aarsleff 1967:233–34. Koerner 1974 says that my book is about 'the historical background which led to the formation of the Philological Society of London in 1842, rather than a history of linguistics.' The book is no more about the Philological Society than *Bleak House* is about Yorkshire because part of the action is set there. Koerner also says that the 'detailed index . . . unfortunately does not seem to include the often very informative footnotes.' The index in fact has very close to 200 references to the footnotes, each one clearly indicated

said Bréal, had often been treated to excess by the German school, which, however, had failed to notice that it is stated in Rousseau's *Émile;* 'La raison seule est commune, l'esprit en chaque langue a sa forme particulière; différence qui pourrait bien être en partie la cause ou l'effet des caractères nationaux.' In his theoretical writings, Rousseau credited the main points of linguistic philosophy to Condillac, as did Diderot, de Brosses, and many other contemporaries. Bréal concluded this essay with mention of the problem of the origin of language, 'to which modern linguistics pays little attention,' but which was so important during the previous century. Comparative philology had made the error of believing that early Indo-European roots were close to the primitive form of language, but 'there are centuries of speech behind behind them,' an assertion also made by Madvig against the German school (1879:1009–1010).[36] In this context Bréal again rejected the organic metaphor and the doctrine that linguistics is a natural science.

In the 1890's Bréal again mentioned the problem of the origin of language in a discussion of Renan's early opinions on this subject. As a disciple of German thought, Renan had set himself against the slow and gradual creation of language: 'Il répugne à l'image d'une humanité développant par degrés son intelligence, conquérant un à un ses titres d'honneur. En ceci, il est en opposition directe avec le dix-huitième siècle, avec la philosophie de Condillac, de Maupertuis, de Condorcet, de Volney. Il est l'élève de la philosophie allemande du commencement du siècle, qui s'était précisément proposé comme tâche de contredire et de réfuter l'école de Condillac. Il s'était nourri des écrits de Frédéric Schlegel, de Guillaume de Humboldt, lesquels avaient eux-mêmes recueilli l'héritage et reçu l'impulsion de Herder' (1893:11).[37] There is no

---

Footnote 35 continued

by the letter n after the page number, and thus readily observable even at a hasty glance. This is typical of Koerner's unreliability, whether it is a question of misrepresentation or plain ignorance of the items he reports on (combined with frequent and demonstrable ignorance of the primary literature that alone can inform the judgment about secondary items). In his review of Koerner 1972a, Edward Stankiewicz (1974) has demonstrated its methodological chaos, its random inclusions and omissions, and its vast number of inaccuracies, with a mere selection of examples.

[36] Here Bréal again states the uniformitarian principle: 'Si nous pouvions assister à cette évolution nous trouverions sans doute l'action des mêmes lois que nous constatons dans la transformation des langues modernes' (1879:1010).

[37] Bréal knew that Renan had later substantially changed his position, see, e.g., Renan 1878. Bréal is here referring to Renan's *L'avenir de la science*, written in 1848, but not published until 1890 with a fascinating introduction that shows how profoundly the intellectual context had changed over the intervening forty years. First in 1871, Madvig

doubt where Bréal stands. His reaction against Schleicher and the German
school drew on the classical eighteenth century tradition.

THE REVIVAL OF EIGHTEENTH-CENTURY THOUGHT

In his respect for the previous century Bréal was not alone. A few years
before Bréal in the *Essai* (1897) praised Condillac and les idéologues,
Durkheim had traced the origins of sociology not to contemporary
English and German thought but to Montesquieu: 'Tout cet élan qui
nous porte aujourd'hui vers les problèmes sociaux, est venu de nos
philosophes du XVIII*e* siècle. Dans cette brillante cohorte d'écrivains,
Montesquieu se détache parmi tous les autres' (Durkheim 1892:25).
The revival of the eighteenth century formed part of the turn against
the philosophy of Victor Cousin and his school, which for nearly a
generation ruled as nothing less than the official philosophy. The
hallmark of this school was denigration of eighteenth-century
philosophy and especially of Condillac, based not on the original texts but
on the radical version of Condillac presented by *les idéologues* (Aarsleff
1971; 1975a; Fox 1973:452–58). There were all along writers who did not
accept this version of Condillac, but by the 1850's the turn was evident.

Cournot is credited with the creation of mathematical economics,
and he was in addition a philosopher of science and an intellectual
historian of distinction (Granger 1971). He defended Condillac against
the neglect and disdain he had suffered. In his two great philosophical
works, Cournot devoted several chapters to language (1851:II, 1–89;
1861:II, 53–118). In the first of these chapters, opening 'une langue
est un système des signes,'' Cournot stressed the necessity of instituted
signs; he also devoted a long section to the subject of 'l'ordre linéaire
du discours' (1851:II, 58ff), in which he said: 'Une des imperfections
radicales du discours parlé ou écrit, c'est qu'il constitue une série
essentiellement linéaire; que son mode de construction nous oblige à
exprimer successivement, par une série linéaire des signes, des rapports
que l'esprit perçoit ou qu'il devrait percevoir simultanément et dans un
autre ordre; à disloquer dans l'expression ce qui se tient dans la pensée
ou dans l'objet de la pensée'' (1851:II, 68).[38] A few years later, Cournot

---

Footnote 37 continued
made a similar critique of Renan (1971:288 [331–32]). In 1875, he added footnotes on
the same matter to his earlier writings (1971:88, 124 [58, 109]).
[38] At this point, Cournot continues with this image: 'La chose sera évidente pour tout
le monde s'il s'agit de décrire par la parole, je ne dirai un tableau ou un paysage . . . mais

was joined by Taine (1868 [1857]) in his severe critique of the school of Cousin. Here Taine also criticized the rule of metaphor: 'Ceci peut s'appeler la métaphysique des métaphores; des fautes de style font ici des fautes de science; le langage faux produit la pensée fausse; en comparant des qualités et des pouvoirs à des êtres, on les change en êtres; l'expression pervertie pervertit la vérité' (1876:245). Taine's major philosophical work *De l'intelligence* (1870), opened with 60 pages under the title 'des signes.' In the Preface Taine stated that he had carefully noted his three principal debts: 'La première, très-féconde, esquissée et affirmée par Condillac ... la seconde ... appartient à Stuart Mill; la troisième ... à Bain.' In 1869, Henri Weil's long-neglected book (1844) was re-issued on Bréal's suggestion.[39] By the 1880's Renan remarked that Cousin's philosophy had now been forgotten for twenty years. During these decades there was also a strong reaction against Comtian positivism, forcefully stated by the greatest French scientists of the time, Claude Bernard (1865, see, e.g., 306) and Louis Pasteur (1882). The innovation begun by Bréal during the 1860's formed part of a broad movement in French intellectual life during the latter half of the nineteenth century. It is well known in art and literature. It also found expression in educational reform (in which Bréal was an important figure), in the creation of new chairs and disciplines, and in the publication of a large number of new journals which give the best understanding of the intellectual vitality of the period.

If we now recall the views of the 1890's sketched earlier in this paper, it will I think be evident that these views were not new then. They date

---

Footnote 38 continued

un système composé de parties discontinues, tel qu'une machine d'horlogerie.' On p. 73, Cournot wrote of 'l'ordre linéaire qu'impose l'essence du langage.' The linearity of discourse is central in Condillac's philosophy of language, see Aarsleff 1974, esp. 103–104. Cournot's distinction and importance became increasingly known toward the end of the nineteenth century. The *Revue de métaphysique et de morale* devoted a special issue to him in May 1905 (vol. 13, 291–543); a brief headnote says that the late Gabriel Tarde had planned a new edition of Cournot's works, 'aujourd'hui à peu près introuvables.' Nothing came of it then, but an edition of Cournot's complete works is now being published in response to the same need that Tarde identified seventy years ago. The nature of Cournot's work and the knowledge of him at that time obviously have significant implications for the history of the study of language and its intellectual locale during the nineteenth century.

[39]   There were eleven editions of Taine's *Philosophes* by 1912. The re-issue of Weil 1844 in 1869 appeared in the *Collection philologique*, edited by Bréal, in which the two Schleicher pieces had been published the previous year. Weil's book was re-issued again in 1879. Weil's reference in the title to *grammaire générale* is not casual; the Introduction refers to the discussion between Beauzée and Batteux, 'ces savants estimables.' Weil began teaching in Paris at the École normale and the École pratique in 1861 and taught there until his retirement in 1892. The Taine passage is in the Preface to the 4th edition (1883).

back to the 1860's; their first exponent was Bréal, who in his reaction against Schleicher and the German tradition deliberately reintroduced the philosophy of the eighteenth century. Language serves the needs of communication; it is instituted by man and constantly controlled and modified by the mind's linguistic activity; it is social, and, being instituted, words are arbitrary signs. The origin of language is a legitimate linguistic problem. Language is not an organism that has independent existence, the study of language is not a natural science, but must be pursued with reference to mind, man, and social life. Universal grammar contains principles that are crucial to the success of this study. The mere historical study of language does not constitute its proper domain. The distinction between diachronic and synchronic study emerges naturally in the reorientation that assigns limited efficacy to historical study. This critique of the German tradition was stated by Madvig during a span of thirty years prior to Bréal and Whitney. The interrelations, if any, between the two latter and Madvig are not clear, but it is evident that Bréal precedes Whitney on the points that have been credited to him. Both chronology and the interpretation to which some details are open, raise the question whether Whitney was drawing on Bréal. It seems to me evident that Madvig's and Bréal's work is superior to Whitney's, though Whitney may have stated the same views with more quotable force, so to speak (although not always consistently). In several respects, Whitney is also old-fashioned and doctrinaire compared to Madvig and Bréal, e.g., in his positivism. It seems to me that Madvig gave a good assessment of Whitney when he wrote: 'Whitney behandelt seinen Gegenstand mit grosser Gelehrsamkeit, nüchterner Klarheit und offenem Blicke für die Thatsachen; das Gespinnst falscher Theorien dialektisch aufzulösen und zu vernichten ist minder seine Sache; er geht an den *metaphysics* vorbei und dringt nicht immer tief genug' (1971:395 [v]; 1875).

I do not see that one can accept as historically correct the statement made in the opening chapter of Saussure's *Cours*: 'Une première impulsion fut donnée par l'Américain Whitney, l'auteur de la *Vie du langage* (1875).' This is not surprising, on the contrary; scholars and scientists have often proved mistaken about the history of their discipline and even about the sequence of their own work (e.g., Newton). In the same chapter, Saussure remarked correctly (though somewhat inconsistently with the words about Whitney): 'Ce n'est que vers 1870 qu'on en vint à se demander quelles sont les conditions de la vie des langues. On s'aperçut que les correspondances qui les unissent ne sont qu'un des aspects du phéno-mène linguistique, que la comparaison n'est qu'un moyen, une méthode pour reconstituer les faits.' Madvig and Bréal had said that long ago. But Saussure was inconsistent once more when he said that the neo-grammarian school appeared soon after 1875 and that, 'grâce à eux, on ne vit plus dans la langue un organisme qui se développe par lui-même, mais un produit de l'esprit collectif des groupes linguistiques. Du même coup on comprit combien étaient erronées et insuffisantes les idées de la philologie et de la grammaire comparée.' Madvig, Bréal, and Gaston Paris had said that before 1870. Saussure concluded that one could not say, in spite of their great services, that the neogrammarians had covered the entire field of linguistics. In a footnote to this passage, at the end of the chapter, Saussure restated Bréal's objection to taking metaphors for reality – there was of course never any question of rejecting any use of metaphor, but only the uses that change the nature of the subject and the method.

Meillet said that Saussure taught the principles of the *Cours* in Paris during the 1880's. In that case, we have an illustration of a principle that was well stated by Claude Bernard in 1865: 'Tout en reconnaissant la supériorité des grands hommes, je pense néanmoins que dans l'influence particulière ou générale qu'ils ont sur les sciences, ils sont toujours et nécessairement plus ou moins *fonction de leur temps*' (310). Today this is a view that is widely accepted in the history of science and intellectual history; the innovative ideas of individuals play an important role, but they occur in particular contexts. In that sense it seems to me that Bréal deserves credit – I don't say greater credit, for he has hardly received any. It seems obvious to me that there can be no doubt of his importance; in the linguistic reorientation that occurs in the late decades of the nineteenth century, he is the first innovator (though the problem remains of Madvig's share in these events). Bernard's axiom (also stated in the seventeenth century) undercuts what has been called the 'heroic' theory of science, the notion that great geniuses make discoveries, that ideas pure and simple change the world, and that progress is a linear, cumula-tive succession of such discoveries quite independently of their context. The 'heroic' theory has little use for the intellectual context, except perhaps to set off genius by contrast, and hardly any for such other historical features as social life and conditions.[40] The pure objectivity of science lives in the upper spheres of the life of the mind. To such a

---

[40] To serve the ends of folk-history, a figure is often placed in a benighted context that makes him shine the more in the dark, though this flattering ad-hoc context is pure myth made possible by ignorance. Thus it is often said that in Herder's time it was dangerously unorthodox to believe that the original language was not Hebrew and that the short

view, there cannot be a history of science or of any discipline; there can only be heroes and saints set off against numskulls and perhaps even villains. This is a positivist doctrine; truth was in the nature of things from the beginning, but has lain hidden owing to prejudice, superstition, and the rule of religion; the past has been a conspiracy against the enlightened present. This is a simple-minded view of things, but it is the typical nineteenth-century version of science and its history; it is the view that makes it possible to accept the absurd belief, doctrinal in the history of linguistics, that with Bopp and a few Germans the study of language, at a stroke, became 'scientific,' or if you wish with Bloomfield in the 1930's (though having more than one contender seriously weakens the doctrine). The decisive innovation that occurred in the study of language during the latter half of the nineteenth century, chiefly in France, shows how false that version of history is. What happened cannot be spun out of the German tradition, whether by positive development or reaction. The postulate that the study of language became 'scientific' with Bopp is equivalent to saying that there is no history of science before Newton or whomever one may choose as god. This is so absurd that one must ask why it should be necessary even to talk about the matter, silly things usually going away by themselves.

THE HISTORY OF LINGUISTICS

Why haven't they gone away in the history of linguistics as they have in the history of science? It cannot merely be because the history of science is older than that of linguistics. The latter has the benefit of the example of the former, yet has not taken the lesson. With only slight simplification, it is true to say that the history of science was created by Paul Tannery and George Sarton (Taton 1976; Merton 1975). Both were committed to the positivist progress doctrine of pure science,

Footnote 40 continued

Mosaic chronology was not authoritative; the result is to make Herder shine. It is possible that such beliefs were held by some Lutheran country pastors, but that is not the claim which is made about the intellectual context. It is nonsense. Mersenne, for instance like the majority in the seventeenth century, rejected both. Another strategy is to claim that a particular figure is so unique that he suffered no influence at all; this attempt to safeguard claims for originality is of course self-defeating, for such claims are empty unless the possibilities of influence have been examined. It is not the aim of intellectual history to reduce individual originality, but to make it possible to identify it. It is no slur on Newton to know what he owed to Kepler. See Aarsleff 1975a.

but they were also admirable scholars who set standards that have
never been known in the history of linguistics. Alexandre Koyré (Gillispie
1973) placed the history of science firmly in the context of intellectual
history on the principle that insight and understanding are subverted
if the work of the past is judged by current doctrines. His ground rule
was that 'la manie de la recherche des "précurseurs" a bien souvent
irrémédiablement faussé l'histoire de la philosophie.' The progress
doctrine is methodologically useless. As method it cannot even reveal
what progress has in fact occurred.[41] The notion that the 'scientific'
study of language began only with Bopp turns all previous work into
what is at best unscientific anticipations. The chief reason for the failure
of the history of linguistics lies elsewhere. The history of science has
shown something that is also open to observation around us: as soon as
a discipline has become institutionally successful, usually in the universities as was the case of philology in nineteenth-century Germany, it
tends to create a history that meets the ideological needs of its practitioners. A good example occurred in the seventeenth century; the Royal
Society was barely half a dozen years old when it created such a story in
Sprat's *History of the Royal Society* (1667). Quite contrary to facts
that were well known to contemporaries, it established the myth that the
new science was almost wholly an English creation, that Bacon was its
father, and that Mersenne, Gassendi, and Descartes had nothing to do
with it; it also failed to mention that the early English scientific meetings
followed French example (Aarsleff 1975b, 1976a). Sprat's work satisfied
the need for a sense of institutional identity that demanded ceremonial
affirmation of the exclusive Englishness of the new science. Benfey's
and von Raumer's great histories (1869, 1870) celebrated the scientific-
ness and Germanness of comparative philology; they are still the best
general histories we have and nearest to what Tannery and Sarton did
for the history of science. It is this self-serving institutional folk-history
that has been believed, as we see, for instance, in the notion that all
later study of language must be spun out of the Bopp tradition. One of
the consequences is that we have the claim that there is a powerful
'Schleicherian paradigm,' something that is rather like saying that the
final codification of the phlogiston theory was the great, forward-looking

---

[41] Another sort of ad-hoc strategy is the claim, ridiculed by Madvig and many others,
about 'das Tiefe und Geheimnisvolle.' Thus when it is suggested that Herder owes much to
Condillac, it is claimed that Herder's theory 'ist doch viel tiefer und konsequenter durch-
gedacht,' without any attempt whatever to demonstrate what this means. The words are
merely hortatory.

principle in chemistry. The phlogiston theory played a fruitful role in the history of chemistry, but the future of chemistry depended on its rejection. In this sense, Bréal was the Lavoisier of linguistics.

But if the history is false, what made and still makes it possible? There are, in fact, several competing histories of linguistics; the Bloomfieldians had their comforting version, and the later orthodoxy waited barely ten years for its retrospective historical construction. Linguistics seems to have a special need for such comforts, which may suggest a certain insecurity about its own status. This variety of incompatible histories is good evidence that something is wrong. It might be argued that the problem is lack of knowledge and scholarship; this is true, just as it is true that good work is enough even in the absence of grandiloquent talk about methodology, which remains empty without good examples of its practice. Many works in history, intellectual history, the history of art, and the history of science have had deep methodological significance without saying a word about method but merely illustrating it. If matters are not so simple in linguistics, the chief reason is that its history is still wedded to the typical nineteenth-century positivist faith in progress, in Baconian induction, in the 'heroic' theory of science as the work of geniuses who make discoveries of long-hidden truths. This is an unsophisticated view by any standard.

The matter of Boppian philology and linguistics after Schleicher has much in common with problems posed by science in the nineteenth century. According to the Baconian orthodoxy, theory was not respectable; the collection of facts was the heart of the matter, followed by description and classification. Claude Bernard's teacher and predecessor, the physiologist François Magendie met disappointment in theoretical work, so he said to Bernard that he compared himself 'to a ragpicker: with my spiked stick in my hand and my basket on my back, I traverse the field of science and I gather what I find' (Grmek, 1974). Darwin made frequent public avowals of respect for plain induction, but in their work both Magendie and Darwin fortunately ignored it. The history of linguistics is dominated by very simple views of the nature both of history and of science. For general orientation in intellectual history, the choice will typically fall on such inferior guides as Loren Eisely.[42] So long as

---

[42]   In 1972b:274, Koerner referred to a passage in Wilhelm Scherer (1875) that related Darwin to Malthus. Koerner, however, doubted 'very much that this is correct, since Malthus was mainly concerned with the economic considerations influencing the growth or decline of the population, not with ideas of selection, survival of the fittest, and the like.' Thus Koerner, who wishes to instruct the world in the history of science and intellectual

the search for knowledge is guided by such method, the result will fit the conventional expectation. Arens' useful anthology (1969) is heavily biased toward German work, as is indicated, for instance, by the astonishing omission of Turgot's influential essay on etymology, the total misrepresentation of Condillac and the French tradition, and the omission of Madvig.[43] Borst's great *Turmbau* undertakes to fit linguistic events into broad conventional categories, without the least indication that those events may not be merely derivative of their intellectual contexts, but themselves have contributed toward the making of those contexts. The work that is done in the history of linguistics is almost without exception the product of linguists working on the side. The history of science did not become what it is until it was no longer the work of scientists. The difference is not a question of finding enough time; it is primarily a question of orientation.

Let me give a few examples. The 'heroic' theory of science reveres discovery and invention, and by the same token plays down or ignores the context. Thus Sir William Jones gets credit for the discovery of Sanskrit and its affinity with certain other languages; an easily detachable

---

Footnote 42 continued

history in relation to the study of language, at one stroke showed elementary ignorance of both Darwin and Malthus. He also demonstrated that he had not read the Scherer passage with much care, for it says that Darwin has 'eingestandermassen, den Kampf ums Dasein aus dem Malthus'schen Bevölkerungsgesetze entlehnt.' As any reader of the *Origin of species* and other writings by Darwin (e.g., the *Autobiography*) knows, Darwin's reading of Malthus played a crucial role in the inception of evolutionary theory. When Koerner published a revised version of his 1972 essay, he tried to correct his error, now saying that Scherer's suggestion 'has been confirmed in recent years' (1976:694). For this confirmation, Koerner refers to Young 1969:110, n. 3. But that footnote is not on that subject at all, and Young naturally does not give confirmation of a fact that has been known not only by scholars but by ordinary readers for more than 100 years. Later in the same essay (125–28), Young does in fact give some of the relevant passages for the sake of analysis. Thus Koerner's effort to correct the error becomes an expanding display of continuing ignorance and misrepresentation regarding an elementary matter to which he seems to attach importance. This also shows that neither Koerner 1972b nor 1976 were submitted to qualified referees before publication, since even small knowledge of the subject would have been sufficient to notice this gross ignorance. Koerner is also of the opinion that Darwin was 'in the final analysis really nothing more than a synthesizer and popularizer of ideas prevailing in the natural sciences of his time' (1973:4). One can only wonder how such things get into print.

[43]   It is notable, however, that Arens says: 'Der Schweizer de Saussure war unstreitig das Haupt der französischen Linguistik, wenn man auch als ihren Begründer Bréal (1832–1915) annehmen will, der seit 1862 mit zahlreichen Schriften als Mythenforscher, Philologe und Linguist hervorgetreten war" (1969:443).

and quotable passage from the second 'Anniversary Discourse' is one of the fixtures of histories of linguistics. The story then goes that this passage presents all that he did for the study of language, that it really contains no proof, that it was merely a lucky, impressionistic insight, and that in any event others before him had said much the same thing. Indeed they had. Jones's achievement is not the 'discovery,' but the lucid presentation of the method of comparative language study within the full sequence of his 'Anniversary Discourses,' all carefully structured as a single argument. Concentration on his 'discovery' not only simplifies the story, but it also has made it possible to give F. Schlegel credit for what Jones did. This is the version of history that has become gospel, so successful that the 'Discourses' are evidently not read even by those who write as if they know them. Comparative philology becomes 'eine deutsche Wissenschaft.' A quotation from Bréal given above said bluntly that Schlegel drew on the *Asiatic Researches,* in which, of course, the 'Discourses' were first published.

The problem raised by the case of Jones is this: if he was not the first to make some such discovery, why is he almost universally associated with it? Why was he successful at least to that small degree? The chief reasons would seem to be these: Firstly, he was already before he went to India and took up Sanskrit a man of recognized intellectual stature in several subjects, including linguistics; thus much was expected of him. Secondly, he presented his 'discovery' in a systematic context that gave it abundant meaning and implications; he created a method. And thirdly, he had the means and foresight to see that without a learned society to promote the study of India and without a publication to make this new knowledge available, the world would not be any the wiser. None of the previous proponents of the discovery came anywhere near meeting these conditions. It may be argued that the impact also came at the right time; that certainly counts for something, but it is not a sufficient explanation. If Leibniz, for instance, had made a similar statement in an equally rich methodological context and published it in, say, the *Journal des Sçavants,* would it have been ignored? This example reveals not only the consequences of the discovery fixation, but also how historical facts that can be quite readily known are ignored in order to make possible, create, and then maintain the ad-hoc mythical history that satisfies the ideology: Schlegel gets credit for what he learned from others. The history of English science in the seventeenth century performed a similar vanishing trick on its debt to France. Like patriotic and even chauvinist history, such distortions and vanishing tricks are not uncommon. But it is surely unusual and rather distressing that the history of linguistics remains so attached to its old folk-history, often stated with great solemnity as befits ceremony.[44]

Just as the 'heroic' theory causes the failures that result from the discovery fixation, so it cannot take account of recurrences and repetitions, that is, the statement of closely similar or even identical arguments and principles at widely separated periods. Since the theory demands that achievement is not forgotten if publicly known, counter-examples must be explained away by some ad-hoc story. Recurrences are embarrassing; if unrelated, they question the progress doctrine; if related, they cast doubt on the originality of the most recent proponent. Seeming instances of the former sort will often on closer inspection prove to belong with the latter. It is the unrelated recurrences that are the most interesting, for they raise illuminating questions about the intellectual contexts and the reasons for the repetition. Were the contexts similar, and if so how similar? And if not seemingly similar, why the repetition? The history and sociology of science have called attention to this problem, to what Robert K. Merton with references to multiple discoveries calls

---

[44] Since I wrote that chapter, Paul Diderichsen informed me that Louis Hjelmslev 'on many occasions in lectures and discussion with great emphasis maintained that it is Jones (and not the Germans) who deserves the honor of being the founder of comparative philology' (see Aarsleff 1976b). For advancing that argument with documentation that I should think would have gone some way toward making the argument at least plausible, a German reviewer, writing in a reputable German journal, accused me of 'prejudice' pure and simple, without the slightest effort to examine what I offered in support. This is understandable; the purpose of the accredited story is not to be history, but to ensure that the faith is kept, that the mythical folk-history is respected. See Nickel 1968; cf. Lämmert 1967. It has also been argued that Jones was not followed up with the immediate excitement that is by some taken to be proof of major accomplishment. Even if this doubtful criterion is accepted, the conclusion does not follow in this case. The nine discourses were delivered during the years 1784–92, and published in the annual volumes of the *Asiatic Researches* beginning in 1788 at Calcutta, which was some six months away from Europe. Given the well-known events of European history during those years, it is not difficult to imagine how slowly these volumes got around. Contemporary correspondence testifies to eager but most often frustrated anticipation. A German translation of some pieces came out during the late 1790's, a pirated English edition began to appear in 1798 (followed by at least two more), and finally a French translation of the first seven volumes appeared at Paris in 1805, with notes and commentary by such famous men as Cuvier. Obviously, the argument about failure to elicit reaction does not stand up. The reason might readily have been suspected, but the history of linguistics is not given to such circumspection; besides, it might lose the day for F. Schlegel and the conventional folk-history. Schlegel was lucky to get into print when he did, with Jones's matter at the beginning of the volume and his his own 'thick fog,' as Bréal said, at the back, On the 'heroic' theory and the discovery fixation, see Merton 1973:343–412. I am referring to the chapter on 'Sir William Jones and the New Philology' in Aarsleff 1967:115–61.

a 'strategic research site.'[45] Uniformitarianism would seem to be a case in point. It is characteristic of the history of ideas, of its weakness, that it does not find this principle until the word had been created, that is around 1840. But there is an analogue in the early seventeenth century in the discussion and controversy that followed Galileo's writings on Jupiter's moons, on the surface of the moon, etc. Indeed, the rejection of the hierarchical Aristotelian universe (with its fixed spheres, etc.) marks the assertion of a uniformitarian view of nature. Marin Mersenne was involved in these events, and he also asserted uniformitarian principles with regard to language. The new science demanded the rejection of the Adamic language doctrine in favor of the view that language is man-made, its aim communication, its being social, and that words are arbitrary signs (Crombie 1974; Aarsleff 1976a). The epistemology of the new science could not get along with the essentialism of the Adamic language doctrine – this is what Locke's argument against innate ideas is about. Owing to Mersenne, one of the conferences of Théophraste Renaudot, held during the late 1630's, debated precisely the same problem that was the topic of Herder's prize-essay some 140 years later. Since there is, it seems, no demonstrable connection between the two events, the implications are suggestive and should prove instructive.

During the nineteenth century uniformitarianism again became an issue both in linguistics and in science; two hundred years apart the controversy took much the same form. The issue joined linguistics and science because the doctrine that words somehow have natural meaning cropped up again in romantic linguistic philology, reflected in renewed interest in Boehme. Darwinian theory faced opponents committed to essentialism. Both in science and linguistics as well as in their interrelations the nineteenth century is in large measure a re-play of the seventeenth; there are a good many more examples than I can mention here. Thus the reassertion of the arbitrariness of the linguistic sign and all that goes with it (that languages are institutions, social, etc.) is perhaps the central theme of the linguistic innovation that took place in the later decades of the nineteenth century. This is also true of the seventeenth century; Mersenne and Locke both (without any direct connection)

---

[45]   There is a rich and recent literature on the sociology of science; Merton 1973 is among the most important, a collection of essays published over the last decades. Among others may be mentioned Ben-David 1960, 1964, 1970, and 1971, as well as Ben-David and Zloczower 1962; the early chapters of Ben-David 1971 should be ignored. The two items by Clark (1968a and 1968b) suggest that a similar investigation of the competing publications of the Société linguistique de Paris and the *Revue de linguistique* could prove fruitful.

made the arbitrariness of the linguistic sign a cardinal principle, a principle that is best known from Locke's *Essay*, which was the chief source of eighteenth century linguistic philosophy. It is therefore not surprising that there are evident similarities between Locke and the eighteenth century on the one hand and what we read in Saussure on the other.

To return to the intellectual history of the nineteenth century, let me examine two principles that occupy Claude Bernard in the *Introduction* (1865); both are related to the matter discussed in the previous pages. We have seen that both Magendie and Darwin ignored the rules of classical Baconian induction just as it was at the peak of its reputation. There is a rich literature on this subject; an understanding of this problem and how it was debated and worked out during the middle stretch of the century is fundamental to achieving a grasp of the intellectual history of that century, including the study of language.[46] Bernard addressed himself to his problem with great boldness. He argued that no worthwhile observation occurs without imagination and prior hypothesis, that method alone is barren, 'et c'est une erreur de certains philosophes d'avoir accordé trop de puissance à la méthode sous ce rapport' (a reference to the positivists), that excessive commitment to preconceived theories and ideas blocks discovery and causes poor observation, that induction and deduction cannot be separated, and finally that (as was to be expected) 'l'induction baconienne est devenue célèbre et on en a fait le fondement de toute la philosophie scientifique . . . Cependant Bacon . . . n'a point compris le mécanisme de la méthode expérimentale' (54, 67, 71, 79, 86). The reaction against Schleicher and the German school was similar to this critique of mere method, of simple induction. Bernard and Bréal stand in the same relation to the traditions that reigned in their disciplines.

The second principle in Bernard parallels the argument that philology is not all of linguistics. Writing of the interrelations of anatomy and physiology, Bernard said that the anatomical perspective had hitherto dominated; he granted that anatomical study would naturally appear

---

[46]   Darwin has for a number of reasons attracted great attention during the last ten years; this distinguished literature is important both as intellectual history and for its methodological example and insight. Ghiselin 1969 is excellent and basic. Hull 1973 has an introduction that is especially illuminating on Darwin's scientific method in the context of the time, e.g., on essentialism. It also reprints fifteen contemporary reviews by well-known figures. Robert M. Young has written a large number of fascinating essays that are also methodologically significant; among these may be mentioned his essays 1969, 1971, 1973. The *Dictionary of Scientific Biography* is the indispensable and authoritative reference work. For a cogent critique of the history of ideas, both method and results, see Skinner 1969.

first, 'mais je crois que ce principe est faux en voulant être exclusif, et qu'il est devenu aujourd'hui nuisible à la physiologie, après lui avoir rendu de très grands services, que je ne conteste pas plus que personne. En effet, l'anatomie est une science plus simple que la physiologie, et, par conséquent, elle doit lui être subordonnée, au lieu de la dominer. . . . En un mot, je considère que la physiologie, la plus complexe de toutes les sciences, ne peut pas être expliquée complètement par l'anatomie' (157–58). What especially marked physiology was the study of living things, 'en un mot, pour savoir quelque chose des fonctions de la vie, il faut les étudier sur le vivant' (160). It is obvious that Bernard's defense of physiology and the study of living specimens against the anatomical tradition and its advocates closely resembles the case of language study around 1870, also in so far as there is a well-known historical link between the early history of comparative philology and anatomy – Sir William Jones had attended John Hunter's famous Croonian lectures and makes reference to them several times in the *Anniversary Discourses*. Both physiology and Bréal's linguistics are linked to the philosophy of science which Bernard stated more openly than Darwin ever did, though both gained eminence by following it. There are perhaps few legacies of the nineteenth century that have had a greater impact on the twentieth than Darwinism and the ideas that found expression in Saussure's *Cours*. There are affinities between their historical situations. It is perhaps not entirely idle, therefore, to note that both have had their greatest impact concurrently during the last generation.

No purely internal history of a science or a discipline can achieve coherence and lead to the sort of understanding that yields a sense of explanation. It is only by inclusion of external factors that genuine intellectual history becomes possible. The prerequisite is disengagement from the conventional patterns and from subservience to the institutional bias of folk-history. This argument is presented with great cogency in Ravetz's excellent book on *Scientific knowledge and its social problems* (1970). Let me quote a suggestive passage from that book: 'Until the nineteenth century, no field of natural science had such internal and social strength that its leaders could, or even wished to, reject all external components of value from its work. The "purity" of science seems to have been developed first in the university environment of nineteenth-century Germany, where the natural sciences struggled to win a place alongside the established humanistic and philological disciplines. With the eventual establishment of university science on a large scale in all advanced countries in the earlier part of this century, the ideology of purity also became a convenient means of preserving the autonomy of an increasingly expensive social activity. By the entirely natural processes of the formation of folk-history, the tradition of the purity of science was extended back in time to the origins of modern science, and across to all fields of scientific inquiry' (164–65).[47]

In the first part of this paper I have tried to illustrate, and in the latter part I have argued that the history of linguistics is rather out of it if we set its conceptual framework, its understanding of history and science, against the method, practice, and achievement of intellectual history and of the history of science. This problem was also the subject of my Introduction to *The study of language in England 1780–1860* (1967). It was clear to me then that the available histories were of little use as to substance and that they followed a method (if one can call it that) which had all the deficiencies I have described above. I argued, consequently, that if the history of the study of language was to be more than a largely unconnected record of events, it would need to expand its territory, that the study of language in any period is so closely bound up with the intellectual context – such as science, philosophy, theology, and ruling ideology – that this context must be known and related to language study, and that the history of linguistics must both relate to the results of the history of science and learn from its example. The terms internal and external history were not then around, but that was what my argument was about. I also pointed to the chief obstacle to a viable history by referring to the consequences of 'a positivist conception of the forward march of history, of progress, a conception that will invariably give less than the history that is my concern. With this sort of outlook, no history of learning or scholarship can ever achieve more than a deceptive coherence.' I illustrated by giving examples from the seventeenth to the nineteenth centuries, including an example to which I have also referred in this paper: 'Even natural science did not have its origin in unalloyed, disinterested, nearly angelic objectivity about the phenomena of nature, though it is still widely believed, indeed often dogmatically asserted against the testimony of the evidence, that the early Royal Society had only the purest of scientific motives.' My book was, I said, 'an essay in the application of that method.' The method for which I argued has general import, and I presented it in those terms. In the body of the book

---

[47]   The great importance of Ravetz 1970, just quoted, needs to be emphasized. Both for knowledge and method, see also Ravetz 1972, 1973. The items listed in notes 45, 46, and 47 lead on to additional literature.

I showed how intimately language study was bound up with events in physics, chemistry, geology, religious thought, church politics, and the philosophical controversies of the time. I also cited Alexandre Koyré's words quoted earlier in this paper. I am eager to call these facts to the readers' attention; they are easy to check. The reason is this: In recent years my argument about the method – clearly noted in several reviews – has made repeated appearances in the writings of E. F. K. Koerner in contexts that not only leave my Introduction unmentioned but also misrepresent what the books does and is about; this can only tend to prevent his readers from knowing what my Introduction says and what my book is about. The most recent version of his misrepresentation says this: 'It seems . . . that the author hoped the reader would, through some kind of osmosis, absorb the "method" from the thicket of positivistically gleaned historical facts . . . nowhere in the book are guidelines of procedure mapped out which could, *mutatis mutandis*, apply to any other period in the history of the linguistic debate.'[48] Let me repeat, I did not leave the method to osmosis, and I did not confine my examples to a narrow time-span. That this sort of misrepresentation can get into print not once but several times is a serious liability for the history of the study of language.

Princeton University

REFERENCES

Abbreviations: *BSL*   *Bulletin de la Société de Linguistique de Paris. Paris.*
                 DSB   *Dictionary of Scientific Biography*
                 RC   *Revue critique d'histoire et de littérature*
Aarsleff, Hans 1967. *The study of language in England 1780–1860.* Princeton University Press.

[48]   Koerner 1976:387. Thus this revised version substitutes equally patent misrepresentation for what appeared in the first version, 1972b. In November of 1972, I spoke to Koerner about the misrepresentation of my book in his essay; I received no answer. Thinking that I might hear by letter, I waited till the end of January 1973, then wrote up the facts in a letter; I quickly received the reply that Koerner hoped I would forgive him that he did not have time to answer. I then wrote Aarsleff 1973, which was immediately published in the same journal that had published Koerner 1972. (Aarsleff 1973 contains essentially what I had said in my letter.) The editor of the volume in which Koerner 1976 has recently appeared was told of Aarsleff 1973 and the misrepresentations of Koerner 1972b. One of the important aspects of Ravetz 1970 is that it discusses honesty and integrity in writing, citation, and editing, not merely as a matter of personal obligation, but as a duty to the subject and the discipline. See esp. pp. 176–83 and 245–59.

— 1971. 'Locke's reputation in nineteenth-century England.' *The Monist* 55:392–422.
— 1973. 'A word on Koerner's historiography of linguistics.' *Anthropological Linguistics* 15 (March), 148–50.
— 1974. 'The tradition of Condillac: The problem of the origin of language in the eighteenth century and the debate in the Berlin Academy before Herder.' *Studies in the History of Linguistics*. ed. by Dell Hymes (Bloomington, Indiana). pp. 93–156.
— 1975a. 'Condillac's speechless statue.' *Studia Leibnitiana. Supplementa XV – Akten des II. Internationalen Leibniz-Kongresses Hannover*, 17–22. Juli 1972. Vol. 4:287–302.
— 1975b 'Thomas Sprat.' *DSB* 12.580–87.
— 1976a. 'John Wilkins.' *DSB* 14.361–81.
— 1976b 'Thoughts on Scaglione's *Classical theory of composition*: The survival of 18th century French linguistic philosophy before Saussure.' *Romance Philology* 29:522–38.
Arens, Hans 1969. *Sprachwissenschaft*. 2nd ed. Freiburg/München, Alber.
Ben-David, Joseph 1960. 'Scientific productivity and academic organisation in nineteenth-century medicine.' *American Sociological Review* 25:828–43.
— and A. Zloczower 1962. 'Universities and academic systems in modern societies.' *European Journal of Sociology* 3:45–84.
— 1964. 'Scientific growth: A sociological view.' *Minerva* 2:455–76.
— 1970. 'The rise and decline of France as a scientific centre.' *Minerva* 8:160–79.
— 1971. *The scientist's role in society. A comparative study*. Englewood Cliffs, Prentice-Hall.
Benfey, Theodor 1869. *Geschichte der Sprachwissenschaft und orientalischen Philologie in Deutschland seit dem Anfange des 19. Jahrhunderts, mit einem Rückblick auf die früheren Zeiten*. München, Cotta.
Bernard, Claude 1865. *Introduction à l'étude de la médecine expérimentale*. Collection Garnier-Flammarion Brochée 1966.
Bopp, Franz 1866–1874. *Grammaire comparée des langues indo-européennes*, tr. by Michel Bréal. Paris. 5 vols. I 1866; II 1868; III 1869; IV 1872; V 1874.
Borst, Arno 1957–63. *Der Turmbau von Babel*. Stuttgart, Hiersemann.
Bréal, Michel 1866a. 'Introduction' to Bopp 1866:I:i-vii.
— 1866b. 'De la forme et de la fonction des mots.' Bréal 1877:243–66. First publ. in *Revue bleue* 1866.
— 1868a. See Schleicher 1868.
— 1868b. 'Les progrès de la grammaire comparée.' Bréal 1877:267–94. First publ. in *Mémoires de la Société de Linguistique de Paris* I (1868), 72–89. Given at Collège de France 9 Dec. 1867.
— 1868c. 'Les idées latentes du langage.' Bréal 1877:295–322. Separately published 1868.
— 1869. Review of Benfey 1869. *RC* 8 (18 Dec.), 385–89.
— 1873. Review of Whitney 1873. *RC* 13 (22 Feb.), 113.
— 1876. 'Les racines indo-européennes.' Bréal 1877:375–411. First publ. *Journal des savants* 1876:632–52, as a review with subtitle 'Examen critique de quelques théories relatives à la langue mère indo-europénne.'
— 1877. *Mélanges de mythologie et de linguistique*. Paris, Hachette.
— 1879. 'La science du langage.' *Revue scientifique*, 2nd ser., vol. 8 (26 April 1879), 1005–11.
— 1883. 'Les lois intellectuelles du langage: Fragment de sémantique.' *Annuaire de l'Association des études grecques en France*, 17:132–42.
— 1884. *Excursions pédagogiques*. Paris, Hachette. First ed. 1882.
— 1886. *Quelques mots sur l'instruction publique en France*. Paris, Hachette. 5th ed. (410 pp.). First ed. 1872 (151 pp.).
— 1893. Review of Renan 1890. *Journal des savants*, January 1893, 5–17. Republished in *BSL* 8 (1894), lviii–lxviii, as Obituary with title 'M. Ernest Renan et la philologie indo-européenne.'

— 1896. Review of Jespersen 1894. *Journal des savants* 1896, 381–89, 459–70.
— 1897. *Essai de sémantique (Science des significations)*. Paris, Hachette.
—1900. Obituary of Max Müller. *Académie des inscriptions et belles-lettres. Comptes rendus.* 2 Nov. 1900, 558–64.
Clark. Terry N. 1968a. 'Émile Durkheim and the institutionalization of sociology in the French university system.' *European Journal of Sociology* 9:37–71.
— 1968b. 'The structure and functions of a research institute: the *Année sociologique*.' *European Journal of Sociology* 9:72–91.
Collin, Carl S. R. 1914. *A bibliographical guide to sematology*. Lund, Blom.
Cournot, Antoine-Augustin 1851. *Essai sur les fondements de nos connaissances et sur les caractères de la critique philosophique*. 2 vols. Paris.
— 1861. *Traité de l'enchaînement des idees fondamentales dans les sciences et dans l'histoire,* 2 vols. Paris.
Crombie, A. C. 1974 'Marin Mersenne' *DSB* 9:316–22.
Darmesteter, Arsène 1887. *La vie des mots étudiée dans leurs significations*. Paris, Delagrave.
De Mauro, Tullio 1969. *Une introduction à la sémantique*. Paris, Payot. Original Italian 1966.
— 1973. See Saussure 1916.
Dionisotti, Carlo 1972. 'A year's work in the seventies.' *Modern Language Review* 67:xix-xxviii.
Durkheim, Émile 1892. *Montesquieu et Rousseau, précurseurs de la sociologie*. Note introductive de Georges Davy. Paris: Les Classiques de la Sociologie, 1953. Original Latin thesis, Bordeaux 1892.
Egger. E. 1873. Review of Bopp 1866–74. vols. 1–4. *Journal des savants* 1873. 473–88.
Fox, Robert 1973. 'Scientific enterprise and the patronage of research in France 1800–70.' *Minerva* 11:442–72.
Friis Johansen, Karsten 1971. 'Einleitung,' in Madvig 1971. 1–46.
Gerbod, Paul 1965. *La condition universitaire en France au XIXe siècle*. Paris.
Ghiselin, Michael T. 1969. *The triumph of the Darwinian method*. Berkeley, California.
Gillispie, Charles C. 1973. 'Alexandre Koyré.' *DSB* 7:482–90.
Godel, R. 1954. See Saussure 1954.
Granger, G. 1971. 'Antoine-Augustin Cournot.' *DSB* 3:450–54.
Grmek, M. D. 1974. 'François Magendie.' *DSB* 9:6–11.
Henry, Victor 1887. Review of A. Darmesteter 1887. *RC*, n.s. 23:282–85.
— 1894. Review of Jespersen 1894. *RC* n.s. 38:501–04.
— 1896. *Antinomies linguistiques*. Paris, Alcan.
Hjelmslev, Louis L. 1937. 'An introduction to linguistics. Inaugural lecture on appointment to the Chair of Comparative Linguistics at the University of Copenhagen.' *Essais linguistiques. Travaux du Cercle Linguistique de Copenhague* 12 (1959), 9–20.
Hovelacque, A. 1876. *La linguistique*. Paris.
— 1877. 'La vie du langage.' *Études de linguistique et d'ethnographie*. Paris. Pp. 1–13.
Hull, David L. 1973. *Darwin and his critics: The reception of Darwin's theory of evolution by the scientific community*. Cambridge, Mass., Harvard.
Jakobson, Roman 1971. 'The world response to Whitney's principles of linguistic science.' Silverstein 1971:xxv–xlv.
Jensen, Povl Johs. 1963. 'Madvig som Filolog.' *Johann Nicolai Madvig. Et Mindeskrift.* 2 vols. Copenhagen 1955–1963. II.1–209.
Jespersen, Otto 1891. *Studier over Engelske Kasus. Med en Indledning: Fremskridt i Sproget*. Copenhagen, Klein.
— 1894. *Progress in language with special reference to English*. London, Swan Sonnenschein.
Koerner, E. F. K. 1972a. *Bibliographia Saussureana 1870–1970*. Metuchen, N. J., Scarecrow Press.

— 1972b. 'Towards a historiography of linguistics. 19th and 20th century paradigms.' *Anthropological Linguistics* 14, no. 7:255–80.

— 1973. *Ferdinand de Saussure. Origin and development of his linguistic thought in western studies of language. A contribution to the history and theory of linguistics.* Braunschweig, Vieweg.

— 1974. 'Annotated chronological bibliography III, 1962–1972.' *Historiographia linguistica* 1:351–84.

— 1976. Revised version of Koerner 1972b. Herman Parret, ed. *History of linguistic thought and contemporary linguistics.* Berlin, De Gruyter. Pp. 685–718.

Lämmert, Eberhard 1967. 'Germanistik eine Deutsche Wissenschaft.' In book under that title. Edition Suhrkamp no. 204, pp.7–41.

Madvig, J. N. 1843. *Bemerkungen über verschiedene Puncte des Systems der lateinischen Sprachlehre und einige Einzelheiten derselben.*

— 1875. *Kleine philologische Schriften.* Vom Verfasser deutsch bearbeitet. Leipzig, Teubner.

— 1971. *Sprachtheoretische Abhandlungen.* Im Auftrage der Gesellschaft für Dänische Sprache und Literatur, hrsg. von Karsten Friis Johansen. Copenhagen, Munksgaard.

Maher, John P. 1966. 'More on the history of the comparative method: The tradition of Darwinism in August Schleicher's work.' *Anthropological Linguistics* 8, no. 3, part. II. 1–12.

Mauss, M. 1900. Review of J. Deniker, *Les races et les peuples de la terre* (Paris 1900). *Année sociologique* 4:139–43.

— 1937. 'In memoriam Antoine Meillet (1866–1936).' *Oeuvres* III (1969) 548–53. First publ. in *Annales sociologiques* sér. E, fasc. 2 (1937) 1–7.

Meillet, A. 1893. 'Les lois du langage.' *Revue internationale de sociologie* 1:311–21, 860–70.

—1898. Review of Bréal 1897. *RC* n.s. 45:141–43.

—1900–1901. Review of Wilhelm Wundt, *Völkerpsychologie,* I *Die Sprache* (Leipzig 1900). *Année sociologique* 5:595–601.

—1903–1904. Review of Bréal 1897, 3rd ed. (1904). *Année sociologique* 8:640–41.

—1913–1914. 'Ferdinand de Saussure.' Meillet 1951:174–83.

—1915. 'La linguistique.' *La science française.* 2 vols. *Exposition universelle et internationale de San Francisco.* 2:117–24.

— 1916a. Obituary of Michel Bréal. *BSL* 20:10–19.

— 1916b. Review of Saussure 1916. *BSL* 20:32–36.

— 1930. 'Michel Bréal et la grammaire comparée ou Collège de France.' Meillet 1951:212–27.

— 1951. *Linguistique historique et linguistique générale.* vol. II. Nouveau tirage. Paris, Champion.

Merton, Robert K. 1973. *The sociology of science. Theoretical and empirical investigations,* ed. by Norman W. Storer. University of Chicago Press.

—1975. 'George Sarton.' *DSB* 12:107–14 (with Arnold Thackray).

Nickel, Gerhard 1969. Review of Aarsleff 1967. *Anglia* 86:163–66.

Paris, Gaston 1868a. Review of *Mémoires de la Société de Linguistique de Paris,* 1 (1868). *RC* 5:248.

— 1868b. Review of Schleicher 1867. *RC* 6:241–44.

— 1887. Review of A. Darmesteter 1887. *Journal des savants* 1887:65–77, 149–58, 241–49.

Pasteur, Louis 1882. *Discours de réception à l'Académie française.* 27 April 1882.

Poliakov, Léon 1971. *Le mythe aryen. Essai sur les sources du racisme et des nationalismes.* Paris, Calman-Lévy.

Raumer, Rudolf von 1870. *Geschichte der germanischen Philologie, vorzugweise in Deutschland.* München, Oldenburg.

Ravetz, Jerome R. 1900. *Scientific knowledge and its social problems.* Oxford University Press.

— 1972. 'Francis Bacon and the reform of philosophy.' *Science, medicine and society in the renaissance. Essays to honor Walter Pagel,* ed. by Allen G. Debus. 2 vols. New York, Watson, 2:97–119.

— 1973. 'Tragedy in the history of science.' *Changing perspectives in the history of science. Essays in honour of Joseph Needham.* London. Ed. by Mikuláš Teich and Robert Young. Pp. 204–22.

Renan, Ernest 1878. 'Des services rendus aux sciences historiques par la philologie.' *Oeuvres complètes,* ed. by Henriette Psichari, 8 (1958), 1213–32. First publ. in *Revue bleue* 1878.

— 1890. *L'avenir de la science.* Paris, Calman-Lévy.

Renaud, Paul 1898. Review of Bréal 1897. *Revue de linguistique* 31:60–67.

Saussure, Ferdinand de 1916. *Cours de linguistique générale,* ed. by Tullio de Mauro. Paris 1972, Payot.

— 1954. 'Notes inédites de F. de Saussure,' ed. by R. Godel. *Cahiers Ferdinand de Saussure* 12:49–71.

Scherer, Wilhelm 1875. Review of German version of Whitney 1867 (München 1874). *Preussische Jahrbücher* 35:106–11.

Schleicher, August 1863. *Die Darwinsche Theorie und die Sprachwissenschaft.* Weimar, Böhlau.

— 1865. *Über die Bedeutung der Sprache für die Naturgeschichte des Menschen.* Weimar, Böhlau.

— 1867. Translation of Schleicher 1863, 1865, in *Collection philologique,* ed. by Michel Bréal.

— 1869. *Die deutsche Sprache,* 2nd ed. Stuttgart, Cotta. First ed. 1860.

Siesbye, O. 1887. 'Nogle ord til minde om Johan Nicolai Madvig.' *Nordisk Tidskrift for Filologi.* n.s. 8:81–150.

Silverstein, Michael, ed. 1971. *Selected writings of William Dwight Whitney.* Cambridge, Mass. and London, MIT Press.

Skinner, Quentin 1969. 'Meaning and understanding in the history of ideas.' *History and Theory* 8:3–53.

Stankiewicz, Edward 1974. Review of Koerner 1972a. *Semiotica* 12:171–79.

Taine, Hippolyte 1868. *Les philosophes classiques du XIX siècle en France.* Paris. First ed. 1857 entitled *Les philosophes français du XIXe siècle.* 12 editions by 1912.

— 1870. *De l'intelligence.* 2 vols. Paris, Hachette.

Tarde, Gabriel 1896. 'L'idée de l'"organisme social"' *Revue philosophique* 41:637–46.

Taton, René 1976. 'Paul Tannery.' *DSB* 13:251–56.

Thackray, A. See Merton 1975.

Thomsen, Vilhelm 1902. *Sprogvidenskabens Historie. En kortfattet Fremstilling.* University, Copenhagen.

Thurot, Charles 1870. Review of Madvig, *Grammaire latine. RC* 9:380–87.

— 1875. Review of Madvig 1875. *RC* 18:241–45.

Weil, Henri 1844. *De l'ordre des mots dans les langues anciennes comparées aux langues modernes: Question de grammaire générale.* Re-issued 1869 and 1879.

Wells, Rulon 1973. 'Uniformitarianism in linguistics.' *Dictionary of the History of Ideas. Studies of Selected Pivotal Ideas.* 4:423–31.

Whitney, W. D. 1867. *Language and the study of language.* New York, Scribner.

— 1868. Review of *Mémoires de la Société de Linguistique de Paris.* vol. 1. *Nation* 6:331.

— 1869. Obituary of August Schleicher. *Nation* 8:70.

— 1871. 'Schleicher and the physical theory of language.' Whitney 1873:298–331. First publ. in *Transactions of the American Philological Association for 1872* under the publ. in *Transactions of the American Philological Association for 1872* under the title 'Strictures on the views of August Schleicher respecting the nature of language and kindred subjects.'

— 1873. *Oriental and linguistic studies.* New York, Scribner Armstrong.

— 1875a. *The life and growth of language: An outline of linguistic science.* New York, Appleton.

— 1875b. 'Are languages institutions?' *The Contemporary Review* 25:713–32. Also publ. under the title 'Streitfragen der heutigen Sprachphilosophie.' *Deutsche Rundschau* 4 (1875) 259–79.

— 1876. Review of Hovelacque 1876. *Nation* 22.98

Worms, René 1894. Obituary of James Darmesteter. *Revue internationale de sociologie* 2:745–47.

Young, Robert M. 1969. 'Malthus and the evolutionists: The common context of biological and social theory.' *Past and Present* No. 43:109–45.

— 1971. 'Darwin's metaphor: Does nature select?' *The Monist* 55:442–503.

— 1973. 'The historiographic and ideological contexts of the nineteenth-century debate on man's place in nature.' *Changing perspectives in the history of science. Essays in honour of Joseph Needham,* ed. by Mikuláš Teich and Robert Young. London. P. 344–438. London, Heinemann.

Zloczower. See Ben-David 1962.

[Since this essay was written, I have completed two pieces that relate to the subject and argument of the present essay. 'Guillaume de Humboldt et la pensée linguistique des idéologues' (*La Grammaire générale: des modistes aux idéologues,* eds. André Joly & Jean Stéfanini [Publications de l'Université de Lille III], 1977, pp. 217–241) shows that Humboldt was deeply indebted to the idéologues, especially to Destutt de Tracy. It is for this reason that Humboldt gains sympathetic mention in the midst of the revival of eighteenth-century linguistic philosophy, e.g., by Bréal and Jespersen. The second essay, on 'Taine and Saussure' (*Yale Review* 1978), deals with the importance of Taine (see pp. 87–88 above), a large subject I deliberately kept out of the present essay. It argues that such well-known Saussurean concepts as value, system and structure, synchrony and diachrony, and the analysis of the linguistic sign (including the illustrative metaphor of the sheet with two sides) are derived from Taine, who was also, as noted by contemporaries, the source of the revival of eighteenth-century philosophy, not least of Condillac. 'Taine and Saussure' is a brief statement of the thesis of a monograph in progress.]

ASPIRATIONS, ORGANIZATION, ACHIEVEMENT

YAKOV MALKIEL

In addressing you within this particular segment of our Society's Golden Anniversary Symposium, I am very much aware of the uniqueness not only of the occasion but also of the situation. Assuming that our planet will still be inhabited by man in the year 2024 and that linguistics will then be a flourishing, universally-recognized discipline, I venture to predict two major deviations from the pattern of events surrounding our own lives. First, it will not be possible to polarize, in linguistic research, Europe and North America to the virtual exclusion of other continents. Stirrings of linguistic curiosity – indeed, important accomplishments – are already at this point in history, observable in South America, in Asia, in Africa, in Australia, to say nothing of the distinctly early start of linguistic thinking on the Asiatic scene. Second, it is most unlikely that there will develop in the next half-century hermetically-sealed schools or circles, each with its own terminology and implied scale of values, in, say, Reykjavik, Luxembourg, Tel Aviv, or Kabul. The period of prolonged isolation of certain communities of linguists is, for better or worse, approaching its end. The balance sheet we are drawing this year may thus involve far more than the assessment of a half-century of research and teaching, viewed in nostalgic retrospect.

The specific topic assigned to me is 'Aspirations, organization, achievement'; I shall try to divide my quota of time as evenly as possible among these three themes.

As regards ASPIRATIONS, we can, I believe, distinguish among three phases: an opening period of almost excessive modesty, with the entire strategy predicated on the assumption that the initiative in linguistics lies with some other country, usually with Germany; a second period of strident, tumultuous search for identity and originality, occasionally accompanied by militant rejection of the European heritage; and a third period, which definitely includes the year 1974, of strong leadership devoid of any isolationist overtones.

To appreciate the timidity of the early Americans, overawed by the accomplishments of the giants among the Central European comparatists (and I include, for the purpose of this talk, Copenhagen and Milan in Central Europe), it suffices to quote a few lines from Whitney's representative *Life and growth of language* (1900:318–9), written and published almost exactly a century ago: 'In truth, to Germany belongs nearly the whole credit for the development of comparative philology; the contributions made to it from other countries are of only subordinate value'. With uncanny foresight Whitney went on to qualify his praise of the Indo-Europeanists by remarking: 'But while Germany is the home of comparative philology, the scholars of that country have, as was hinted above, distinguished themselves much less in that which we have called the science of language [by this Whitney meant linguistic theory]. There is among them ... such discordance on points of fundamental importance, such uncertainty of view, such carelessness of consistency that a German science of language cannot be said yet to have an existence'. This discrimination between two unequal performances abroad implies perhaps the hope for America some day to fill the void.

Whitney was of course a 19th-century figure, but this attitude of near-subservience did not become entirely extinct even after the First World War. Here is a brief corroborative passage from the preface to a book titled *From Latin to Italian*, by the Harvard pioneer in Romance linguistics Charles H. Grandgent (true, in 1927, when the book appeared, its author was no longer a young man); in fact, the chosen lapidary remark is the opening statement of the entire book: 'This work, the result of over thirty years' collecting, classifying, and speculation, after many reconstructions is at last offered to fellow-scholars in the hope that it may render service, in America and perhaps in England, to the study of Romance philology'. The author, clearly, did not expect specialists on the European continent to sink their teeth into the fruits of thirty years of his own gropings.

Such occasional displays of modesty and admissions of pessimism obviously do not mean that American scholars were hesitant to strike out in new directions – directions germane to the geographic, social, and intellectual conditions prevailing in their own country. It was difficult to aim at such originality, even more so to achieve it, in fields such as Sanskrit, Homeric Greek, Gothic, and Old French, which all four fascinated an intellectual élite in this country at the turn of the century. But the young Johns Hopkins scholar C. Carroll Marden, in the mid-nineties, surprised the world of scholarship by submitting a brilliant doctoral dissertation on the phonology of the Spanish dialect of Mexico City based on original field work – a monograph not only published but later expanded and translated into Spanish. Some research, of uneven quality, was conducted on Canadian French and Louisiana French. William Read, a far-sighted and long-lived professor of English at Baton Rouge, visualized the prospect of a Caribbean linguistics, involving the blend of research in pidgins, creoles, overseas varieties of French, Spanish, and Portuguese as well as colonial English and Dutch plus investigations of Amerindian and West African languages, that is to say, an areal linguistics, insular and circummaritime, comparable in sheer sweep and intricacy to the finest traditions in Mediterranean studies. Americans were, already at that stage, showing greater independence than their British cousins, whose conservatism in the Romance field, for instance, hindered them from straying from continental models much farther than did Mildred K. Pope in slanting her historical grammar of Old French, excellent by the standards of her time, at a peculiarly British angle; witness the title: *From Latin to Modern French, with especial consideration of Anglo-Norman* (1934).

In appraising the relationship between the Old and the New World we should remember that in the late 19th and the early 20th century some of the most prominent figures on the American scene were immigrants or long-term visitors from Europe, who came over and struck root under widely varying sets of conditions but certainly had no reason for hiding this fact, which stood them in excellent stead. This qualification applies to Indo-Europeanists, such as Maurice Bloomfield, an expert in Sanskrit and Greek, and Hermann Collitz, a specialist in Germanics and in Greek dialects; to Americanists, such as Franz Boas; to comparative Germanists, like Eduard Prokosch; and, later, Werner Leopold, an innovator in the study of child language and bilingualism; to Anglists, like Hans Kurath; to Romanists, like Karl Pietsch in Chicago and Henry R. Lang at Yale; and no doubt to a long procession of Orientalists. The reverse was not true; native American linguists, at that stage, were not normally invited to teach at European institutions of higher learning, or to hold positions at trans-Atlantic research centers. Then again, it was customary for an aspiring American linguist to spend a year or two of his post-doctoral leisure in Europe; Leonard Bloomfield made a pilgrimage to Leipzig to meet some patriarchs of the Neogrammarian movement, and this trip strongly colored his thinking, while the Johns Hopkins Romanist David S. Blondheim impressed Parisian scholars so favorably that they commissioned him to edit the

Judeo-French glosses transcribed twenty years before by Arsène Darmesteter. Again there was no reciprocity; before Jerzy Kurylowicz's memorable research trip to Yale, around 1931, young European scholars would come as short-term visitors to America only for the sake of opportunities of field-work, as was the case with the older Uhlenbeck. The only real recognition that an American pioneer could expect to win across the Atlantic was to have a book of his translated into German or into French – in 1876 August Leskien did publish the German version of Whitney's *The life and growth of language*, nine years later there appeared Heinrich Zimmer's adaptation of the same Yale scholar's *The roots, verbal forms, and primary derivatives of the Sanskrit language*, while the 20th century witnessed the adoption, by Carl Winter's prestigious publishing firm, of Carl D. Buck's *Grammar of Oscan and Umbrian* (1904). Minor successes could be scored when American scholars were invited to contribute to a European *Festschrift* or vice versa. Around 1911, two such miscellanies were organized for American Romanists, one to honor the Johns Hopkins trailblazer Marshall Elliott, the other to commemorate Elliott's former student John Matzke, who had had the courage to establish himself in the Far West, at Stanford. Then again, Europeans, somewhat paternalistically, could show their benevolence by contributing a note to an American learned journal; by reviewing, in one of their own media, an American monograph; or by taking into account, in their major research projects, articles published in trans-Atlantic periodicals. Thus, Graziadio Isaia Ascoli's miscellany *Zigeunerisches* (1865) – second in importance only to Pott's pioneering book on the Gypsies – contained, as its opening piece, a critical 'Auseinandersetzung' with a memoir from the pen of Alexandre G. Paspati (also known as Paspates), which had appeared in Vol. 7 of the *Journal of the American Oriental Society*.

The most ambitious and hardest-working American scholars of that era (or those imbued with this *Zeitgeist*, even though they reached their peak later) tried, in emulating Europeans, to beat their task-masters at their own game. Through the *Corpus Inscriptionum Latinarum*, which the Berlin Academy had launched at Mommsen's behest, the study of Latin epigraphy went into high gear, and a young Hugo Schuchardt used this new evidence in piecing together provincial Vulgar Latin; thirty years later, under the aegis of Columbia, Cowper started studying suffixal derivation in racy varieties of literary Latin and, soon thereafter, Olcott extended this analysis to inscriptions, doing an even better job than the Germans. At Harvard, Jeremiah D. M. Ford, in his

1897 dissertation, attacked the thorny problem of Old Spanish sibilants with neater tools than the Colombian Cuervo, a resident of Paris, who had raised the issue in the first place. Another Harvard-trained scholar, but one who went to Michigan, Edward L. Adams, prepared a monograph on word-formation in Old Provençal which surpassed in thoroughness, if not along the axis of imagination, anything European predecessors and contemporaries had achieved. In the authoritative opinion of Leonard Bloomfield, an American Germanist, namely, Edwin Roedder, prepared the best available dialect monograph (1936) of German – obviously against the stiffest competition.

In the *inter bella* period, the climate of opinion changed abruptly. With isolationism coloring all facets of American life, linguistics, if it was to survive and to attract the young, had to steer its own course rather than moving in the groove of a foreign, transoceanic culture. The old ties were not immediately cut, but suddenly the truly tone-setting linguists turned out to be those who were ready to offer a program of research free from any heavy dependence on Europe. The 'liberation', if that is the right word, was both topical and methodical.

The rise of a distinguished school of Amerindian studies is closely connected with the flowering of ethnography in the English-speaking countries and has, *prima facie*, nothing to do with cultural isolationism. Edward Sapir's earliest published work on Upper Chinook goes back to the year 1907; he was also, as is well known, at that juncture deeply involved in the study of Indian religious ideas, mythology, and folk belief, all of which, as is less frequently remembered, did not prevent him from occasionally cultivating Indo-European etymology as well. But the conjunction of personal talent and inclination with the mood prevailing in the country impelled Sapir, immediately after World War I, to offer his bold and scintillating synthesis, *Language*, over which his expertise in Indian languages so clearly presided and which ignited an enormous enthusiasm even outside the headquarters of ethnographers – something that the highly specialized research in Algonquian of a Michelson Truman had not accomplished.

Leonard Bloomfield was still in his late twenties and a confirmed paleo-Indo-Europeanist when he sallied forth with his first attempt at a book-length synthesis, *An introduction to the study of language* (1914). Subsequently, his first major venture in the description of an exotic tongue, with the help of an informant, was, as is common knowledge, the 1917 Illinois monograph, *Tagalog texts, with grammatical analysis*, which involved the utterances of a native speaker of a Filipino language.

But in the early 'twenties, a radical change took place: By 1922, Bloomfield reviewed, incurring the author's displeasure, Michelson's book *The Owl Sacred Pack of the Fox Indians*; two years later, he presented at the Twenty-First International Congress of Americanists held at The Hague, his paper on 'The Menomini Language', which initiated a powerful trend in his *œuvre* and eventually influenced his own outlook – an outlook, needless to say, which he succeeded in transmitting to his followers. After 1925, the study of indigenous American languages became before long a front-line (not, as before, a side-line) in American linguistics.

In a different way, a stubbornly nativist tradition asserted itself in the American spokesmen's refusal to follow European leaders along paths – suspected to be primrose paths and therefore angrily rejected – conducive to humanistic and esthetic speculation – and to any kind of unscientific amenity or nebulosity. A succession of book reviews and position papers by an increasingly irascible Bloomfield became the clearest expression of this mood; the victims were, in turn, Jespersen, Ries, Hermann, Havers, Swadesh for good measure, and, in the end, Leo Spitzer, an émigré scholar. In the last analysis, Bloomfield was, clearly, attacking his own Wundtian, thoroughly mentalistic past, after having resolutely espoused behaviorism in psychology, a school of thought which, whatever its merits and flaws in the perspective of 1974, at that moment gave the impression of American authenticity if not orthodoxy through honest, truthful observation of verifiable facts, to the exclusion of idle speculation – or so it seemed.

A separate manifestation of objectivity in the best tradition of American pragmatism was the new reliance on statistics, for a wide variety of not closely integrated purposes. On the most elementary, didactic level, frequency counts of words, idioms, and syntactic constructions promised to buttress the graded approach to language teaching, under the guidance of a level-headed linguist. Since the new language in most American curricula, starting with 1917, was Spanish, which spread like wildfire, at the cost of German and the classics, it was Hayward Keniston's statistical approach to sixteenth- and twentieth-century Spanish that caught everyone's attention. On a higher plateau of sophistication, statistics was applied to the measurement of time depth by A. L. Kroeber, in a move which eventually, in the fifties, was to trigger glottochronology and lexicostatistics. Yet another application, equally controversial, of the statistic principle was the web of theories launched by the maverick Harvard sociologist and psychologist George K. Zipf, between 1929 and 1949 (he died relatively young) on the principles, to use his own idiosyncratic jargon, of dynamic equilibrium, relative frequency, least effort, as well as on psycho-biology and on human ecology; from here a thin thread may have led to Joshua Whatmough's distinctly later key-concept of selective variation.

It cannot be my responsibility here to assess all these gropings, but it is not inaccurate to characterize their common denominator as an energetic recoil from the European tradition, occasionally to the tune of strident militancy, and, in the process, as a switch from the precarious alliance with the humanities, characteristic of German scholarship ('Geisteswissenschaften'), to an equally delicate integration with the social sciences, which French scholarship – a Saussure, a Meillet – had at all times advocated. The estrangement from Europe reached its peak when the revival of the stimulating Sapir-Whorf hypothesis, spearheaded by anthropological linguists, failed to take into account the crucial fact that the hypothesis goes back to a conjecture by Humboldt which in turn refracts, rather than reflects, the thinking of Herder and the further, clinching circumstance that its earliest, embryonic formulation on American soil is traceable, of all sources, to one of Sapir's juvenilia – a paper published as early as 1907, titled 'Herder's *Ursprung der Sprache*'.

Not unexpectedly, this cultural divorce, related to World War II (including that war's prelude and repercussions), had its human dimension. European linguists who came to the shores of America between 1935 and 1950, usually in a state of anguish and distress, in some instances received a warm welcome (I am thinking of Albrecht Götze and Eva Fiesel, among many peers), while in others they were exposed to a politely cool reception and in still others encountered aloofness or downright repudiation. They certainly were no longer lionized in any quarters. One close-knit group felt so acutely left out that its spokesmen were instrumental in founding a separate society, with its own journal, in metropolitan and cosmopolitan New York.

This articulate separatist movement became stunted by the mid-fifties. While the most vociferous American linguists, for twenty long years, had seen their primary goal in awakening an indifferent and, in part, prejudiced local society to the true nature of language, to the diversity of languages, and to the challenge of linguistics, a self-imposed triple task which required a closing of ranks and the acceptance of a common creed, to the virtual exclusion of foreign heresies, the situation began to change radically around 1955. The conversion of American society in the direction of linguistic tolerance, relativism, and rationalism became a commitment less and less urgent; the younger and more resilient European intellectuals who had struck root in America served as mediators between the two hemispheres and acquired a small, but rapidly growing following; European scholarship on its home ground underwent a thorough and merciless re-appraisal, conceivably more so in guilt-ridden, remorseful Germany than elsewhere; and, in America herself, there occurred several splits, on doctrinal grounds, so that the concept of 'American linguistics', displaying the dubious sense with which the sloganeers of the 'forties had endowed it, not the irreproachable sense that Franz Boas had associated with it, simply no longer made sense and no longer was fun. As a result of these multiple shifts, the polarization America vs. Europe, so far as linguistics was concerned, itself rapidly became obsolete.

The discussion of ORGANIZATION can be presided over by two *leitmotivs*: first, the original primacy of reading (and writing) over discussion, and second, the gradual overcoming of the handicap of long distances. Both *leitmotivs* pertain to the issue of smooth and effective communication.

In the 19th century, linguistic research was embodied (a) in books, including monographs, textbooks, and memorial or testimonial volumes; (b) in memoirs and transaction volumes (the famous *Abhandlungen* [orig. *Denkschriften*] and *Sitzungsberichte*) issued by practically all respectable academies, several learned societies, and a few research institutes, including ethnographic museums; (c) in University-sponsored journals, e.g., on this side of the Atlantic, the *American Journal of Philology* launched by Johns Hopkins and the [*Harvard*] *Notes and Studies in Philology*; and (d) in Society-sponsored journals: Oriental, Classical, neophilological, anthropological (or ethnographic, or folkloristic), and theological. Peripherally, there developed in certain countries, e.g. Italy, the custom of making commercially available an outline of well-attended lectures, as drafted by the professor in charge – not, under any circumstances, by top-notch students. There were relatively few journals on the market, and these were subscribed to and read avidly by everyone eager to attain professional status. Except for the class-room experience, linguistic research was conducted silently: by reading, annotating, reviewing books and by writing in legible longhand elaborate, exegetic letters, epistles running to ten or more pages, the celebrated *Gelehrtenkorrespondenz* of a leisurely age.

Of course scholars of like tastes, backgrounds, and intellectual commitments would meet privately, especially in major centers, such as Paris, Vienna, Berlin, Oxford, and, in their wake, Philadelphia and Baltimore; and from such private nuclei there would sprout, here and there, circles, groups, and even small-sized urban associations, organized around monthly meetings involving, as a rule, one lecture or the reading of two shorter papers, or of one paper and one report, the whole followed by discussions of varying degrees of formality. One paradigm of this kind of activity has been, over a century, the 'Société de linguistique de Paris', created by Bréal, influenced by Saussure during his ten-year tenure of a position at the École des Hautes Études, strengthened by Meillet, and kept at a high level by Benveniste. An alternative type of society was national, responsible for the issuance of a quarterly (or yearbook) and geared to annual meetings; witness Germany's 'Indogermanische Gesellschaft'. International congresses in our field were not organized before the First World War; linguists were thus far behind Orientalists and other groups of scholars.

The Linguistic Society of America – whose creation, in the mid twenties, must be credited almost entirely to Leonard Bloomfield, at least on the level of inspiration – was, then, something of a late-comer, and its founding fathers wisely adopted several of the features which European models had bequeathed: the journal, two monograph series attached to it, the annual meeting, the hierarchy of elected officers, the choice of foreign honorary members, etc. The novelty consisted in the birth of a national society in a country of such vast dimensions. Another distinctive feature which Bloomfield correctly stressed in his opening remarks was the chance given for the first time to linguistically-oriented classicists, Orientalists, medievalists, etc. to meet with one another rather than facing, as they had done for decades with frustrating results, other classicists, Orientalists, medievalists, etc. indifferent or hostile to analysis of language. With rare exceptions, everyone in this country was, at best, a part-time linguist; there existed no full-fledged, properly budgeted departments of linguistics. It was, all told, a heroic age; ours was a discipline for enthusiasts, idealists, and would-be martyrs, not one for opportunists and small-time hedonists.

The first truly great innovation was the addition, to the responsibilities of our Society, of a summer institute which, at the pioneering stage, in the late twenties, was usually conducted at the City College of New York and, in the thirties, reached its first peak on the Ann Arbor campus. Workshops, seasonal institutes, and artistically or pedagogically flavored summer sessions have, of course, from time immemorial been a hallmark of American education – not one whit less than campuses, dormitories, commons eating facilities, commencements, football games, and the like. An intensive course of Latin or Greek, at the undergraduate level, would hardly have constituted anything sensationally new. But a program with graduate courses in Hittite and Sanskrit and Amerindian languages and linguistic theory was something different again, especially if the instructors in charge were persons like Franklin Edgerton, or Leonard Bloomfield, or – the most sparkling of all – Edward Sapir.

How did the Linguistic Institute sponsored by our Society (not the only one, but the most important of its kind) influence the delicate interplay of relations between American and European linguistics? I think one can single out three consequences of its functioning. First, a mechanism was created which made it possible to invite foreign linguists of high distinction not only to visit this country for reasonably extended periods of time, but to meet, in addition to meritorious fellow scholars, and to more or less casual auditors attending public lectures, also highly select groups of qualified advanced students capable of appreciating a first-rate teaching performance. The roster of these visiting professors is impressive; it includes such names as Émile Benveniste from France, J. R. Firth from England, Louis Hjelmslev from Denmark, Jakob Jud from Switzerland, Manfred Mayrhofer from Austria. Certain disciplines, such as linguistic theory and Indo-European comparatism, seem to have been heavily favored over others.

A second influence, conceivably flowing from the first, has been sporadic attempts, in the Europe that has emerged from the shambles of World War II, to adopt some of our Society's procedures – a deviation from past *hauteur* understandable only against the background of current general curiosity, in the Old World, about the visibly successful American *modus operandi*. The best example of such emulation in reverse direction is, I take it, the 'Societas Linguistica Europaea', whose executive secretary, characteristically, spent several years at a succession of American universities and has thus acquired an enviable body of experience at first hand.

The third facet of the process under study is the growing number of young doctoral candidates or Ph.D.'s from Europe who, under one arrangement or another, as beneficiaries of their respective national or of an American fellowship program or else on their own, have derived keen satisfaction from attending our summer institutes.

As I come to the concluding theme of my talk, namely ACHIEVEMENT, which implies the task of drawing a balance sheet, I confess that the motto under which this section of the symposium has been given itself invites a brief comment. To a student of diachrony, the European background of American Linguistics is a topic whose treatment, to a crucial extent, depends on one's answer to this question: Has there occurred, as with the supposed disintegration of certain language families, a sudden 'sharp split' between the two traditions, or has a certain kind of osmosis continued to prevail, the membrane at issue being the Atlantic Ocean? The answer, undeniably, is the alternative possibility. Young American theorists and practitioners of linguistics judge the European ingredient of their own tradition not only by what they learn about Leibniz, and Vico, and Verner, and Saussure, and Trubetzkoj, but also by what they see and hear when observing, on their own ground or while travelling abroad, live specimens of European scholarly *engagement*. They are not least concerned with present-day European responses to imaginative American challenges.

As soon as we reject the hypothesis of a sharp split and residual heritage, and accept instead the formula of European background plus continued, indeed renewed contacts with European scholarship, which, incidentally, is once more in high gear, we gain a more realistic view of the total situation. The next question awaiting us may be phrased thus: Granted that differences in real-life conditions, including educational opportunities and chances of employment, are discrepant in many sectors of the Old World and in North America, should these differences be allowed to thicken into incompatibilities? Should inevitable minor irritations at contact or upon impact give nourishment to ideological superstructures that might encourage American linguists to extirpate their European legacy and, by the same token, stimulate Europeans to bar entry to American innovative ideas? Every single test shows that, on both sides of the Atlantic, this way of thinking is rapidly evaporating.

The reasons for this peculiar development, which exceeds by a wide margin the domain of linguistics and which, by way of free variation on a provocative book title of recent vintage, I am tempted to call one of 'Converging Parallels', can be presented in various, perhaps equally persuasive ways. Let me try out one approach. Linguists the world over, as a result of a cultural caprice or in overreaction against a hidden feeling of inadequacy, have, ever since Saussure, tried almost desperately to establish the autonomy of their discipline: There have arisen among them priests of 'pure linguistics'. In reality, linguistics has always, quite properly, been in alliance with other disciplines; the remarkable circumstance is not this ever-present possibility of integration, but the quick switch executed from one alliance to another. For a while there was in existence a humanistic confederacy, with historical linguistics representing little more than the backbone of philology and remaining, through this link, loosely associated with literary studies. The next phase was marked by the emergence of an alliance with the social sciences, including the conglomerate of sociology, ethnography, demography, and anthropology. Now we have reached the point where certain vociferously advertised varieties of linguistics encroach upon the domain of logico-mathematical inquiries. Whatever the ultimate wisdom of these reorientations, it is clear that national or continental traditions, including certain unavoidable substantive biases and idiosyncrasies of terminology and styling, are very powerful and, up to a certain point, conceivably legitimate in humanities; should be less strong, but are artificially buttressed through political and ideological pressures, in the realm of social sciences; and are almost non-existent in the rarefied air inhaled by logicians and mathematicians. The progressive move toward increased abstractness, whether of itself beneficial or baneful, certainly has had the advantage of making it less painful for American linguists to be reminded of the European background of their discipline and more palatable for them to maintain liaison with European counterparts, on condition of reciprocity.

Within certain limits, the craving for relative independence from earlier and present-day European models makes excellent sense. The élan with which Amerindian studies have been conducted and allowed to yield fresh theoretical insights is a case in point: The emotional need of a country in search of self-identification and the yearning for intellectual enlightenment were satisfied at once, and both the earlier and the concurrent European investments in this kind of research were before long eclipsed. Today, with the all-pervasive new awareness of its essentially multicultural structure, America, a classic melting-pot, is, understandably, far ahead of Europe in the meticulous study of immigrants' speech and bi- or tri-lingualism, a study once more fed by an inexhaustible supply of sentimental resources. Meanwhile, European research continues to be superior in other domains, e.g. in etymology, for which the relevant prerequisites are patience, precision work, command of and respect for sources, joint application of several techniques, ability to read numerous languages, and a certain sensibility for a three-thousand-year continuum, a receptiveness which cannot be created overnight.

Perhaps, if William Dwight Whitney were to visit us today, coming to Manhattan on a train from New Haven as he surely often did, he would not completely disapprove of our composite record of aspirations, organization, and even achievement.

University of California, Berkeley

REFERENCES

Ascoli, Graziadio Isaia 1865. *Zigeunerisches.* Halle, E. Heynemann, etc.
Bloomfield, Leonard 1914. *An introduction to the study of language.* New York, Holt; London, G. Bell.
— 1922. Review of *The Owl Sacred Packs of the Fox Indians*, by Truman Michelson, *AJPh* 43:276–81.
— 1924. 'The Menomini language', Proceedings of the 21th Congress of Americanists, 336–43.
Buck, Carl Darling 1904. *A grammar of Oscan and Umbrian.* Boston, Ginn & Company.
— 1905. *Elementarbuch der oskisch-umbrischen Dialekte* (translated and edited by Eduard Prokosch). Heidelberg, Carl Winter.
Grandgent, Charles H. 1927. *From Latin to Italian.* Cambridge, Mass., Harvard University Press.
Paspati, Alexandre G. 1862. 'Memoir on the language of the Gypsies as now used in the Turkish Empire' (translated by C. Hamlin), *JAOS* 7:143–270.
Pope, Mildred K. 1934. *From Latin to modern French, with especial consideration of Anglo-Norman.* Manchester University Press.
Sapir, Edward 1907. 'Herder's *Ursprung der Sprache*', *MPh* 5:109–42.
— 1921. *Language: An introduction to the study of speech.* New York, Harcourt Brace.
Whitney, William Dwight 1885. *The roots, verbal forms, and primary derivatives of the Sanskrit language.* Leipzig, Breitkopf & Härtel. Reprinted 1945 as American Oriental Series Vol. 30.
— 1900. *The life and growth of language.* [Presumably a reprint of the 1875 *princeps*.] New York, D. Appleton & Company.

LINGUISTICS IN AMERICA 1924–1974
A DETACHED VIEW

E. M. UHLENBECK

I

In spite of valuable work done in the recent past, one cannot escape the conclusion that the history of linguistics of the first three quarters of the twentieth century is still to be written. Balanced and authoritative accounts of these turbulent years can only emerge from historical research conducted by scholars who, apart from broader qualifications, are equally at home in linguistics and in history.

However, this conclusion does not free the linguist from the obligation to evaluate what is happening in his field through the years of his own scientific activity. His progress as a scholar depends on his readiness to assess the value of new proposals and new points of view and on his flexibility to act accordingly. If they contain a promise of an advance, the linguist should adopt and assimilate them forthwith. If not, it still remains his duty, especially when he acts as a teacher entrusted with the task of providing guidance to others, to explain why what is presented as new will not lead to improvement. By this continuous assessment the linguist, like every scientist, becomes over the years a critical observer and an active participant in the recent history of his discipline. It is my awareness of this double role which has given me the courage to accept the invitation to present here some thoughts on the development of American linguistics and the problems it faces at present. Later historical studies based on systematic use of all the available evidence will certainly have to correct as well as to amplify the picture I am going to draw. However, I do hope that at least its main contours will be able to stand the test of historical scrutiny.

The organisation of my paper is as follows. In the first section the emergence of phonology and its general importance for the later development of linguistics will be briefly discussed. It is intended to provide the background for the second section which will be devoted to Bloomfield and the Post-Bloomfieldians: that is, those linguists who accepted his conception of language and developed further certain aspects of his views. As it is my contention that the Post-Bloomfieldians take up a pivotal position in American linguistics, I will try to determine their position in three respects: (1) in relation to linguistics in Europe as a unique variant of structural linguistics, different from other, European, forms of structuralism, (2) in relation to other linguistic work done in the United States in the same period, and (3) as a background for understanding transformational generative grammar. In a third section the main lines of development within this school of thought will be presented. The fourth and final section deals with the actual present and with the future. In this section I will try to indicate some fundamental problems which confront American linguistics in its present stage of development.

It is clear that this is a large and ambitious program, difficult to realize in a short paper. A certain amount of simplification and subjectivity is unavoidable. Again, let us hope that the distortion of historical realities, if not absent, remains within tolerable limits.

II

The founding of the Linguistic Society which we are celebrating with this symposium took place in a period of fundamental change in linguistics. There is no better way to appreciate this change than by contrasting Sapir's 'Sound patterns in language', the leading article of the very first issue of *Language*, with Panconcelli-Calzia's *Die experimentelle Phonetik in ihrer Anwendung auf die Sprachwissenschaft*, of which a second impression had come out just a year before Sapir's epoch-making study. In this treatise which reflected widely held views, Panconcelli-Calzia, director of the then well-known phonetic laboratory in Hamburg, conceded that linguists for purely practical reasons might find it useful to set up classifications of speech-sounds, but he warned that such classifications could not have any scientific value. According to the German phonetician, experimental phonetics was the only scientific approach to the study of speech sounds. As a natural science, phonetics had to study what he called 'sich in der Gegenwart vollziehende, vom Orte unabhängige Phonationsvorgänge im normalen Organismus' (Panconcelli-Calzia 1924:136). For this study it was totally irrelevant in what language these sound-producing processes took place, how they had historically developed, and what their semantic function was.

It is against this view that Sapir's article was directed. Sapir emphasized that the nature of speech sounds cannot be properly understood in purely phonetic terms. It may be that there is a physical similarity or even identity between the sound that accompanies the blowing out of a candle, and the initial sound of words like *whisky, wheel* and *when*. Nevertheless, there is an essential difference between the two. It is only the sound used in speech which is part of a pattern, or as Sapir wrote 'of a definite system of symbolically utilizable counters'. In short, it is part of the phonemic system of English, and therefore can only be described as a function of this system.

The insight that the study of the sounds of speech was first of all a task of the linguist which could not be relegated to others, an insight expressed in various ways in the contemporaneous writings of Jakobson, Trubetzkoy, Pos, Hjelmslev, and others, had wider implications. First of all it helped to acquire for linguistics recognition as an autonomous science and to dispel the old notion of linguistics being merely a composite of parts of physics, physiology and psychology. But still more important, it gave direction to the further development of linguistics. Phonology, or to use the American equivalent: phonemics, set an example for the way a language had to be described, as it showed – be it only for a restricted and subordinate part of language – how language could be studied as a system of which in De Saussure's words 'toutes les parties peuvent et doivent être considérées dans leur solidarité synchronique' (Saussure 1916:124). As Van Wijk indicated by the choice of the subtitle for his monograph which summarizes the results of phonological study in the interwar period, phonology was only a first chapter of structural linguistics.

The best minds in linguistics understood that the concepts underlying phonology were valid for a wider area than the one in which they were initially applied. Consequently the task of the future became progressively clear. It could not but consist in a program of extrapolation, that is, one had to try to describe language in its synchronic totality making use of the principles applied by the phonologist in describing phonemic systems, of course with due regard for the specific characteristics of the prospective fields of application. A great amount of linguistic activity during the following decades in Europe and in the United States can be understood from this point of view. Jakobson's early articles on morphology (Jakobson 1932; 1936), morphemics as developed by the Post-Bloomfieldians, Pike's pioneering study of intonation of American English (Pike 1945) and De Groot's *Structural syntax* (De Groot 1949) may be seen – in spite of deep-seated differences in theoretical background – as examples of extrapolatory efforts.

It is not at all my intention to give a historically tenable account of the origin and rise of structural linguistics in Europe or in the United States. Such an account would at least require a careful appraisal of the role played by Baudouin de Courtenay, by De Saussure's *Cours de linguistique générale*, by Sapir's *Language* and of course by their predecessors. In any case it is certain that with the advent of phonology linguistics definitely entered a new phase, as a successful beginning was made in carrying out the task set for linguistics by De Saussure. According to the second chapter of the *Cours de linguistique générale*. De Saussure was of the opinion that what linguistics had to do was: (1) to describe all languages synchronically as well as diachronically, (2) to study the factors which play a permanent and universal role in all languages, and to derive from this study general laws, (3) to delimit and to define itself (Saussure 1916:20). Before De Saussure the second and the third task had been largely neglected. This was changing now. Also because new data from languages outside the familiar circle of Indo-European and Semitic languages became available and leading linguists such as Trubetzkoy, Sapir, Bloomfield, Firth and Hjelmslev had first hand knowledge of such languages, linguistics could begin to carry out De Saussure's program.

Accordingly three types of activity characterized the years following the advent of phonology:
(1) intensive discussion of the theoretical and practical problems posed by phonology itself;
(2) widely varying endeavors to extend structural descriptive methods to other subsystems of language;
(3) attempts to develop general conceptions of language consonant with the new insights brought about by phonology.

As to the study of phonology, the main results – reached only after the second world war – were a new understanding of the complementary role of phonology and phonetics, and closely related with it, the development of the distinctive feature theory of Roman Jakobson, which succeeded – and this is its crucial importance – in explaining, at least for a limited area of language, how the fact of the individuality of each language can be reconciled with the equally undeniable fact of the universality of language past and present.

It is impossible within the compass of a single paper to survey the multifarious attempts made to extrapolate notions from phonology. Even a discussion of these notions themselves has to be kept at a minimum. The most prominent of them seem to be (1) the concepts of opposition or contrast, and complementary distribution, (2) the concept of functional relevance, (3) a reluctance to introduce into a description a priori distinctions from other languages, from logic or from traditional grammar, (4) the requirement that distinctions made in a description should have psycholinguistic reality, (5) the requirement that a complete inventory of the elements of each subsystem had to be made in order to describe the relations between them.

However, for the understanding of the further development of linguistics and certainly also of American linguistics, it is necessary to point out that the main difficulty in all these efforts at extrapolation was a lack of clarity as to what the other provinces of linguistic structure actually comprised. This was largely caused by the fact that the study of syntax had lagged behind for centuries. It is well known that Delbrück in preparing his comparative syntax for the *Grundriss*, deplored in the long preface to his book the fact that descriptions of the syntax of the languages to be compared, were largely absent and that therefore his task was much heavier than Brugmann's who could base his comparative studies on reasonably reliable morphological and phonetic descriptions (Delbrück 1893:vi). In 1894 Ries published his *Was ist Syntax?*, one of the first innovative works on syntax of the nineteenth century which may be said to have determined De Saussure's views on syntax. In 1927, more than thirty years later, it proved to be still worthwhile to reproduce the text of the book virtually unchanged. This neglect of syntax and the uncertainty about its object is not accidental. It is related to the fact that in syntax – in contrast with morphology – the linguist is confronted not only with the question of the relation between language and logic, but also with the difficult problem of how to distinguish between the obligatory and the optional. The solution of these fundamental questions required understanding of the nature of the semantic aspect of language and – as Weinreich has pointed out in his valuable survey (Weinreich 1963:115) – in this area too progress had in most places been slow. It is therefore understandable that in Europe as well as in the United States it was in the first place morphology with its obligatory distinctions on which most extrapolational effort was spent.

It is not difficult to understand that the more general aspects of phonology briefly mentioned earlier may be incorporated in widely different structural conceptions of language. Theoretically this is related to the fact that phonemics only involves the description of a very limited part of language. The central problems of semantics are hardly involved in it, and the province of grammar poses questions never met in phonemics. However, for realizing to what extent acceptance of basic tenets of phonology is compatible with quite different attitudes towards language, it is enough to take note of the quite differently oriented monographs which began to appear, such as Gardiner's *Theory of speech and language*, Bally's *Linguistique générale et linguistique française*, Bühler's *Sprachtheorie*, and Reichling's *Het woord*, all published between 1932 and 1935, and of the later work of scholars such as Hjelmslev, Martinet and Firth. Again I have to refrain from characterizing the approaches followed and the contributions made by each of the centers of structural linguistics, such as Prague, Copenhagen, Geneva, London, and Amsterdam, where scholars were engaged – along quite different lines – in realizing a common aim: the gradual discovery of the synchronic structure of language. It is important to add, in view of the later development of linguistic theory, that it was soon understood – thanks to Mathesius, Karcevski and Jakobson – that one should not follow De Saussure in his identification of synchronic with static. A morphological description is simply impossible without making use of the concept of productivity as Karcevski in his monograph on the Russian verb of 1927 had already proved convincingly.

It is within this period of cautious extrapolation and renewed attention for linguistic theory that a book appeared which was different from all others and which was destined to be instrumental in the development of a special brand of structural linguistics: Leonard Bloomfield's *Language*.

III

Bloomfield's monumental handbook has many qualities not found in other works of the same period. The book as a whole was refreshingly new and sober-minded, important qualities which can be only fully appreciated by comparing it with the abstruse and vague psychologistic treatises on language of which the Germans seemed to hold a monopoly. The synchronic part of *Language* may be regarded as an original attempt to extrapolate from phonemics and to present – also terminologically – one coherent treatment of grammar. In its diachronic part Bloomfield summarized in a way unsurpassed in competence and lucidity of exposition, the results of historical and comparative linguistics and of dialect geography. As a handbook provocative, because of its newness and at the same time reliable as to its account of past achievement, it remained for years the book chosen by teachers inside and outside of the United States as obligatory reading.

At this moment, however, another feature of the book, and a truly distinctive one, should occupy all our attention: its acceptance of the behaviorism of A. P. Weiss. For understanding the far-reaching consequences of this decisive move, a passage taken from Bloomfield's review of Havers' *Handbuch der erklärenden Syntax* is particularly illuminating. It runs as follows: 'The simple correlations of language consist of the linking of MEANINGS (stimuli) with LINGUISTIC FORMS (speech-responses). In everyday life we assume the existence of these correlations: when anyone says anything, we proceed, in one way or another, to reckon with the meaning of his speech . . . As a matter of scientific study, however, we are unable to demonstrate this correlation between the stimulus acting on a speaker (the meaning) and the speech form which he utters' (Bloomfield 1934:35). Three closely related elements in this passage stand out clearly: (1) a strong belief that only an inquiry into perceptible entities can be a scientific inquiry, (2) the conviction that the fact that users of a language are certain that they mean something when they speak, does not have to be taken into account in a scientific study of language, and last but far from least (3) the assumption that the linking of linguistic forms with meaning has to be understood as an association of these forms with things and situations.

I believe that this set of assumptions, more than anything else, is responsible for the deep gap which after the second world war separated Post-Bloomfieldian linguistics from the forms of European structuralism, which had developed on the European mainland and which had all accepted in one form or another the Saussurean conception of the bipartite nature of the linguistic sign. In the Post-Bloomfieldian period semantics was considered to be outside of language, or at best as something which takes up a peripheral position in language. Which of these alternatives one preferred was, according to *A course in modern linguistics*, rather a matter of personal taste, and in any case an unimportant issue (Hockett 1958:138). The really scientific study of language was held to be first of all concerned with sound shapes and their distribution. It is in this last area – neglected by European structuralists who were inclined to pay attention chiefly to paradigmatic relationships – that important advances were made. Post-Bloomfieldian linguistics then was essentially: phonemics + morphemics. Meaning was, according to Joos, an area to be studied not by linguists but by sociologists (Joos 1950:701). On syntax little effort was spent. It is remarkable, however, that although traditional grammar was held in contempt, the only method of syntactic analysis which was taken over from Bloomfield's conception of syntax, namely immediate constituent analysis, was similar to, if not identical with, traditional parsing procedures taught in school. This means that there existed a conceptual discrepancy between phonemics and morphemics on the one hand and syntax on the other, and a conceptual void as to the relation between syntax and semantics.

There has been in recent years a tendency to belittle the achievement of Bloomfield and those linguists who followed in his tracks. However, everybody who rereads for instance Greenberg's moderate and sensible essay on the definition of linguistic units of 1957 will realize how much present-day descriptive practice owes to their careful and systematic observations within well-defined areas of a great variety of languages. Such a positive appreciation does not have to make us blind to less satisfactory aspects. Three of them have to be mentioned here because they explain at least partly the later developments. Many Post-Bloomfieldians – among them influential linguists such as Joos, Trager and Hockett – were genuinely convinced that their behavioristic approach, which put sound in the center, and meaning as much in the background as possible, represented the only truly scientific one. There are many symptoms of this feeling of scientific superiority. In *A course in modern linguistics* the statement is made that "linguistics has always concentrated on the three central subsystems (the grammatical, the phonological, and the morphophonemic system) without much concern with the peripheral systems" (the semantic and the phonetic system) (Hockett 1958:138). Such a statement can only be made when 'linguistics' is equated with 'linguistics in America' and when 'always' is considered equivalent with 'since Bloomfield'. Such a point of view is of course not very conducive to taking note, let alone for making use, of, advances made by colleagues in Europe, as their work was not to be taken seriously in view of its mentalistic orientation and because it seemed not to satisfy self-styled canons of scientific rigor. In this way Post-Bloomfieldian linguistics tended to isolate itself from others. Many symptoms of this disregard for other views could be mentioned. From Hockett's 'Two models of grammatical description', an article which by its title already indicates its confinement to linguistics in the United States, one can conclude that the notion of process in a synchronic sense was difficult to appreciate for the author (Hockett 1954:211) as it was also for Harris (Harris 1951:289–292) and Wells (Wells 1963:41). This proves that, for instance, the work of Bally and Karcevski, in which a clear distinction is made between the diachronic French term *procès* and the synchronic term *procédé*, had remained unknown. Fruitful and in my opinion even indispensable distinctions such as between 'marked' and 'unmarked', and between 'center' and 'periphery', introduced by the Prague school, shared this fate. Karl Bühler's important achievement, his *Sprachtheorie*, was never reviewed in *Language*, and its author, sometimes called the theoretician of the Prague school, did not exert any perceptible influence on the course of American linguistics, although he lived in this country since the outbreak of the second world war (see Garvin 1964). This isolationist tendency and lack of interest in achievements elsewhere were not easily overcome and remained characteristic also during the later period of generative grammar. Bühler's treatment of deixis (Bühler 1934:79–148), the studies on the topic-comment distinction by the Prague school (Mathesius 1924; 1928; 1929, Firbas 1959; 1964; 1967; 1971; 1974), Ducrot's important work on presupposition (Ducrot 1966; 1968; 1969; 1972) are rarely taken into account in American studies on the same topics.

The dislike of generalizations, of theorizing, and in general of anything which seemed unduly removed from the directly perceptible facts of individual languages, is another characteristic, indirectly reflected in Trager's words of welcome extended to the newly founded journal *Lingua*, in which he confessed 'to be disturbed by the vast and vague generalizations indulged in by his European colleagues' and deplored that Reichling in his inaugural lecture – which served, in translation, as the leading article of the first issue – had been 'a bit too much concerned with universal categories of speech and with general laws of language', at a time when according to Trager so much 'specific work' still had to be done (Trager 1948:207).

Language was defined in a rather narrow way. It was maintained that 'as linguistic science uses the term language, it is restricted to (phenomena of the order of) systems of arbitrary acoustic symbols by which human beings interact' (McDavid 1949:69), a definition which required little modification to become suitable for communication systems found among other species. In harmony with this restricted view of the nature of language, linguistics seemed to be a dry subject of limited scope, cut off from the study of literature, cut off from the study of the human faculty of speech and from the study of language in society. Lévi-Strauss' well-known dictum: 'Qui dit homme, dit langage, et qui dit langage, dit société' (Lévi-Strauss 1955:421) would not have met with enthusiastic approval, except of course in those quarters which continued in adhering to Sapir's view that language, being a cultural product, should be studied as such (Sapir 1929:214).

One would make a serious mistake if – misled by Joos' one-sided anthology – one identified linguistics in America with Bloomfield and the Neo-Bloomfieldians. The Boas-Sapir tradition, although somewhat in the background and better represented in the West than in the East, had remained very much alive. It is enough to mention linguists such as Newman, Haas, Hoijer and Pike. After the second world war the journal *Word* provided a forum for a more internationally oriented group of linguists and gave American linguists a much-needed opportunity to get acquainted with a broader spectrum of linguistic views. The arrival of eminent linguists from abroad stimulated the dialogue with the reigning Item-Arrangement orthodoxy and conveyed through their academic teaching and through their writings, often in *Word*, a broader conception of language than could be derived from the sole reading of *Language* and *Studies in Linguistics*. There was a growing pluriformity and Hamp's statement that American linguistics was not a monochrome (Hamp 1963:166), certainly contains an element of truth, although Haugen's presidential warnings of 1951 against parochial attitudes were by no means superfluous (Haugen 1951:211).

It may be true – as Jakobson rather optimistically stated in his elegant closing speech at the Bloomington conference of 1952 – that in the early fifties the reluctance to discuss 'meaning' was somewhat lessening (Jakobson 1953:19–21), but it is hard to find signs of a serious attempt to ANALYZE the semantic facts or even to study what had been done in semantics so far. It would have been natural for linguists favoring behaviorism to pay attention to the similarly oriented semiotic theory of Charles Morris, but neither of his two monographs (Morris 1938; 1946) was reviewed in *Language*, while the reviewer of his second book in *Studies in Linguistics* deplored, instead of welcomed, its broadening of the definition of language (McDavid 1949:68). The influence of Morris only became visible in American linguistics in 1956 when Goodenough and Lounsbury introduced componential analysis of conceptually determined lexical domains. It is also remarkable that semantic insights found in the work of Boas and Sapir remained unexplored. Boas, for instance, had emphasized the obligatory nature of grammatical categories in contrast to the essentially non-obligatory character of lexical meaning (Boas 1938:132), while Sapir, through his informants, had grasped the psycholinguistic reality of the word as a linguistic unit (Sapir 1921:34). Sapir's three semantic studies reprinted in the Mandelbaum reader in 1949, although sympathetically mentioned by Zellig Harris in his review of this monumental anthology (Harris 1951b:300–301), did not exert any perceptible influence.

As to syntax, the main progress lay in the reintroduction of a functional approach by Pike (Pike 1954; 1958), while Harris' discourse analysis (Harris 1952) may be appreciated as a first attempt to transcend the limits of the framework of the sentence. However, the widely used handbooks by Gleason, Hill, and Hockett did not go beyond I.C. analysis, as worked out by Wells (Wells 1947). It was in this situation, here very sketchily described, with omission of everything that does not seem to be of direct relevance, that Chomsky's *Syntactic structures* appeared. Although in several important aspects much more a continuation of Post-Bloomfieldian linguistics than its author and his followers initially assumed, the book constitutes in other, equally important aspects such a clean break with it, that it seems natural to consider the year of its appearance as the beginning of a new period in American linguistics.

IV

Like the Post-Bloomfieldians, Chomsky and his followers were convinced of the scientific superiority of their linguistic conception. They were certain that they could also prove it in a way which they considered to be quite conclusive. There were at least five interrelated arguments. First of all, there was the argument based on recursiveness as a necessary property of grammar. The reasoning was simple and compelling if one was willing to accept some assumptions. If a language consists of an infinite number of sentences, if a grammar is finite, as it must be because it is assumed to be mastered by a normal child in a few years, and if a grammar has to specify all the sentences in the language, then the grammar, conceived as a system of rules, must possess some kind of recursive mechanism. This implies that grammars without such a mechanism, are necessarily defective, remaining for ever unable to do the descriptive job required from them. No grammar in existence could be shown to have the property of recursiveness. Therefore, our only hope could be a transformational generative grammar, of which recursive rule application is a design feature.

Already this argument, if valid, would be sufficient to cast strong doubts on the viability of Post-Bloomfieldian structuralism. But there were more, and I believe also more decisive ones. A second criticism – of particular importance as we shall see later – was directed against immediate constituent analysis, which was shown to be inadequate as a sole descriptive device and had to be supplemented by a quite different type of operation, namely transformations, which had the advantage that syntactic structures, felt to belong together, could also be described in close relation to each other.

Apart from the argument against an independent phonemic level developed somewhat later by Halle on the basis of certain phonological and morphonological facts of Russian (Halle 1959) there were three more criticisms against American structuralism based on general considerations. The first of them was particularly strong. As Bloch himself had admitted in 1953, Post-Bloomfieldian linguistics had not developed "a unified theory of structural description" (Bloch 1953:43). In general it had insufficiently realized the crucial importance of the adoption of a theory, although linguists in Europe such as Paul (Paul 1920⁵:5) and De Saussure (Saussure 1916:20) and later Bühler and Reichling had insisted on this point time and again (Bühler 1934:1–24; Reichling 1948:14). It is one of the lasting merits of Chomsky that he has made American linguistics aware of the fact that only on the basis of an explicit theory can scientific progress be made, as it allows a real and exact confrontation with the facts, so that whenever this proves to be necessary, changes in the theory can be made which can then again – in its revised form – be applied and further tested.

In the second place American structuralism was criticized for not having had a clear view of what a linguistic description had to achieve. It had contented itself with stating certain regularities on the basis of a limited amount of language material, had never formulated any explicit rules, and was therefore not in a position to work towards what was gradually seen by Chomsky to be the real goal of grammar, namely providing a scientific description of the lingual capabilities of the native speaker.

Finally, American structuralism had occupied itself only with the surface of the linguistic facts. It had not developed, and was essentially also unable to develop, descriptive mechanisms for portraying the deeper structural relations which play an essential role in the understanding of sentences, as reflection on sentences such as *John is easy to please, John is eager to please, They are flying planes* and the like seemed to prove.

In a few years the climate of American linguistics seemed to have changed completely. A kind of Umwertung aller Werte was taking place. Traditional school grammar, at best ignored by American structuralists, was now found to have been basically correct in its syntactic analyses (Chomsky 1965:64). There was a striking preference for extreme positions in order to make clear how different one was from the older generation of linguists who had only tried to describe but had rarely arrived at explanations. While Joos had stressed the differences between languages (Joos 1957:96), now all languages were supposed to be nearly identical; their differences only pertained to unimportant details of surface structure. Virtually overnight there was a complete switch from a mechanistic to a mentalistic position, although it soon appeared that it was easier to confess to be a mentalist than to act like one, as was shown by the uncertain attitude towards the semantic aspect of language. In the past one studied different languages; now English, the native language of the linguist, was supposed to be enough. While collecting a large amount of lingual material was formerly considered to be a prerequisite for arriving at descriptive results, and attention to linguistic theory was held at a minimum, now there was a tendency to be long on theory, but short on facts.

This moving to extremes, characteristic for the early years of transformational grammar but now, fortunately, lessening gradually, tended to prevent appreciation of the large measure of continuity between American structuralism and the new linguistics which has been seeking to replace it.

The continuity was discernible in at least five respects. First of all, and most important of all, the attitude concerning the semantic aspect of language did not change materially. The grammatical model of *Syntactic structures* had no place for semantics, an area still viewed in the usual way: parallel to, but outside of language. Secondly, immediate constituent analysis, although found wanting by Chomsky, was nevertheless incorporated into the model. Like Post-Bloomfieldian linguistics, early generative grammar was hardly interested in the study of paradigmatic relations, did not consider the word as a central unit of linguistic structure, and devoted little attention to the analysis of the act of speech, considered by many European linguists to be a natural starting point for the development of basic theoretical notions.

Comparing a textbook such as *A course in modern linguistics* with Chomsky's early work, one becomes aware how one approach developed out of the other, how certain views basic for transformational generative grammar also in later years, are already adumbrated in some Post-Bloomfieldian writings. This is particularly true for the distinction between surface and deep structure tentatively introduced by Hockett in a chapter of his textbook and briefly illustrated with the help of some English, Chinese and Latin sentences. There is a short passage in this chapter which deserves to be quoted here. It runs as follows: 'This most apparent layer constitutes, we shall say, surface grammar. Beneath it lie various layers of deep grammar, which have much to do with how we speak and understand but which are still largely unexplored, in any systematic way, by grammarians' (Hockett 1958:249). This is a remarkable passage in many ways. It admits that in Post-Bloomfieldian linguistics little attention was being paid to the way people speak and understand each other, and also gives the impression that linguists have been using most of their energy so far to the study of the more superficial aspects of language. However, the main observation I want to make concerning this passage is that the idea that the really important things about language lie deep beneath the surface, comes natural only to those who are accustomed to view sentences as surface-phenomena, that is as sequences or strings of sound forms, of empty shapes. The discovery of deep structure is their way of discovering that there is something more in language than sound shapes and their distribution and also that language is used in conjunction with situational data. For those linguists who from the beginning accept as a cornerstone for their linguistic conception the presence in sentences of meaning-bearing units, there is little reason to develop a concept of deep structure. For those linguists what others call deep structure is largely, if not completely, identical with what they consider to be the semantic aspect of language. The discovery in American linguistics that semantics was a part, and a constitutive part, of language, could only be made via a tortuous route, namely via a syntactic concept of deep structure. This route is determined by the behavioristic point of departure which prevented appreciation of the basic insight that linguistics is concerned with facts which owe their existence to the simultaneous presence of a perceptible and a cognitive aspect. To this very day it remains difficult for those who have been fed on a behavioristic diet to grasp this very fundamental datum. A telling example is Chafe's book on *Meaning and the structure of language*. This work, admirable because of the sensitivity of its author in analysing minute but very real semantic differences such as between: *any elephant, an elephant, elephants, the elephant*, and the like, nevertheless contains the statement that words are of course not meaningful units (Chafe 1970:74), a statement eloquently refuted by the best pages of the book itself.

It is not too difficult to indicate the turning points in the development of transformational generative grammar. By far the most important one was when in 1963 generative grammar began to change its stance towards semantics. The second one was in 1967, when a conference of dissenters took place which led to the publication of the well-known Bach-Harms volume (Bach-Harms 1968). This conference marks the fact that transformational generative grammar ceased to be a single theory and began to develop into a field of competing alternatives.

As is generally known, Katz and Fodor are largely responsible for the change in attitude towards semantics through their article on 'The structure of a semantic theory'. The importance of their article does not reside in the actual semantic proposals it contained, but in the fact that it convinced generativists that if a grammar had to give a full account of all lingual abilities of a native speaker, then it could be shown that such a speaker also possesses certain semantic abilities which an asemantic grammar of the *Syntactic structures* type could never describe. Katz and Fodor's article led to a period of experimentation with the familiar triangular models consisting of a syntactic component as the generative component, flanked by two interpretative components, a phonological and a semantic one. In *Aspects of the theory of syntax* two of such triangular models were introduced, one of which was soon discarded in favor of the other, more simple one, which became known later as the Standard Theory.

This triangular model formed a short, transitional stage within the development of generative grammar. Although the inclusion of a semantic component led to important changes in the organization of the syntactic component as it necessitated acceptance of the far from unproblematical principle that transformations are meaning-preserving (cf. Partee 1971), still one could maintain that in the *Aspects* model no basic principle of transformational generative theory had been sacrificed. The grammar as a whole was still meant to be an explicit account of the competence of the native speaker. It was still conceived as a self-contained device consisting of rules, presumably ordered rules, which could produce structural descriptions of the sentences of the language. One continued to assume that it was possible to arrive at such a device without having recourse to the data of performance, as introspective reports of the linguist in his capacity of native speaker were deemed to furnish sufficient factual information.

However, this attempt to cope with the semantic facts by means of an additive strategy failed. In the following years it became clear that the decision to accept a semantic component as part of a linguistic description, had a disruptive influence on the rest of the transformational generative edifice, in the end also affecting some of the foundations of generative theory itself.

Around 1965 semantics was for most generative grammarians a largely unknown subject. It was – to borrow a picturesque but rather unsavory expression from McCawley – 'the hairy mess that remains to be talked about after one has finished with linguistics proper' (McCawley 1968: 125). The difficulty was that one cannot finish with linguistics proper before turning to the semantic facts, for the very solid reason that there is no linguistics proper in abstraction from the semantic facts. In other words, generative grammar faced the problem how to make semantics a really integrated part of linguistics. Since about 1967 two strategies have been followed: one – the more conservative strategy – is adopted by interpretive semantics, which tries to preserve in its extended standard theory as many features of the old conception as is still considered compatible with semantic exigencies, while the other – the more revolutionary and radical one – is followed by the generative semanticists, who have done away with some long cherished principles such as a purely syntactic concept of deep structure and the generative principle itself, which has recently been explicitly rejected by McCawley in his detailed review of Chomsky's *Studies on semantics in generative grammar* (McCawley 1973a).

It might seem that in this section too much space has already been given to transformational generative grammar at the expense of the various other types of linguistic study which are being carried out under a bewildering variety of labels such as computational linguistics, mathematical linguistics, ethnoscience, anthropological linguistics, sociolinguistics, psycholinguistics, paralinguistics, semiotics, stratificational grammar and tagmemic theory. As I have to be selective as well as brief, I will conclude this section with the following remarks.

Diversity – a striking characteristic of the present linguistic scene – has to be appreciated in a positive way. The linguistic phenomena are of such dazzling complexity and at the same time of such central importance for the understanding of man, that scientific progress is only possible if these phenomena are studied from widely different angles and with different aims. Concentrating on general linguistic theory it seems to me that the sociolinguistic work of Labov and associates and that of Schank in computational linguistics (Schank 1972a; 1972b) are holding the greatest promise for theoretical advances. Since Labov's fundamental study of 1966 and since the impressive article written by my much regretted friend Weinreich in collaboration with Labov and Herzog on 'The empirical foundations for a theory of language change' of 1968, with its fruitful concept of ordered heterogeneity, our insight into the position of language in society has been considerably deepened and enriched. These studies which have been followed by others (Labov 1972a; 1972b) present a much-needed corrective to the extreme emphasis placed on the purely psychological aspect of language and on its cognitive function by Chomsky and his associates with their focus on an ideal speaker-listener in a homogeneous language community. The importance of the work of Schank and Wilks lies in the first place in the fact that they recognize the necessity of a study of 'meaning with respect to the actual usage of speakers' (Schank-Wilks 1974:312). With them I am convinced that the study of 'performance' is the only way for arriving at a satisfactory account of the semantic facts.

V

It is time now to conclude this paper with some short final observations on the present situation. In recent publications by Postal and Lakoff, feelings of disappointment and pessimism are being expressed about the results of fifteen years of descriptive effort within a transformational framework. Postal, for instance, complained in his contribution to Peters' volume of studies on *Goals of linguistic theory*, that 'proposal after proposal, from the auxiliary analysis to selectional features, to nounphrase-conjunction, to cyclic pronominalization, to cross-over constraints, has collapsed or slid into the murk of competing claims and contradictory evidence' (Postal 1972:160; cf. also Postal 1971:3–4). Postal's only consolation seems to be that at least one has been led to the discovery that 'natural languages are fantastically vast, complex, and mysterious systems whose principles have so far largely eluded specification' (Postal 1972:160). In my opinion, however, there is no room for despair about our ignorance, nor is there any reason to consider the complexity of language a recent discovery. The fact that the proposed rules fail (cf. Lakoff 1972a) should be interpreted differently, namely as an indication that the conception behind those rules, i.e. the conception of a grammar as one integrated and closed system of rules by which one expects that the semantic aspect of language can also be described, is inadequate; I see in the recent linguistic literature some encouraging signs of a realization that important changes in the current transformational paradigms have to be made, just because the semantic facts are being recognized as part and parcel of language.

In order to get things in the right perspective, it is necessary to return to my earlier conclusion that around 1925 phonology set in motion a series of extrapolatory efforts. These efforts remained limited to morphology. Transformational generative grammar can also be viewed as a certain form of structural linguistics, as it also tries to arrive at a complete synchronic language description, but – and this is an important difference – it started where the others left off: with syntax. After a few years it was understood that a syntactic description needs an understanding of the semantic aspect of language, that is, not only of lexical meaning but of the entire spectrum of the semantic phenomena including, for instance, deixis, the meaning of proper names, and the semantic value of morphological categories.

One cannot but positively appreciate the fact that studies within the transformational generative framework occupied themselves seriously with the whole set of interrelated phenomena which constitute the fields of grammar and semantics. This is definitely progress, but – and this is the present trouble – in exploring these phenomena some unfortunate moves have been made which are largely responsible for the present feeling of uncertainty and discontent. First of all it was bad strategy to take over immediate constituent analysis from one's predecessors and, although understanding its insufficiencies, to build upon this analysis a supplementary descriptive device, the transformational operations. With Willy Haas I am convinced that in this way the syntactic investigation of the relational structure of the sentence was arrested (Haas 1973b:107–110), and to this very day there are in American linguistics few signs of progress in this area since Longacre's article on 'String constituent analysis' (1960). Secondly, progress has been held back because of the drastic decision in favor of assuming that syntactic and semantic phenomena are in a direct line with each other, instead of realizing – and this is in my opinion crucial for one's conception of language – that they constitute entirely different but correlative dimensions of language. It is certainly to be deplored that Boas' insight into the obligatory nature of syntax against the essential freedom of lexical meaning was lost, as recent studies of readings of lexical items such as those on *remind* (Postal 1970; Kirsner 1972) and *kill* (McCawley 1968b; 1971; Fodor 1970; Shibatani 1972) prove. If it is realized that the *raison d'être* of grammar is to provide a framework of rules within which the semantic aspect of language can function freely and creatively in actual language use, then the best descriptive strategy seems to be to begin with the study of what is essentially obligatory, and to try to describe these obligatory phenomena of morphology and syntax in terms of exhaustive and explicit rules. Implicit in this suggestion is that one should not a priori assume the presence of rules of one single type, as it is more than likely that we will need, next to strict rules, also rules of relative preference and avoidance.

There has been another questionable practice which seems responsible for the arbitrariness with which deep sources are being posited for various constructions, namely the persistent habit of studying sentences in isolation without taking into account the fact that sentences are spoken and interpreted with the help of various types of extra-lingual information. Since about 1969, however, generative semanticists and others have begun to realize that this practice should be abandoned as it was based on the doubtful assumption that the study of competence should and could take place before and without paying attention to the data of performance (Lakoff 1969; 1974). In recent years one notices a quite healthy return of interest among linguists to the study of speech acts and to what Morris has called pragmatics. This is shown, for instance, by the intense occupation with the varied phenomena of presupposition, entailment and implication, in the past mainly studied by philosophers. It is to be hoped that still one more step will be taken towards a more realistic study of sentences, by proceeding to study them with constant attention to their intonational component. It is a good thing that, as Léon's recent survey shows (Léon 1972), there is in the last few years a rapidly increasing amount of knowledge becoming available concerning these very complex and multilayered phenomena.

Fourthly and finally, serious doubts have to be raised against the view that 'the underlying structure of a sentence is the logical form of that sentence, and consequently that the rules relating logical form to surface form are exactly the rules of grammar' (Lakoff 1972b:559). Linguists cannot leave the study of the semantic aspect of language to logicians. It is their specific task to analyse this unique form of knowledge which is different from conceptual knowledge. In general I believe that Lotz in 1951 and the Chomsky of the *Language* article of 1955 were right in their conclusion that there is an essential difference between artificial and natural languages. However, as this opinion is based on knowledge of artificial languages existing at that time, and as at present more sophisticated formal languages are being developed than those of first order predicate logic (Montague 1970a; 1970b; Martin 1971; Cresswell 1973) one must perhaps leave open the possibility that in the future such formal systems may serve linguistic purposes.

Looking at the present situation, then, one may arrive at a twofold conclusion. Linguistics is still engaged – and will remain engaged for many years to come – in a struggle to get a closer view of what the structure of a language really comprises and how universal and individual characteristics are interrelated. There is some reason to expect that in the following decades it will be generally understood that to give an answer to these fundamental questions requires a full investigation of the way language functions within a speech community. There is also some reason to assume that the various linguistic approaches in this country as well as abroad, although at present still largely working in isolation from each other, can find in this goal a common ground for cooperation and mutual exchange of results.

University of Leiden

REFERENCES

Bach, Emmon and Robert T. Harms (eds.) 1968. *Universals in linguistic theory*. New York, Holt.
Bally, Charles 1932[1], 1944[2]. *Linguistique générale et linguistique française*. Berne, Francke
Bloch, Bernard 1953. 'Linguistic structure and linguistic analysis', *Report of the Fourth Annual Round Table Meeting on Linguistics and Language Teaching*, Washington D.C.: Georgetown University. 40–44.
Bloomfield, Leonard 1933. *Language*. New York, Holt.
— 1934. Review of W. Havers. Handbuch der erklärenden Syntax. *Language* 10:32–40.
Boas, Franz 1938. *General anthropology*. Boston, D. C. Heath.
Bühler, Karl 1934. *Sprachtheorie. Die Darstellungsfunktion der Sprache*. Jena, Fischer.
Chafe, Wallace L. 1970. *Meaning and the structure of language*. University of Chicago Press.
Chomsky, Noam 1955. 'Logical syntax and semantics: Their linguistic relevance.' *Language* 31:36–45.
— 1957. *Syntactic structures*. The Hague, Mouton.
— 1962. 'Introduction to the formal analysis of natural languages', in: *Handbook of Mathematical Psychology*, vol. 2.
— 1965. *Aspects of the theory of syntax*. Cambridge, Mass., M.I.T. Press.
— 1972. *Studies on semantics in generative grammar*. The Hague, Mouton.
Cresswell. M. J. 1973. *Logics and languages*. London, Methuen.
De Groot, A. W. 1949. *Structurele syntaxis*. Den Haag, Servire.
Delbrück, B. 1893. *Vergleichende Syntax der indogermanischen Sprachen* 1 (= K. Brugmann und B. Delbrück, *Grundriss der vergleichenden Grammatik der indo-germanischen Sprachen* 3) Strassburg, Trübner.
Ducrot, Oswald 1966. 'Le roi de France est sage, Implication logique et présupposition linguistique'. *Etudes de linguistique appliquée* 4:39–47.
— 1968. 'La description sémantique des énoncés français et la présupposition'. *L'homme* 8:37–53.
— 1969. 'Présupposés et sous-entendus'. *Langue française* 4:30–43.
— 1972. *Dire et ne pas dire: Principes de sémantique linguistique*. Paris, Hermann.
Firbas, Jan 1959. 'Thoughts on the communicative function of the verb in English, German and Czech.' *Brno Studies in English* 1:39–68.

— 1964. 'On defining the theme in functional sentence analysis', *Travaux de linguistique de Prague* 1:267–80.

— 1967. 'On the prosodic features of the modern english finite verb as means of functional sentence perspective', *Brno Studies in English* 7:11–48.

— 1971. 'On the concept of communicative dynamism in the theory of functional sentence perspective', *Studia Minora Facultatis Philosophicae Universitatis Brunensis* A 19:135–44.

— 1974. 'Some aspects of the Czechoslovak approach to problems of functional sentence perspective', *Papers on Functional Sentence Perspective*, Prague, Akademia, pp. 11–37.

Fodor, Jerry A. 1970. 'Three reasons for not deriving 'kill' from 'cause to die'', *Linguistic Inquiry* 1:429–38.

Gardiner, Alan H. 1932[1], 1951[2]. *The theory of speech and language*. Oxford, Clarendon Press.

Garvin, Paul 1964. 'Karl Bühler', *Language* 40:633–34.

Gleason, H. A., Jr. 1955[1], 1961[2]. *An introduction to descriptive linguistics*. New York, Holt.

Goodenough, Ward H. 1956. 'Componential analysis and the study of meaning', *Language* 32:195–216.

Greenberg, Joseph H. 1957. 'The definition of linguistic units', *Essays in linguistics*, Viking Fund Publications in Anthropology 24. New York.

— (ed.) 1963. *Universals of language*. Cambridge Mass., M.I.T. Press.

Haas, W. 1973a. 'Meanings and rules', *Proceedings of the Aristotelian Society*. New Series vol. 73.135–55.

— 1973b. 'John Lyons' ''Introduction to theoretical linguistics''', *Journal of Linguistics* 9:71–113.

Halle, M. 1959. *The sound pattern of Russian*. The Hague, Mouton.

Hamp, Eric P. 1961. 'General linguistics – The United States in the fifties', *Trends in European and American Linguistics 1930–1960*. Utrecht, Spectrum, pp. 165–95.

Harris, Zellig S. 1951a. *Methods in structural linguistics*. University of Chicago Press.

— 1951b. Review of David G. Mandelbaum (ed.), *Selected Writings of Edward Sapir in Language, Culture and Personality*, *Language* 27:288–333.

— 1952. 'Discourse analysis', *Language* 28:1–30.

Haugen, Einar 1951. 'Directions in modern linguistics', *Language* 27:211–22.

Hill, Archibald A. 1958. *Introduction to linguistic structures*. New York, Harcourt Brace.

Hockett, Charles F. 1954. 'Two models of grammatical description', *Word* 10:210–34.

— 1958. *A course in modern linguistics*. New York, Macmillan.

Jakobson, Roman 1932. 'Zur Struktur des russischen Verbums', in: *Charisteria Guilelmo Mathesio quinquagenario oblata*. Prague, Cercle linguistique de Prague, pp. 74–84.

— 1936. 'Beitrag zur allgemeinen Kasuslehre', *Travaux du cercle linguistique de Prague* 4:240–88.

— 1939. 'Observation sur le classement phonologique des consonnes', *Proceedings of the Third International Congress of Phonetic Sciences*, 34–41.

— 1944. 'Franz Boas' approach to language', *International Journal of American Linguistics* 10:188–95.

— 1949. 'The phonemic and grammatical aspects of language in their interrelations', *Proceedings of the Sixth International Congress of Linguists*, 5–18.

— C. Gunnar M. Fant, and Morris Halle 1952. *Preliminaries to speech analysis; The distinctive features and their correlates*. Cambridge, Mass., M.I.T. Press.

— 1953. in: Claude Lévi-Strauss, Roman Jakobson, C. F. Voegelin, and Thomas A. Sebeok, *Results of the conference of anthropologists and linguists*. (Supplement to *International Journal of American Linguistics* 19:2:11–21.

— 1956. 'Serge Karcevski (August 28, 1884–November 7, 1955)', *Cahiers Ferdinand de Saussure* 14: 9–13.
—1959. 'Boas' view of grammatical meaning', *American Anthropologist* 61:139–45.
— 1963. 'Efforts toward a means-ends model of language in inter-war continental linguistics', *Trends in Modern Linguistics*. Utrecht, Spectrum, pp. 104–108.
Joos, Martin 1950. 'Language design', *Journal of the Acoustical Society of America* 22:701–708.
— 1957[1], 1958[2], 1966[4]. *Readings in linguistics; The development of descriptive linguistics in America since 1925*. New York, University of Chicago Press.
— (ed.) 1957[1], 1966[4]. *Readings in linguistics*. New York, American Council of Learned Societies.
Karcevski, Serge 1927. *Système du verbe russe: Essai de linguistique synchronique*. Prague, Imprimerie "Legiografie".
— 1932. 'Autour d'un problème de morphologie'. *Annales Academicae Scientiarum Fennicae*, Ser. B, 27:84–91.
Katz, Jerrold J. and Jerry A. Fodor 1963. 'The structure of a semantic theory', *Language* 39:170–210.
Kirsner, Robert S. 1972. 'About "about" and the unity of "remind"', *Linguistic Inquiry* 3:491–99.
Labov, William 1966. *The social stratification of English in New York City*. Washington, Center for Applied Linguistics.
— 1972a. *Sociolinguistic patterns*. Philadelphia, Univ. of Pennsylvania Press.
— 1972b. *Language in the inner city*. Philadelphia, Univ. of Pennsylvania Press.
Lakoff, George 1969. 'Presuppositions and relative grammaticality', in W. Todd (ed.), *Studies in Philosophical Linguistics*, Series one. Evanston Ill., pp. 103–16.
— 1970. *Irregularity in syntax*. New York, Holt.
— 1972a. *Where the rules fail, an unauthorized appendix to M. K. Burt, From deep to surface structure*. Preprint Indiana University Linguistics Club.
— 1972b. 'Linguistics and natural logic', in: Donald Davidson and Gilbert Harman (eds.), *Semantics of natural language*. Dordrecht, Reidel, pp. 545–665.
— 1974. Dialogue, with H. Parret, in H. Parret, *Discussing language*. The Hague, Mouton.
Léon, P. R. 1972. 'Où en sont les études sur l'intonation?', *Proceedings of the Seventh International Congress of Phonetic Sciences*, pp. 113–56.
Lévi-Strauss, Claude 1955. *Tristes tropiques*. Paris, Plon.
Longacre, Robert E. 1960. 'String constituent analysis', *Language* 36:63–88.
Lotz, John 1951. 'Natural and scientific language', *Proceedings of the American Academy of Arts and Sciences* 80:1:87–88.
Lounsbury, Floyd G. (1956) 'A semantic analysis of the Pawnee kinship usage', *Language* 32:158–94.
Malkiel, Yakov, and Margaret Langdon 1969. 'History and histories of linguistics', *Romance Philology* 22:530–74.
Mandelbaum, David G. (ed.) 1949. *Selected writings of Edward Sapir*, Berkeley-Los Angeles, Univ. of California Press.
Martin, Robert L. 1971. 'Some thoughts on the formal approach to the philosophy of language', in: Yehoshua Bar-Hillel, *Pragmatics of natural languages*. Dordrecht, Reidel, pp. 120–44.
Mathesius, V. 1911. 'On the potentiality of the phenomena of language', in: Josef Vachek 1964. *A Prague school reader in linguistics*. Bloomington, Ind., Indiana University Press. Pp. 1–32.
— 1924. 'Několik poznánzek a funkci podmětu v moderni angličtině' [= Some notes on the function of the subject in Modern English], *Časopis pro moderni filologii* 10:1–6.

— 1928. 'On linguistic characterology'. *Actes du Premier Congrès International des Linguistes* 59–67.

—1929. 'Zur Satzperspektive im modernen Englisch', *Archiv für das Studium der neueren Sprachen und Literaturen* 84:202–10.

McCawley, James D. 1968a. 'The role of semantics in a grammar', in: Emmon Bach and Robert T. Harms (eds.) *Universals in linguistic theory*. New York, Holt, pp. 124–69.

— 1968b. 'Lexical insertion in a transformational grammar without deep structure', in: B. J. Darden et al. (eds.), *Papers from the Fourth Regional Meeting*, Chicago Linguistic Society, pp. 71–80.

— 1973a. Review of N. Chomsky, *Studies on semantics in generative grammar*. Preprint, Indiana University Linguistics Club.

— 1973b. Syntactic and logical arguments for semantic structures. in: Osamu Fujimura (ed.), *Three dimensions of linguistic theory*. Tokyo, TEC Company, pp. 259–376.

McDavid, Jr., Raven I. 1949. Review of Charles W. Morris, *Signs, language and behavior, Studies in Linguistics* 7:67–70.

Montague, R. 1970a. 'English as a Formal Language', in: *Linguaggi nella società e nella tecnica*. Milano, Edizioni di Comunità (= Saggi di cultura contemporanea 87).

— 1970b. 'Universal grammar'. *Theoria* 36:373–98.

Morris, Charles W. 1938, 1953[8]. *Foundations of the theory of signs* (= *Int. Encyclopedia of Unified Science* 1.2.) University of Chicago Press.

— 1946. *Signs, language and behavior*. New York, Prentice Hall.

Panconcelli-Calzia, G. 1924[2]. *Die experimentelle Phonetik in ihrer Anwendung auf die Sprachwissenschaft*. Berlin De Gruyter.

Parret, Herman 1974. *Discussing language*. The Hague, Mouton.

Partee, Barbara Hall 1971. 'On the requirement that transformation preserve meaning,' in Charles J. Fillmore and D. Terence Langendoen (eds.), *Studies in linguistic semantics*, New York, Holt, 1–22.

Pike, Kenneth L. 1945. *The intonation of American English*. Ann Arbor, University of Michigan.

— 1954. *Language in relation to a unified theory of the structure of human behavior*. Glendale, Calif., Summer Institute of Linguistics.

— 1958. 'On tagmemes, née gramemes', *International Journal of American Linguistics* 24:273–78.

Postal, Paul M. 1964. *Constituent structure: a study of contemporary models of syntactic description*. Bloomington and London, Indiana University Press; The Hague, Mouton.

— 1970. 'On the surface verb "remind"'. *Linguistic Inquiry* 1:37–120.

— 1971. *Cross-over phenomena*. New York, Holt.

— 1972. 'The best theory', in Stanley S. Peters (ed.), *Goals of linguistic theory*. Englewood Cliffs, N. J., Prentice Hall. 131–70.

Reichling, Anton 1935. *Het Woord, een studie omtrent de grondslag van taal en taalgebruik* [= The Word, A study of the basis of language and language-use], Nijmegen, Berkhout.

— 1948. 'What is general linguistics?' *Lingua* 1:8–24.

Ries, John 1894, 1927[2]. *Was ist Syntax*? Prag, Taussig.

Sapir, Edward 1921. *Language*. New York: Harcourt Brace.

— 1925. 'Sound patterns in language', *Language* 1:37–51.

— 1929. 'The status of linguistics as a science'. *Language* 5:207–14.

Saussure, F. de 1916. *Cours de linguistique générale*. Lausanne, Paris: Payot.

Schank, R. C. 1972a. 'Conceptual dependency: A theory of natural language understanding', *Cognitive Psychology* 3:552–631.

— 1972b. '"Semantics" in conceptual analysis', *Lingua* 30:101–40.
—and Yorick Wilks 1974. 'The goals of linguistic theory revisited'. *Lingua* 34:301–26.
Shibatani, Masayoshi 1972. 'Three reasons for not deriving "kill" from "cause to die" in Japanese', in John P. Kimball (ed.), *Syntax and Semantics*, vol. 1, New York and London, Seminar Press A. Pp. 125–27.
Teeter, Karl V. 1964. 'Descriptive linguistics in America: triviality vs. irrelevance', *Word* 20:197–206.
Trager, George L. 1948. Review of *Lingua, International Journal of General Linguistics. International Journal of American Linguistics* 14:207–209.
Uhlenbeck, E. M. 1966. Enige beschouwingen over Amerikaanse en Nederlandse linguïstiek [= Some reflections on American and Dutch linguistics], *Forum der Letteren*] 7:1–22.
Van Wijk, N. 1939. *Phonologie, een hoofdstuk uit de structurele taalwetenschap* [= Phonology, A chapter of structural linguistics]. The Hague, Nijhoff.
Weinreich, Uriel 1963. 'On the semantic structure of language', in Joseph H. Greenberg (ed.), *Universals of Language*. Cambridge, Mass., M.I.T. Press. Pp. 114–71.
— W. Labov, and M. I. Herzog 1968. 'Empirical foundations for a theory of language change', in W. P. Lehmann and Yakov Malkiel (eds.), *Directions for historical linguistics*, Austin, University of Texas Press, pp. 98–188.
Wells, Rulon S. 1947. 'Immediate constituents', *Language* 23:81–118.
— 1949. 'Automatic alternation', *Language* 25:99–116.
— 1963. 'Some neglected opportunities in descriptive linguistics', *Anthropological Linguistics* 5:1:38–49.
Wilks, Y. 1974. 'One small head-models and theories in linguistics', *Foundations of Language* 11:77–96.

DISCUSSION OF THE PAPERS BY YAKOV MALKIEL AND BY E. M. UHLENBECK

D. TERENCE LANGENDOEN

In this discussion, I focus on the contributions of Leonard Bloomfield and certain American linguists that have come after him. As a result, I do not comment specifically on those aspects of Professor Malkiel's paper that deal with the pre-Bloomfieldian period in American linguistics. There is very little that I could, or would want, to add to his insightful commentary on that period. We may all be grateful for the fruit of his research.

Today's presentations by both Professor Malkiel and Professor Uhlenbeck remind us that if we are really going to understand the history of modern American linguistics, we must come to grips with the impact of one person in particular: Leonard Bloomfield.[1] This is not to deny the importance of Edward Sapir, Otto Jespersen, and others that contemporary American linguists single out as their pre-Chomskyan intellectual forbears, nor of the many scholars, prominent and obscure, who, as Malkiel has shown us, laid the foundations of linguistic science in America. What Bloomfield accomplished was the establishment of an autonomous American approach to the study of language. Part of his accomplishment was ideological – he gave American linguistics a solidly empiricist and positivist outlook – and part was inspirational – his descriptive and historical work, particularly on American indigenous languages, provided models that it is still difficult to surpass today, even with our much greater theoretical sophistication. There is a certain irony in the fact that Halle and Chomsky (Halle 1959:13–14; Chomsky & Halle 1968:76) have singled out Sapir's phonological work as fore-shadowing their own, since Bloomfield's paper 'Menomini morpho-phonemics' (1939), in my opinion, surpasses anything Sapir ever wrote

---

[1] This point has been most forcefully made by Hockett (1968, chapter 1; 1970). In preparing this discussion, I have greatly benefited from Hockett's account of Bloomfield's career, and of his impact on his colleagues and students.

in phonology, and in its explicitness and rigor practically achieves the status of a notational variant of generative phonology.[2]

In applying the canons of positivistic methodology, Bloomfield had one major blind-spot, his belief that the features that distinguish the phonemes of a language have objective, measurable and invariant status in acoustic reality. This belief was brilliantly refuted by Twaddell in his monograph *On defining the phoneme* (1935). One consequence of this refutation is that there is no general warrant for the use of the principle of complementary distribution in establishing the phonemes of a language. In the short run, Twaddell's point had no impact; when Haugen and he repeated these objections in 'Facts and phonemics' (1942) against the particular phonemicization of English vowels developed by Trager and Bloch (1941), they were ignored, and Twaddell from that time on remained silent on the issue. But in the long run, the point was heeded, so that by the time of Harris' book *Methods in structural linguistics* (1951), one no longer spoke (that is, those who understood what was going on no longer spoke) of the phonemes of a language. Rather, one said that there are as many phonemicizations and corresponding sets of phonemes as there are decisions about whether or not to impose the criterion of complementary distribution. Accordingly, Halle's classic argument against the autonomous phonemic level in *The sound pattern of Russian* (1959) is fallacious, since it is based on the false premise that there is some particular phonemicization of Russian, required by phonemic theory, with respect to which a single phonemenon is treated in part as an alternation among phonemes, and in part as an alternation among phones. However, there are phonemicizations of Russian for which the alternation in question is entirely morphophonemic in nature. Thus, the claim that the interposition of an autonomous phonemic level necessarily leads to a loss of a generalization about Russian phonology is false.[3] Of course, the fact that phonemic theory

---

[2] The importance of Bloomfield as a precursor of generative phonology is acknowledged in Bever (1963, 1967).

[3] In Bloomfield (1939) a problem in Menomini phonology very much like the one that Halle describes in Russian is considered. Among the long-vowel phonemes /ī, ē, ɛ̄, ū, ō, ā/, it turns out that /ū/ is non-contrastive; it alternates with /ō/ in an environment in which /ī/ alternates with /ē/. However, /ī/ and /ē/ contrast, and hence must be separate phonemes. On the basis of pattern congruity, and in order to describe the alternation between /ō/ and /ū/ as morphophonemic, and hence by the same rule that describes an alternation between /ē/ and /ī/, Bloomfield decides to treat /ū/ as a separate phoneme. That he is not entirely happy with this solution is reflected in his decision to say that /ū/ is not a 'full phoneme'. Even so, it is clear that Bloomfield, when faced with the option of reducing the phonemic inventory versus saving a generalization expressed by the system of phonological rules, chose the latter.

should admit of so many alternative descriptions of the same phonomenon is as great a defect as the one that Halle thought he had found in it.

Before passing on to a consideration of the period following Bloomfield's major personal contributions, I should like to comment on Professor Uhlenbeck's list of what he sees as the five defining principles of phonemics, which he claims formed the basis of the extrapolative efforts he discusses. The principles he cites appear to be drawn from at least partially incompatible approaches to phonology, and there is no one, to my knowledge, who can be identified as having held all five. In particular, I know of no one who ever held the first principle – that of contrast and complementarity – and the fourth principle – that of psychological reality – simultaneously.

Like so many others, Uhlenbeck characterizes the period from 1940 to 1957 in American linguistics as 'post-Bloomfieldian', by which he means that a particular mode of analysis that he thinks of as 'Bloomfieldian' gained ascendancy over another that he characterizes as 'Sapirian'. The Bloomfieldian mode he identifies with the static, item-and-arrangement (IA) format; and the Sapirian mode with the dynamic, item-and-process (IP) format. It might, however, be more appropriate to call the former Saussurean and the latter Sapir-Bloomfieldian, since Saussure clearly identified in the *Cours de linguistique générale* (1916, Part I, Chapter 3) the static format with synchronic description and the dynamic format with diachronic description, whereas both Sapir and Bloomfield explicitly used and endorsed a dynamic format for synchronic description. The only essential difference between Sapir and Bloomfield was that Sapir ascribed psychological reality to the entities being described, whereas Bloomfield did not. The development of the IA format furthermore was due, not to Bloomfield, but to a student of Sapir's, Zellig Harris, in a series of review articles during the mid-forties (Harris 1944, 1945a, 1945c, 1947a, 1947b). Throughout this development, Harris was careful to point out that the two modes of analysis are notationally interchangeable, and that any decision to choose one over the other must be based on what the analyst wishes to highlight or focus on in his description. Exactly the same point was made by Hockett in 'Two models of grammatical description' (1954). Thus, I am in disagreement with Uhlenbeck's judgment that: 'From Hockett's "*Two models of grammatical description*" . . . one can conclude that the notion of process in a synchronic sense was difficult to appreciate for the author, as it was also for Harris and Wells.'

Not only did these three linguists have a deep appreciation for the IP format, but Wells was even able to show, in 'Automatic alternation'

(1949), that although the two formats are notational variants, they make different claims about what constitutes automatic alternation. That is, Wells was able to show that, with certain reasonable assumptions about the facts, the alternation that relates morphophonemic *pat + tus* in Latin to phonemic *pas + sus* is automatic (i.e. morphologically unconditioned) when viewed dynamically, but nonautomatic (morphologically conditioned) when viewed statically. This is an extremely important demonstration, even if its significance has gone largely unnoticed, because it shows that two theories can be notational variants, and yet make different claims about what is going on in a given language. With respect to the issue at hand, it reveals the superiority of the Sapir-Bloomfield-Chomsky dynamic format over the Saussure-Harris static one, since one would want to claim that the Latin alternation (given the factual assumption that Wells makes) is an automatic one.

Although the study of phonology and morphology was the dominant concern of American linguistics under Bloomfield and his followers, a great deal of work was done on syntax; so much so, in fact, that the attitude prevailed that syntax was being done really for the first time in the history of linguistics (cf. Hockett 1968:31). Also, I cannot agree with Professor Uhlenbeck's assessment that there is a 'conceptual discrepancy' between the theory of immediate-constituent (IC) analysis that was developed for syntax, and the distributional theory of phonemics and morphemics. One has only to examine Harris' paper 'From morpheme to utterance' (1945b) and Wells' paper 'Immediate constituents' (1947), to see that exactly the same distributional criteria for setting up phonemes and morphemes were used to set up morpheme-sequence classes (or ICs).[4] Any similarity between the technique of IC analysis and traditional parsing procedures is either accidental, or a reflection that both procedures are basically correct.[5] In reading these papers, particularly Wells', one cannot help but admire the degree of precision with which the theory is developed, and the concern for its possible inadequacies (for example in the matter of so-called 'discontinuous constituents', which

[4] Nida (1948:168) argued that distributional analysis is 'only one of the principles which should be employed in determining sets of immediate constituents.' However, these other principles all reduce to distributional analysis.
[5] As Professor James McCawley remarked from the floor, traditional parsing is formalizable in terms of dependency grammar (Hays 1965), whereas IC analysis is formalizable in terms of phrasestructure grammar (Chomsky 1957; Postal 1964). He observes that Bloomfield was aware of this difference.

Chomsky was later so effective in using to reveal exactly what was wrong with the theory).

As for semantics, I think it is an oversimplification to say that the subject was totally neglected by the post-Bloomfieldians. While it is true that in chapter 2 of *Language* (1933), Bloomfield effectively excluded semantics as a proper domain of linguistic study, at least given the then-available tools for its study, he also provided in chapters 9–11 of the same book a framework for a distributional theory of semantics. While the further development of such a theory languished during the way years (but cf. Bloomfield 1943), the postwar period saw a revived interest in it, particularly for the study of kinship semantics. The first surfacing of this interest is a short piece by Greenberg in 1949 in the journal *Philosophy of science;* seven years later, in *Language,* there appeared back-to-back papers by Lounsbury (1956) and Goodenough (1956), setting forth in detail the componential-analysis (CA) theory of kinship semantics. Both papers emphasize that CA theory is based on the same distributional techniques that proved so successful in the analysis of other domains of linguistics, and Goodenough further acknowledges that CA theory is basically just a modification of the semantic theory originally set out by Bloomfield.

Another important paper of the mid-fifties, Wells' 'Meaning and use' (1954), suggests that the approach of the British ordinary-language philosophers is compatible with descriptive semantics, and to return the favor, Quine's theory of semantics can be seen as springing directly out of Bloomfield's conception of language. Thus, while some linguists may have viewed semantics as beyond the pale (a set that did not always include Joos, who in 1958 published a very remarkable and quite insightful discussion of semantic theory in Trager's journal *Studies in Linguistics*), many others did not, and had the advent of generative grammar in the late fifties not wrenched the field of linguistics out of the course set by Bloomfield, Lounsbury-Goodenough-style semantic analysis might very well have become the standard for linguistic semantics today.

Let me conclude my remarks by considering briefly what Uhlenbeck says about the period of American linguistics that dates from the appearance of Chomsky's *Syntactic structures* in 1957 to the present. First of all, Uhlenbeck is correct in seeing the advent of generative grammar as both breaking with and continuing the Bloomfieldian line of development.[6] However, I do not agree with his characterization of

---

[6]   Professor Uhlenbeck could have strengthened his argument on this point by noting

certain aspects of the current scene in American linguistics. I mention the minor ones first.

(1) Chomsky never claimed that what was wrong with previous theories of grammar was their lack of recursiveness; even finite-state grammars can be recursive. Rather, Chomsky was objecting specifically to the conception of grammar as accounting for just a fixed finite corpus of data, a view that was by no means held by all followers of Bloomfield.

(2) I am also not convinced by Professor Uhlenbeck's argument that American linguistics had failed to develop a sufficiently explicit theory of linguistic structure, and that it was Chomsky who made everyone aware of the need for explicitness. Chomsky (1964) and Hockett (1968) have both argued that rigor and explicitness are two of the hall-marks of post-Bloomfieldian linguistics, and it is these that in fact make it possible to demonstrate that the theory is inadequate. Take the matter of 'discontinuous constituents'. Without an explicit theory of IC-analysis, it would not have been possible to show that this notion is a contradiction in terms, and that a theory adequate to account for that notion requires two distinct levels of syntactic analysis, one at which the constituents can be defined, and the other at which their elements are discontinuous; in other words, a generative-transformational theory of the standard sort.

My more serious objections to Uhlenbeck's account of the present state of the field concern his arguments against the way the competence-performance distinction has been used in generative grammar, and his characterization of the relation between semantics and the concept of deep structure.

Concerning competence and performance, Uhlenbeck argues that up to the advent of generative semantics, generative grammarians held that 'the study of competence should and could take place before and without paying attention to the data of performance.' I do not believe that this is correct. Granted that the theory of competence is not a theory about linguistic performance (rather, it is a theory about sentence types, of which tokens may be manifested when people use language to talk to themselves or to one another), it is inconceivable how one could develop such a theory without knowing anything about what people actually say. The relationship between the theory of competence

Footnote 6 continued

the relation of generative-transformational grammar to Harris' taxonomic conception of transformational grammar (Harris 1957).

and the data of performance is simply an indirect one, in which the performance data provide evidence for what we may conclude that people know about the structure of their language. These conclusions, what one might call the data of competence, are what the theory of competence is constructed to account for. In any event, I can see no advantage to be had in denying that there is a difference between competence and performance, or in affirming that there is no point to the study of competence.

Finally, concerning the relation of semantics to deep structure, Uhlenbeck contends that the concept of deep structure would not have been developed if the presence in sentences of meaning-bearing units had been assumed. Quite the contrary. The concept of deep structure was developed under precisely that condition; when Chomsky claimed in *Syntactic structures* (1957) that one could and indeed must do syntax without semantics, he did not thereby deny that the elements of sentences were meaningful. Rather, he claimed, prophetically as it turned out, that should the syntactic descriptions resulting from completely ingoring semantics provide the most adequate basis for then developing semantic descriptions, the syntactic theory so developed receives independent confirmation. If, on the other hand, one builds a theory that blends syntax and semantics together, indiscriminately, then one has a theory of neither domain. The semantic theory that has been developed by Katz (1966; 1972) on the basis of accepting the results of autonomous syntactic investigation hardly can be thought of as a failure.

To conclude: I do not disagree with Professor Uhlenbeck's conclusion that full investigations of the way language functions in a speech community will be necessary to provide answers to such questions as what the structure of language really comprises, and how universal and individual characteristics are interrelated. I only caution that such investigations will only be successful if they are related to conceptually rich and articulated theories of both language structure and language function.[7]

Brooklyn College and Graduate Center
City University of New York

---

[7] A point argued in some detail in Bever (1974); see also Bever, Katz and Langendoen 1976.

REFERENCES

Many of the papers referred to here have, conveniently, been reprinted in one or more of the following three anthologies. Hence I give only the date of the original appearance of those papers that have been so anthologized; page numbers refer to the reprinting.

Harris, Zellig S. 1970. *Papers in structural and transformational linguistics.* Dordrecht, D. Reidel Publishing Company.
Joos, Martin (ed.) 1966. *Readings in linguistics I.* University of Chicago Press.
Makkai, Valerie Becker (ed.) 1972. *Phonological theory: evolution and current practice.* New York, Holt, Rinehart & Winston.

Bever, Thomas G. 1963. 'Theoretical implications of Bloomfield's *Menomini morphophonemics'. Quarterly progress report of the Research Laboratory of Electronics* 68:197–203.
Bever, Thomas G. 1967. *Leonard Bloomfield and the phonology of the Menomini language.* Unpublished doctoral dissertation, Massachusetts Institute of Technology.
— 1974. 'The ascent of the specious, or there's a lot we don't know about mirrors.' In David Cohen (ed.), *Explaining linguistic phenomena,* New York, Halsted Press, pp. 173–200.
Bever, Thomas G., Jerrold J. Katz, and D. Terence Langendoen (eds.) 1976. *An integrated theory of linguistic ability.* New York, T. Y. Crowell.
Bloomfield, Leonard 1933. *Language.* New York, Holt.
— 1939. 'Menomini morphophonemics', Makkai 58–64.
— 1943. 'Meaning', *Monatshefte für deutschen Unterricht* 35:101–106.
Chomsky, Noam 1957. *Syntactic structures.* The Hague, Mouton.
— 1964. *Current issues in linguistic theory.* The Hague, Mouton.
Chomsky, Noam and Morris Halle 1968. *The sound pattern of English.* New York, Harper & Row.
Goodenough, Ward S. 1956. 'Componential analysis and the study of meaning'. *Language* 32:195–216.
Greenberg, Joseph 1949. 'The logical analysis of kinship'. *Philosophy of science* 16:58–64.
Halle, Morris 1959. *The sound pattern of Russian.* The Hague, Mouton.
Harris, Zellig S. 1944. 'Yokuts structure and Newman's grammar'. Harris 188–208.
— 1945a. 'Emeneau's Kota texts'. Harris 209–16.
— 1945b. 'From morpheme to utterance'. Harris 100–25; Joos 142–53.
— 1945c. 'Navaho phonology and Hoijer's analysis'. Harris 177–87.
— 1947a. 'Structural restatements I'. Harris 217–34.
— 1947b. 'Structural restatements II'. Harris 235–50.
— 1951. *Methods in structural linguistics.* University of Chicago Press.
— 1957. 'Cooccurrence and transformation in linguistic structure'. Harris 390–457.
Haugen, Einar and W. Freeman Twaddell 1942. 'Facts and phonemics'. Makkai 91–98.
Hays, David 1965. 'Dependency theory: a formalism and some observations'. *Language* 33:283–340.
Hockett, Charles F. 1954. 'Two models of grammatical description'. Joos 386–99.
— 1968. *The state of the art.* The Hague, Mouton.
— (ed.) 1970. *A Leonard Bloomfield anthology.* Bloomington and London, Indiana University Press.
Joos, Martin 1958. 'Semology: a linguistic theory of meaning'. *Studies in linguistics* 13:53–70.
Katz, Jerrold J. 1966. *The philosophy of language.* New York, Harper & Row.
— 1972. *Semantic theory.* New York, Harper & Row.
Lounsbury, Floyd 1956. 'A semantic analysis of Pawnee kinship usage'. *Language* 32:158–94.

Nida, Eugene A. 1948. 'The analysis of grammatical constituents'. *Language* 24:168–77.
Postal, Paul 1964. *Constituent structure.* Bloomington and London, Indiana University Press.
Saussure, Ferdinand de 1916. *Cours de linguistique générale.* Paris, Payot.
Trager, George L. and Bernard Bloch 1941. 'The syllabic phonemes of English'. Makkai 72–89.
Twaddell, W. Freeman 1935. *On defining the phoneme.* Joos 55–79 (extract).
Wells, Rulon S. 1947. 'Immediate constituents'. Joos 186–207.
— 1949. 'Automatic alternation'. *Language* 25:99–116.
— 1954. 'Meaning and use'. *Word* 10:235–50.

Rejoinder by E. M. Uhlenbeck:

While listening to Dr. Langendoen at the symposium – the author had not sent me his text beforehand – I became painfully aware of the futility of scholarly exchanges, if not sustained by a sincere wish to understand a point of view different from one's own. I must confess that I have little hope that what I am going to say in this rejoinder will have much impact upon the views of my opponent, given the fact that he had been able to familiarize himself with the contents of my paper for about three months before the symposium was held. However, for other readers the following notes may be useful as they may clear up some confusion due to the necessary briefness of my paper or to the uncomprehending remarks made by Dr. Langendoen. While the text of my paper is identical with the version orally presented (except for some minor stylistic alterations), this rejoinder was written after Dr. Langendoen's revised text had been forwarded to me. It is organized in the following way. First I will take up some differences of opinion concerning the period before 1957. In a second paragraph I will briefly go into some of Dr. Langendoen's objections against my view of the development of generative grammar and of the present situation in the United States. In a short final paragraph I will present some general observations about my paper.

I

(1) In my paper I stressed the importance of Bloomfield's adoption of the behaviorism of Weiss, as this sets his form of structural linguistics apart from other forms. Dr. Langendoen is silent on this crucial point, but implicitly plays down its importance by stating that Bloomfield had one major blind spot namely his belief in the acoustic invariance of phonemes. If a blind spot, it was a minor one in comparison with his acceptance of behaviorism, and still more important, one which did not play a role during the period under review, as Dr. Langendoen himself admits. Bloomfield's views concerning the acoustic reality of phonemes were not so different from those of other linguists, and Twaddell's monograph of 1935 was not specifically directed against Bloomfield but was intended to show that neither a psychological nor a physical or physiological definition of the phoneme was possible. Since Twaddell was convinced of the usefulness of the notion of the phoneme, he concluded that it was best to consider the phoneme as a fictitious unit. What Twaddell did not understand at the time, however, was that phonemes are LINGUISTIC units and cannot as such be defined solely either in psychological or in physical terms.

(2) It is simply not the case, as Langendoen states (page 146), that by 1951 one no longer spoke of the phonemes of a language. As a matter of fact most linguists keep doing this to this very day. It is true that Dr. Langendoen makes a restriction by adding between parentheses: that is, those who understood what was going on. However, since no names are mentioned, one remains completely in the dark to whom Dr. Langendoen is referring.

(3) Langendoen's comments about the extrapolations from notions in phonology are partly irrelevant as they have no relation to what I actually wrote, and partly incorrect. I did not speak of defining principles of phonemics. I did not express the opinion that my list of five notions came from one and the same approach to phonology, although it is not difficult at all to mention linguists in Europe as well as in the United States who simultaneously held to the notion of opposition and to the requirement of psycholinguistic reality (Jakobson and in general the members of the Prague school, Sapir, and Dutch linguists such as Pos, De Groot and Reichling).

(4) Langendoen misinterprets my characterization of the pre-Chomskyan period by applying the terms 'static' and 'dynamic' in a way not found at all in my paper. He gives the impression that I characterized 'the Bloomfieldian mode' as static, something I never did. He also gives the impression that I ascribed the development of the IA-model to Bloomfield, which I did not do either. Furthermore, Dr. Langendoen is in error when he states that Hockett and Wells considered the IA and the IP descriptive models as notational variants. This will become clear to whoever takes the trouble to read Hockett's 'Two models of grammatical description' and Wells's article on 'Automatic alternation'. Hockett wrote (1954:213): 'There is partial translatability between IP and IA but the results of translation are apt to seem somewhat strange', and Hockett's final conclusion was: 'In other words, what we have is two main types of model, neither completely satisfactory. We must have more experimentation as much with one model as with the other – and with the devising of further models too, for that matter – looking towards an eventual reintegration into a single more nearly satisfactory model, but not forcing that reintegration until we are really ready for it' (1954:233). As to Wells's article, the author was not even concerned with the question whether or not IA and IP are notational variants. Moreover, the static and dynamic way of describing automatic alternation, as defined by Wells, 'lead to different results in theory and in practice'. (1949:101) and elsewhere he discusses in a separate paragraph (1949:110–11) the non-equivalence of the two conceptions.

(5) My conclusion that Hockett as well as Harris and Wells experienced some difficulty in appreciating the notion of process was based on certain passages found in articles of these three linguists, listed in my bibliography. Hockett for instance wrote in his 'Two models' article: 'For example, if it be said that the English past tense from *baked* is "formed" from *bake* by a "process" of "suffixation", then no matter what disclaimer of historicity is made, it is impossible not to conclude that some kind of priority is being assigned to *bake*, as against either *baked* or the suffix. And if this priority is not historical, what is it? Supporters of IP have not answered that question satisfactorily' (1954:211). In his article on 'Automatic alternation' Wells connected 'the dynamic conception' with the 'predominantly historical interest of most linguists', and concluded that 'for purely descriptive purposes . . . the dynamic conception has the disadvantage of requiring that for every morpheme that has two or more morphs, one of these be treated as basic to all the others' (1949:113).

(6) I am really surprised at Langendoen's contention that in the pre-Chomskyan period 'a great deal of work was done on syntax, so much so, in fact, that the attitude prevailed that syntax was being done really for the first time in the history of linguistics'. Langendoen backs up this statement by referring to a page in Hockett's *State of the art*. But this is surely not adequate. On page 31 of his book Hockett admits that 'very little had been published on the syntax of American Indian languages, with which so many of us had served our apprenticeships'. He points out the existence of vast quantities of excellent data on Latin, Greek, and Sanskrit, but were they collected by American scholars? The only syntactic study by an American scholar mentioned by Hockett, is Bloomfield's *Tagalog texts with grammatical analysis* (1917). It happens that as a student of Indonesian languages, I am quite familiar with this valuable volume. It consists of a collection of texts with translation followed by a grammatical analysis largely based on these texts. The part of the

grammatical analysis which is devoted to syntax (pp. 146–209) consists of a series of remarks, valuable for our knowledge of Tagalog, but certainly not innovative as far as syntactic theory is concerned. The syntactic information given in brief numbered paragraphs is very much ad hoc: it serves to explain certain constructions and other syntactic features found in the texts. The theoretical framework is traditional, and does not deviate in any major way from what we find elsewhere in Europe at the time Bloomfield was writing. As Langendoen neither receives factual support for his claim from Hockett, nor, on his own, mentions important syntactic studies made during the period 1940–57, one cannot but conclude that Langendoen has made a statement for which apparently he can not present any evidence.

(7) As to immediate constituent analysis, I am not the only one who has noticed its parallelism with traditional parsing methods. In his *Constituent structure*, Postal wrote (1964:67): 'The conceptions represented by P-markers are really traditional. The earlier grammatical analysis which spoke of parsing a sentence etc. utilized in essence just these ideas. For example, on the highest level the sentence was not only divided into two parts, but these were named "Subject" and "Predicate". Similarly on a lower level, each word was assigned to one or more labelled constituents called "parts of speech" etc.'

(8) As to the study of semantics, Langendoen considers it 'an oversimplification [apparently on my part] to say that the subject was totally neglected by the Post-Bloomfieldians', and then goes on to mention in support of this view a short article by Greenberg of 1949 and the two *Language* articles by Lounsbury and Goodenough of 1956, all three on kinship semantics, Wells's well-known piece on 'Meaning and use' in *Word* of 1954, and finally Joos's article in *Studies in Linguistics* of 1958. First of all I must point out that in my paper I never made the oversimplification that semantics was 'totally neglected'. In fact, when one has to survey a large body of literature belonging to a field as extensive as linguistics, there is little room for sweeping general statements, and in my paper I carefully observed that 'in the early fifties the reluctance to discuss "meaning" was somewhat lessening' (p. 130 of my paper). Apparently Langendoen has little use or feeling for nuance. Nevertheless I consider it an undeniable CHARACTERISTIC of linguistics as practised by the Post-Bloomfieldians that little attention was given to semantics. The evidence for this is simply overwhelming. Some of it has been presented in my paper. Even the articles mentioned by Langendoen corroborate my point. This is particularly true of Wells's interesting paper on 'Meaning and use' which, by the very cautious, not to say gingerly, way in which he approaches his topic, clearly shows how uncertain at that time many American linguists were about the relationship between semantics and linguistics.

II

Against my treatment of the development of transformational generative grammar Dr. Langendoen has raised four objections, two minor and two major ones. I will take up all four, in the order in which he presents them.

(1) On page 131 of my paper I was concerned with the 'five interrelated' arguments on which the claims of the superiority of generative grammar were based. One of the superior features of such a grammar was the feature of recursive rule application. It cannot be denied that, especially in the early years, recursiveness played a fundamental role. Language was viewed as 'a set (finite or infinite) of sentences, each finite in length and constructed by concatenation out of a finite set of elements' (Chomsky 1962). Accordingly a grammar which had the task of enumerating and describing all the sentences of the language was viewed as a set of rules that '(in particular) recursively specify all the sentences of the language'.

(2) I regret that I have not been able to convince Langendoen that among the Post-

Bloomfieldians there was little interest in linguistic theory, let alone in general and explicit theories. The concept of language universals, nowadays so fashionable a topic, did not attract any attention in the fifties which were in general not prone to speculation. Many linguists still adhered to Bloomfield's opinion that 'the only valid generalizations about language are inductive generalizations'. It is certainly true that the notion that linguists should develop and apply rigorous procedures was widespread, but as Bloch himself explicitely stated, 'no unified theory of structural description had come into existence'; nor can Harris's *Methods in structural linguistics*, one of the major theoretical treatises of the period, qualify as such.

(3) Langendoen does not agree with my contention that generative grammarians have assumed that the study of competence should and could take place before and without paying attention to the data of performance. According to Langendoen it is inconceivable that a theory of linguistic competence could develop 'without knowing anything about what people actually say' (page 150). We have here a (familiar) case in which the theory is not in harmony with actual linguistic practice. There are innumerable statements to be found in the transformational generative literature about the precedence of competence over performance and about the fact that competence constitutes the primary subject of linguistics, and Langendoen must be familiar with them. Hence the deplorable practice of assuming that a linguist could arrive at judgments about sentences just by some kind of introspective activity. Now it has finally been understood (as recently by McCawley; see his interview with Parret 1974) that this activity consists of trying to construct a situation in which the sentence under review could be used. If such a situation is found, the sentence is considered to be 'grammatical'. Therefore, unwittingly, generativists have somehow had to take into account data of performance, BUT this is something quite different from an intentional and systematic study of the factors involved in the act of speech. It is one of the most obvious weaknesses of transformational generative research up till about 1970 that no expertise was developed on this crucial point.

Before I can turn to the last of the four objections raised by Langendoen I have to insist that I never stated that there is no difference between competence and performance, nor that there is no point in the study of competence, as Langendoen seems to intimate on page 151 of his reply. What I want to stress is that the relationship between competence and performance is not at all a simple one and is still in need of further clarification. I expect that the way Chomsky distinguishes between the two will prove to be more of a hindrance to linguistic theory than anything else; for a similar opinion, compare Jacques Bouveresse in Parret 1974).

(4) Langendoen's few critical remarks concerning my conclusions about the reasons why the concept of deep structure came into existence prove that he has not yet grasped what I had to say about the linguistic sign (see page 135 of my paper). He still has confidence in the semantic theory of Katz, without, however, refuting or even paying attention to the fundamental criticisms made against Katz' views on semantics by Bolinger, Lyons, Cohen and others.

III

Langendoen's reaction forced me to reread and rethink the text of my paper. In rejecting his objections I do not want to give the impression that I consider my characterization of the last half century of American linguistics as unassailable and beyond all criticism. In retrospect I regret that important scholars such as Bolinger, Harris, Householder and Pike have not been given the place they ought to occupy in any account of the recent past: Bolinger as a fundamental and persistent critic of generative grammar, Harris as a scholar who forms a bridge between the Post-Bloomfieldians and generative grammar, Householder because of his insightful review of Harris' *magnum opus* and because of his polemic against Chomsky and Halle, and Pike as an early critic of Post-Bloomfieldian doctrine, as a pioneer in the study of intonation and also because of his far-ranging 'unified theory of the structure of human behavior'. There may be other shortcomings. It may be that I have concentrated my attention too much on presenting an overall picture of the historical development of only the dominant groups in American linguistics, but I found that the characterization of the main lines of this development was my first task on this festive occasion. I am fully aware that a complete, balanced and well-articulated account of the remarkable rise of American linguistics in the present century needs the space of a book.

For references, see pp. 140–44.

Surrejoinder by D. Terence Langendoen:

In this surrejoinder, I comment briefly on the specific points made in Professor Uhlenbeck's rejoinder, and then summarize what I take to be the major differences between us. My numbering of sections follows his.

I

(1) I do not believe that Bloomfield's adoption of the radical behaviorism of Weiss seriously affected the development of American linguistics. In fact, I do not find that radical behaviorism affected even Bloomfield's linguistic work (what he said in his polemical articles and reviews is another matter). American linguists on the whole followed, rather, the mediated behaviorism of writers like Tolman and Hull – see, for an interesting discussion of these matters, Schlauch 1946. The differences between American and European linguists of the 1940's and early 1950's, therefore, are not so much differences of theory, but rather ones of emphasis. For example, although studies of paradigmatic relations, one of the primary concerns of European linguistics during this period, did not flourish in America, neither did they totally languish; one need only cite Bloch's work on Japanese morphology (Bloch 1946a) to see that they did not.

Concerning Twaddell and the phoneme, I would maintain that Twaddell did see the phoneme as a linguistic unit. Twaddell's point was that the only way of saving the notion of the phoneme for linguistics was to view it as an abstract entity.

(2) I had in mind particularly Harris and Hockett. The following observation by Miller (1969:xxv) also bears testimony to my claim.

The phonemics article [Bloch 1950] . . . probably represents the apogee of American descriptivist phonemic theory and practice. It was the last such major paper to appear in *Language*, and in the years immediately following the problems and methods with which it concerned itself – as well as the full-blown "phonemics paper" itself as a genre for linguistic publication – would begin to hold less and less interest for many linguists.

(3) I see that I did misunderstand Uhlenbeck's point in his listing of five prominent notions of the phonological theories of the period; I also stand corrected on the matter of the existence of those who held the notions of contrast and complementarity, and that of psychological reality simultaneously, although I believe that Sapir's name should be dropped from the list, since he explicitly rejected what later came to be called the principle of complementary distribution (Sapir 1924, note 2).

(4) I derived my alleged misinterpretation primarily from the two paragraphs on pp. 129–30. By 'notational variants', a technical term not found in the literature under discussion, I meant 'notations in which one can express the same properties and relations for a given

class of phenomena, but which do not necessarily classify any given phenomenon the same way'. I am sorry for the misunderstanding that my failure to define this notion in my discussion gave rise to.

(5) With this clarification, I withdraw my disagreement with Uhlenbeck's judgment concerning Hockett's, Harris's, and Wells's difficulties in appreciating the notion of process in a synchronic sense.

(6) I present as evidence such well-known and major studies on syntax as Nida (1943), Harris (1945b), Bloch (1946b), and Wells (1947).

(7) The issue is not whether IC-analysis has its roots in traditional syntax, but whether there is any discrepancy between it and the distributional analysis that was proposed for phonology and morphology. Uhlenbeck has not presented any substantiation for his claim that such a discrepancy exists.

(8) My objection to Uhlenbeck's discussion of post-Bloomfieldian semantics centers on the last part of the following passage (p. 130).

It may be true . . . that in the early fifties the reluctance to discuss 'meaning' was somewhat lessening, but it is hard to find signs of a serious attempt to ANALYZE [emphasis his] the semantic facts of even to study what had been done in semantics so far.

The semantic studies I cited represent serious attempts during that period to analyse semantic facts, which do contain considerations of what had been done in the field previously.

II

(1) What Uhlenbeck says here is true, but concerns, perhaps, another point. Recursiveness is implicit in IC-analysis.

(2) Here, we simply disagree.

(3) I accept Uhlenbeck's protestation that he does not wish to do away with the competence-performance distinction. It is still not clear to me, however, that Uhlenbeck wishes to make the distinction, which I take to be crucial with respect to the development of an adequate competence-based theory of semantics, between 'what is said' and 'what is meant'. For example, an utterance of 'Can you pass the salt?', on normal occasions of its use around a dinner table, literally inquires about the addressee's ability to pass the salt. This is what must be represented as the meaning of the sentence. The fact that such tokens of the sentence-type communicate the speaker's desire to have the salt passed to him can be accounted for in a performance theory that considers the semantic representation of that sentence, together with principles of language use (pragmatic principles) that are not themselves incorporated in the grammatical system.

(4) Again, we simply disagree. This is not the place to go into a detailed consideration of semantic theory.

III

My reading of the recent history of American linguistics differs from Uhlenbeck's primarily in that I do not recognize that radical behaviorism had any important impact on the development of linguistics in America, and that work in American linguistics was almost exclusively devoted to phonology and morphology. Rather, I hold that linguistic theory in America, as it applied to phonology, morphology, syntax, and semantics, developed organically during this period into a full-fledged theory of language. By the mid-fifties that theory included the notion of syntactic transformations, and the rise of generative grammar shortly afterwards should be viewed as a reinterpretation of that theory, not as a replacement of it.

ADDITIONAL REFERENCES:

Bloch, Bernard 1946a. 'Studies in colloquial Japanese I. Inflection;' 'III. Derivation of inflected words'. *Journal of the American Oriental Society* 66:97–108; 304–15.
— 1946b. 'Studies in colloquial Japanese II. Syntax'. Joos 154–84.
— 1950. 'Studies in colloquial Japanese IV. Phonemics'. Joos 329–48.
Miller, Roy Andrew (ed.) 1969. *Bernard Bloch on Japanese.* New Haven, Yale University Press.
Nida, Eugene A. 1943. *A synopsis of English syntax.* Doctoral dissertation, University of Michigan.
Sapir, Edward (1924). 'Sound patterns in language'. Joos 19–25.
Schlauch, Margaret (1946) 'Early behaviorist psychology and contemporary linguistics'. *Word* 2:25–36.

THE TWENTIETH CENTURY IN EUROPEAN AND AMERICAN LINGUISTICS: MOVEMENTS AND CONTINUITY

ROMAN JAKOBSON

Dear friends! I was asked to speak at the present Symposium devoted to the European background of American linguistics about the science of language in America and in Europe in the twentieth century. Apparently this topic was suggested because I witnessed the international development of linguistic thought through the long period of six decades – I followed this development first in the upper classes of the Lazarev Institute of Oriental Languages, afterwards as a student of linguistics and subsequently as a research fellow at Moscow University, then from 1920 in Prague and in other West-European, especially Scandinavian, centers of linguistic thought, and since the forties in America, with frequent visits to other areas of intense linguistic research.

As my eminent colleague Einar Haugen said in his recent paper, 'Half a Century of the Linguistic Society' (Haugen 1974), 'each of us treasures his own memories'. Thus, may I turn refer to my first, though indirect, acquaintance with the LSA. In March of 1925, the pioneering Czech scholar expert in both English and general linguistics, Vilém Mathesius, together with his younger devoted collaborator in these two fields, Bohumil Trnka, invited Sergej Karcevskij and me to a consultative meeting. Mathesius began by citing two events. The first of them was the tenth anniversary of the Moscow Linguistic Circle, which, let us add, was already dissolved at that time, yet whose creation in 1915 and whose vital activities were a durable stimulus in the Russian and international development of linguistics and poetics. On my arrival in Prague in 1920, Mathesius questioned me about the make-up and work of the Moscow Circle and said, 'We will need such a team here also, but now it is still too early. We must wait for further advances.' At the outset of our debates of 1925, he announced the most recent and impelling news – the formation of the Linguistic Society of America. Mathesius was one of those European linguists who followed with rapt attention and sympathy the impressive rise of American research in the science of language.

In October 1926, the Prague Linguistic Circle had its first meeting. It is wellknown that this Prague association, which, strange as it seems at first glance, has also been dissolved, gave in turn a powerful and lasting impetus to linguistic thought in Europe and elsewhere. From the beginning, there was a close connection between the Linguistic Society of America and the Prague Linguistic Circle. I don't know whether the young generation of scholars realizes how strong these relations were. N. S. Trubetzkoy's letters (Jakobson 1975) reveal some new data on the manifold ties between American linguistics and the 'école de Prague'. At the end of 1931, Trubetzkoy, at that time immersed in the study of American Indian languages, emphasized that 'most of the American Indianists perfectly describe the sound systems, so that their outlines yield all the essentials for the phonological characteristics of any given language, including an explicit survey of the extant consonantal clusters with respect to the different positions within or between the morphemes.' Trubetzkoy had a very high opinion of the American linguist whom he called 'my Leipzig comrade'. This was Leonard Bloomfield, who in 1913 shared a bench with Trubetzkoy and Lucien Tesnière at Leskien's and Brugmann's lectures. Bloomfield (Hockett 1970:247) praised 'Trubetzkoy's excellent article on vowel systems' of 1929 and devoted his sagacious 1939 study on 'Menomini Morphophonemics' (Hockett 1970:351–62) to N. S. Trubetzkoy's memory.

The Prague Circle had very close ties with Edward Sapir. When we held the International Phonological Conference of 1930, Sapir, though unable to attend, kept up a lively correspondence with Trubetzkoy about this Prague assembly and the development of the inquiry into linguistic, especially phonological, structure. Almost nothing remains of this exchange. Those of Sapir's messages which had not been seized by the Gestapo were lost when the Viennese home of Trubetzkoy's widow was demolished by an air raid. In their turn, Trubetzkoy's letters perished when Sapir, at the end of his life, destroyed his entire epistolary archive. However, some quotations from Sapir's letters have survived in Trubetzkoy's correspondence, and others were cited by Trubetzkoy at our meetings. It is noteworthy that Sapir underscored the similarity of his and our approaches to the basic phonological problems.

These are not the only cases of the transoceanic propinquity between linguists of the American and of the Continental avantgarde. We may recollect and cite a remarkable document published in *Language* (vol. 18, pp. 307–9). In August 1942 the Linguistic Society of America received a cable forwarded by the Soviet Scientists' Anti-Fascist Committee. This was a telegraphic letter of more than 4,000 words sent from Moscow and signed by a prominent Russian linguist, Grigorij Vinokur, the former secretary of the Moscow Linguistic Circle. In this cabled report Vinokur emphasized the particular affinity of the young Russian linguists, especially the Moscow phonologists, with the pursuits and strivings of the LSA. He noted how profoundly Sapir was valued by the linguists of the USSR. Apparently the first foreign version of Sapir's *Language* was an excellent Russian translation of this historic handbook by the Russian linguist A. M. Suxotin, with interesting editorial notes about the parallel paths in international linguistics.

In the light of all these and many other interconnections, the question of purported hostility between American and European linguists comes to naught. Any actual contact puts an end to the belief that these were two separate and impervious scientific worlds with two different, irreconcilable ideologies. Sometimes we hear allegations that American linguists repudiated their European colleagues, particularly those who sought refuge in this country. I was one of those whom the second world war brought to the Western hemisphere, and I must state that the true scholars, the outstanding American linguists, met me with a fraternal hospitality and with a sincere readiness for scientific cooperation. If there were signs of hostility and repudiation – and they were indeed evident – they occurred solely on the side of a few inveterate administrators and narrow-minded, ingrained academic bureaucrats and operators, and I am happy to acknowledge the unanimous moral support and defence which came from such genuine men of science as Charles Fries, Zellig Harris, Charles Morris, Kenneth Pike, Meyer Schapiro, Morris Swadesh, Stith Thompson, Harry V. Velten, Charles F. Voegelin, and many others.

One of the first American linguists whom I met on my arrival in this country and who became a true friend of mine was Leonard Bloomfield. Both orally and in writing, he repeatedly expressed his aversion to any intolerance and he struggled against 'the blight of the odium theologicum' and against 'denouncing all persons who disagree' with ones interest or opinion or 'who merely choose to talk about something else' (in 1946). The fact that one, Bloomfield wrote, 'disagrees with others, including me, in methods and theories does not matter; it would be deadly to have one accepted doctrine' (in 1945). I recollect our cordial and vivid debates; Bloomfield wanted me to stay and work with him at Yale, and assured me that he would be happy to have someone with whom he could have real discussions. The great linguist severely repudiated any selfish and complacent parochialism.

From my first days in this country in June 1941 I experienced the deep truth of Bloomfield's later obituary judgment on Franz Boas: 'his kindness and generosity knew no bounds' (Hockett 1970:408). The fundamental role in American linguistics played by this German-born scholar, 28 years old at his arrival in the United States, was wisely appraised by Bloomfield: "The progress which has since been made in the recording and description of human speech has merely grown forth from the roots, stem, and mighty branches of Boas' life-work." As to the founder and skilful director of the *Handbook of American Indian Languages* himself, I recall his amiable, congenial house in Grantwood, New Jersey, where the host, with his keen sense of humor, used to say to his sister in my presence: 'Jakobson *ist ein seltsamer Mann!* He thinks that I am an American linguist!'

Boas strongly believed in the international character of linguistics and of any genuine science and would never have agreed with an obstinate demand for a regional confinement of scientific theories and research. He professed that any analogy to a struggle for national interests in politics and economics was superficial and far-fetched. In the science of language there are no patented discoveries and no problems of intertribal or interpersonal competition, of regulations for imported and exported merchandise or dogma. The greater and closer the cooperation between linguists of the world, the vaster are the vistas of our science. Not only in the universe of languages, but also throughout the world of creative linguistic science, Boas liked to detect eloquent instances of convergent development or bilateral diffusion.

One may add that isolationist tendencies in the scientific life of the two hemispheres were mere transient and insignificant episodes and that the international role of American linguistics and, in particular, the transoceanic influence of the American achievements in the theory of language appear as early as the European models do in American linguistics.

During the second half of the past century it was Germany which witnessed the widest progress and expansion of comparative Indo-European studies. Yet the new and fecund ideas in general linguistics emerged outside the German scholarly world. Toward the end of the nineteenth century Karl Brugmann and August Leskien, the two leading German comparatists and proponents of the world-famed Leipzig school of neogrammarians, emphatically acknowledged the immense stimulation which the American linguist William Dwight Whitney gave to the European research in the history of languages by his original treatment of general principles and methods. At the same time, Ferdinand de Saussure (Jakobson 1971:xxviii–xliii) stated that Whitney, without having himself written a single page of comparative philology, was the only one 'to exert an influence on all study of comparative grammar,' whereas in Germany linguistic science, which was allegedly born, developed, and cherished there by innumerable people, in Saussure's (as also in Whitney's) opinion never manifested 'the slightest inclination to reach the degree of abstraction necessary to dominate what one is actually doing and why all that is done has its justification in the totality of sciences.' Having returned at the end of his scholarly activities to the 'theoretical view of language', Saussure repeatedly expressed his reverence for 'the American Whitney, who never said a single word on these topics which was not right.' Whitney's books of general linguistics were immediately translated into French, Italian, German, Dutch, and Swedish and had a far wider and stronger scientific influence in Europe than in his homeland.

For many years American students of language, absorbed in particulars, seemed to disregard Whitney's old warning to linguists in which he adjured them not to lose 'sight of the grand truths and principles which underlie and give significance to their work, and the recognition of which ought to govern its course throughout' (1867). Leonard Bloomfield was actually the first American scholar who from his early steps in linguistic theory endeavored to revive Whitney's legacy in the study of language.

As a parallel to the earlier and deeper naturalization of Whitney's *Principles of Linguistic Science* in the Old World one may cite the reception of Saussure's *Cours de linguistique générale* in the New World. Although it opened a new epoch in the history of linguistics, the appearance of this posthumous publication found, at first, only a few linguists ready to accept the basic lessons of the late Genevan teacher. Originally most of the West-European specialists outside his native Switzerland showed restraint toward Saussure's conception, and, strange to say, France was one of the countries particularly slow in assimilating his theory. One of the earliest open-minded appraisers and adherents of the *Cours* was an American scholar. Its first two editions were commented on by Bloomfield not only in the separate review of the *Cours* for the *Modern Language Journal* (1923–24; Hockett 1970:106–109), but also in Bloomfield's critiques of Sapir's *Language* (1922; Hockett 1970:91–4) and of Jespersen's *Philosophy of grammar* (1927; Hockett 1970:141–3), and in a few further texts, all of them made easily available by Charles F. Hockett in his magnificent anthology (1970).

According to the aforesaid review, the nineteenth century 'took little or no interest in the general aspects of human speech,' so that Saussure in his lectures on general linguistics 'stood very nearly alone,' and his posthumous work 'has given us the theoretical basis for a science of human speech.' In reviewing Sapir's *Language*, Bloomfield realizes that the question of influence or simply convergent innovations is 'of no scientific moment,' but in passing he notes the probability of Sapir's acquaintance with Saussure's 'book, which gives a theoretical foundation to the newer trend of linguistic study.' In particular, he is glad to see that Sapir 'deals with synchronic matters (to use de Saussure's terminology) before he deals with diachronic, and gives to the former as much space as to the latter.'

Bloomfield subscribes not only to the sharp Saussurian distinction between synchronic and diachronic linguistics, but also to the further dichotomy advocated by the *Cours*, namely a rigorous bifurcation of human speech *(langage)* into a perfectly uniform system *(langue)* and the 'actual speech-utterance' *(parole)*. He professes full accord with the 'fundamental principles' of the *Cours* (Hockett 1970:141–42; 107): 'For me, as for de Saussure . . . and, in a sense, for Sapir . . ., all this, de Saussure's *la parole*, lies beyond the power of our science. . . . Our science can deal only with those features of language, de Saussure's *la langue*, which are common to all the speakers of a community, – the phonemes, grammatical categories, lexicon, and so on. . . . A grammatical or lexical statement is at bottom an abstraction.' But in Bloomfield's opinion, Saussure 'proves intentionally and in all due form: that psychology and phonetics do not matter at all and are, in principle, irrelevant to the study of language.' The abstract features of Saussure's *la langue* form a 'system, – so rigid that without any adequate physiologic information and with psychology in a state of chaos, we are,' Bloomfield asserts, 'nevertheless able to subject it to scientific treatment.'

According to Bloomfield's programmatic writings of the twenties, the 'newer trend' with its Saussurian theoretic foundation 'affects two critical points.' First, and once more he underscores this point in his paper of 1927 'On recent work in general linguistics' (Hockett 1970:173–90), Saussure's outline of the relation between 'synchronic' and 'diachronic' science of language has given a 'theoretical justification' to the present recognition of descriptive linguistics 'beside historical, or rather as precedent to it' (1970:179). In this connection it is worth mentioning that even the striking divergence between the search for new ways in Saussure's synchronic linguistics and his stationary, nearly neogrammarian attitude toward 'linguistic history,' was adopted by Bloomfield, who was disposed to believe that here one could hardly learn 'anything of a fundamental sort that Leskien didn't know' (see Hockett 1970:177–78 and 542).

Referring to the second critical point of the 'modern trend' in linguistics. Bloomfield commends two restrictive definitions of its sole attainable goal: he cites the Saussurian argument for '*la langue,* the socially uniform language pattern' (Hockett 1970:177) and Sapir's request for 'an inquiry into the function and form of the arbitrary systems of symbolism that we term languages (Hockett 1970:92–93, 143).

When maintaining that this subject matter must be studied 'in and for itself,' Bloomfield literally reproduces the final words of the *Cours.* Strange as it seems, here he shows a closer adherence to the text of Saussure's published lectures than the lecturer himself. As has since been revealed, the final, italicized sentence of the *Cours* – '*la linguistique a pour unique et véritable objet la langue envisagée en elle-même et pour elle-même'* – though never uttered by the late teacher, was appended to the posthumous book by the editors-restorers of Saussure's lectures as '*l'idée fondamentale de ce cours.'* According to Saussure's genuine notes and lectures, language must not be viewed in isolation, but as a particular case among other sytems of signs in the frame of a general science of signs which he terms *sémiologie.*

The close connection between Bloomfield's (and, one may add, Sapir's) initial steps in general linguistics and the European science of language, as well as Whitney's significance in the Old World, exemplify the continuous reciprocity between the linguists of the two hemispheres.

In his first approach to the 'principle of the phoneme' Bloomfield pondered over the concepts developed by the school of Sweet, Passy, and Daniel Jones, and when we met, he cited his particular indebtedness to Henry Sweet's 'classical treatise' on the *Practical study of languages* (1900). From the very outset of his concern for phonemic problems, Bloomfield confronted the difference between the discreteness of phonemes and 'the actual continuum of speech sound' and Saussure's opposition of *langue/parole* (Hockett 1970:179) and he found 'explicit formulations' in Baudouin de Courtenay's *Versuch einer Theorie der phonetischen Alternationen* of 1895 (Hockett 1970:248). In this book he also got the fruitful concept and term MORPHEME, coined by Baudouin (Hockett 1970:130). Upon the same label, likewise borrowed from Baudouin's terminology, French linguistic literature mistakenly imposed the meaning 'affix'.

There are certain classical works in the European linguistic tradition which have constantly attracted special attention and recognition in the American science of language. Thus, the two books which so captivated Noam Chomsky, one by Humboldt and one by Otto Jespersen, have more than once since their appearance evoked lively and laudatory responses from American linguists: thus, in Sapir's estimation, 'the new vistas of linguistic thought opened up by the work of Karl Wilhelm von Humboldt,' and the latter's treatise *Über die Verschiedenheit des menschlichen Sprachbaues* compelled Bloomfield to admire 'this great scholar's intuition'; as to Jespersen's masterpiece, Bernard Bloch in 1941 praised 'the greatness of the *Philosophy of grammar*,' and Bloomfield's review of 1927 pointed out that by this book 'English grammar will be forever enriched' (Hockett 1970:143, 180).

The widespread myth of a sole and uniform American linguistic school and of its exclusive control throughout the country, at least during certain periods in the development of the science of language in the United States, is at variance with the actual situation. Neither the geographical nor the historical significance of one or another scientific trend can be based on the excessive number of students who, as Martin Joos neatly remarked (1957:v), 'accept the current techniques without inquiring into what lay behind them.' What really counts is the quality alone, both of theoretical and of empirical attainments.

In America, as well as in Europe, there has fortunately always been an imposing variety of approaches to the foundations, methods, and tasks of linguistics. In its initial output, the Linguistic Society of America displayed a remarkable diversity of views. Its first president Hermann Collitz of the Johns Hopkins University, in his inaugural address (December 28, 1924; Collitz 1925) on 'The scope and aims of linguistic science', spoke about the rapidly improving conditions for a new advancement of 'general or "philosophical" grammar', which for a while 'had to be satisfied with a back seat in linguistics.' Collitz laid stress on the principal problems of general linguistics, one of which concerns 'the relation between grammatical forms and mental categories.' He referred in this connection to 'an able study written by an American scholar, namely: *Grammar and thinking*, by Albert D. Sheffield' (New York, 1912; Hockett 1970:34),' a book, let us add, 'heartily welcomed' in Bloomfield's review of 1912 as 'a sensible volume on the larger aspects of language.' The other concern of general linguistics was defined by Collitz as 'uniformities and permanent or steadily recurring conditions in human speech generally.' The latter item shortly thereafter became a subject of controversy in the gatherings and publications of the LSA: skeptics were disposed to deny the existence of general categories, as long as no linguist can know which of them, if any, exist in all languages of the world, whereas Sapir with an ever growing persistence worked on a series of preliminaries to his *Foundations of language*, a wide-ranging program of universal grammar that he cherished till the end of his life.

The passage of the aforementioned inaugural address on the 'mental categories' as correlates of external forms hinted at a question about to become for decades an enduring *casus belli* between two linguistic currents in America, where they have been nicknamed respectively 'mentalism' and 'mechanism' or 'physicalism'. With regard to the pivotal problems of general linguistics touched upon by Collitz, Bloomfield's prefatory article – 'Why a Linguistic Society?' – for the first issue of the Society's journal *Language* (Hockett 1970:109–12) adopted a conciliatory tone: 'The science of language, dealing with the most basic and simplest of human social institutions, is a human (or mental or, as they used to say, moral) science. . . . It remains for linguistics to determine what is widespread and what little is common to all human speech.' Yet the two integral theoretical articles which made up the second issue of the same volume – Sapir's 'Sound patterns in language' and 'Linguistics and psychology' by A. P. Weiss – brought to light a major scientific dissent. Sapir's epochal essay (1925), one of the most farsighted American contributions to the apprehension and advance of linguistic methodology, asserts from its first lines that no linguistic phenomena or processes, in particular neither sound patterns nor sound processes of speech (for instance 'umlaut' or 'Grimm's law', so-called), can be properly understood in simple mechanical, sensorimotor terms. The dominant role was said to pertain to the 'intuitive pattern alignment' proper to all speakers of a given language. According to the author's conclusion, the whole aim and spirit of the paper was to show that phonetic phenomena are not physical phenomena *per se* and to offer 'a special illustration of the necessity of getting behind the sense data of any type of expression in order to grasp the intuitively felt and communicated forms which alone give significance to such expression.'

Sapir's assaults against mechanistic approaches to language run counter to the radical behaviorism of the psychologist Albert Paul Weiss.

The latter's article appeared in *Language* thanks to the sponsorship of Bloomfield, who taught with Weiss at Ohio State University, 1921–27, and who was increasingly influenced by his doctrine. In this paper of 1925 Weiss envisions a 'compound multicellular type of organization' produced by language behavior, and he assigns to written language the rise of an even 'more effective sensorimotor interchangeability between the living and dead.' Bloomfield's wide-scale outline of 1939, *Linguistic aspects of science*, with its numerous references to Weiss, picks up and develops this image: 'Language bridges the gap between the individual nervous systems. . . . Much as single cells are combined in a many-celled animal, separate persons are combined in a speech community. . . . We may speak here, without metaphor, of a social organism.'

What, however, most intimately fastens Bloomfield to the works of Weiss is the latter's demand that human behavior be discussed in physical terms only. 'The 'Relation between structural and behavior psychology,' examined by Weiss in the *Psychological Review* (1917), rejects the structuralist's aim 'to describe the structure of the mind or consciousness' and denies the possibility of cooperation between structuralism and behaviorism, so far as the fundamental conceptions underlying both methods and the theoretical implications of either method are subjected to a close scrutiny.

In conformity with these suggestions, any "mentalistic view" was proscribed by Bloomfield as a 'prescientific approach to human things' or even a 'primeval drug of animism' with its 'teleologic and animistic verbiage': will, wish, desire, volition, emotion, sensation, perception, mind, idea, totality, consciousness, subconsciousness, belief, and the other 'elusive spiritistic-teleologic words of our tribal speech.' In the mentioned *Linguistic aspects of science* (Bloomfield 1939:13) one chances to come across a paradoxically phrased confession: 'It is the belief [!] of the present writer that the scientific description of the universe . . . requires none of the mentalistic terms.' Bloomfield's presidential address to the Linguistic Society of America in 1935 prophesied that 'within the next generations' the terminology of mentalism and animism 'will be discarded, much as we have discarded Ptolemaic astronomy' (Hockett 1970:322).

It is this drastic dissimilarity between the two leading spirits of the Linguistic Society in the very essence of their scientific creeds which found its plain expression in Sapir's oral remarks on 'Bloomfield's sophomoric psychology' and in Bloomfield's sobriquet for Sapir, 'medicine man' (Hockett, 1970:540). A diametrical opposition between both of them with regard to such matters as 'the synthesis of linguistics with other sciences' was deliberately pointed to in Bloomfield's writings (Hockett 1970:227, 249).

This difference between two methods of approach deepened with the years and greatly affected the course and fortunes of semantic research in American linguistics. On the one hand, the inquiry into the 'communicative symbolism' of language in all its degrees and on all its levels, from the sound pattern through the grammatical and lexical concepts, to the 'integrated meaning of continuous discourse,' was becoming of still higher import in the work of Sapir, and with an avowed reference to his enlightening teaching, it was said in 1937 by Benjamin L. Whorf that 'the very essence of linguistics is the quest for meaning' (1956:79). On the other hand, Bloomfield, though realizing perfectly that the treatment of speech-forms and even of their phonemic components 'involves the consideration of meanings,' admitted at the same time in his paper 'Meaning' of 1943 that 'the management of meanings is bound to give trouble' as long as one refuses to adopt 'the popular *(mentalistic)* view' and to say 'that speech forms reflect unobservable, non-physical events in the *minds* of speakers and hearers' (Hockett 1970:401).

The difficulty in considering meaning while negating any 'mental events' provoked repeated efforts by some younger language students to analyze linguistic structure without any reference to semantics, in contradistinction to Bloomfield's invocation of meaning as an inevitable criterion. Bloomfield himself was ready to deny not only the validity of such claims, but even the possibility of their existence (cp. Fries 1954). Nonetheless, experiments in antisemantic linguistics became widespread toward the late forties. I was invited in the summer of 1945 to give a series of lectures at the University of Chicago. When I informed the University of my title for the planned cycle – 'Meaning as the pivotal problem of linguistics' –, there came a benevolent warning from the faculty that the topic was risky.

It would be fallacious, however, to view the avoidance of semantic interpretation as a general and specific feature of the American linguistic methodology even for a brief stretch of time. This tentative ostracism was an interesting and fruitful trial accompanied by simultaneous and instructive criticisms, and it has been superseded by an equally passionate and acclaimed striving for the promotion of semantic analysis first in vocabulary, then also in grammar.

Yet, finally, what bears a stamp of American origin is the semiotic science built by Charles Sanders Peirce from the 1860's throughout the late nineteenth and early twentieth centuries, a theory of signs to which, as was justly acknowledged (under Charles Morris' influence) by Bloomfield, 'linguistics is the chief contributor,' and which in turn has prepared the foundations for a true linguistic semantics. But in spite of this, Peirce's *semiotic* remained for many decades fatally unknown to the linguists of both the New and the Old World.

Now to sum up. In America the science of language produced several remarkable, prominent, internationally influential thinkers – to mention only some of those who are no longer with us, Whitney, Peirce, Boas, Sapir, Bloomfield, Whorf. What we observe at present, and what proves to be timely indeed, is an ever higher internationalization of linguistic science, without a ludicrous fear of foreign models and of 'intellectual free trade'.

One can still reproach American students and scholars, as well as those in diverse European countries, for a frequent inclination to confine the range of their scientific reading to books and papers issued in their native language and homeland and particularly to refer chiefly to local publications. In some cases this propensity results merely from an insufficient acquaintance with foreign languages, which is a debility widely spread among linguists. It is for this reason that important studies written in Russian and other Slavic languages have remained unknown, although some of them provide new and suggestive approaches.

One should finally mention the most negative phenomenon of American linguistic life. Bloomfield, who in 1912 had expressed 'a modest hope . . . that the science of language may in time come to hold in America also its proper place among the sciences' (Hockett 1970:33), returned to this question in his notable survey, 'Twenty-one years of the Linguistic Society', shortly before the end of his scholarly activity. He was certainly right in concluding that 'the external status of our science leaves much to be desired, though there has been some improvement' (Hockett 1970:493). Now, however, this improvement is rapidly vanishing. Once again we observe that the blame does not lie with linguists, but with those bureaucrats who, under the pretext of scarcity and restraint, are prone to abolish or reduce departments and chairs of general linguistics, of comparative Indo-European studies, of Romance, Scandinavian, Slavic, and other languages. In Sapir's pointed parlance, efforts are being made to establish and perpetuate the 'very pallid status of linguistics in America,' because this science seems to be hardly 'convertible into cash value' (1925:4–150). Such antiscientific measures are most deplorable. In spite of the present crisis, America still remains more prosperous than most of the European countries, but even under their economic recession, none of them has dismantled its graduate schools and their linguistic programs. Nevertheless, permit me, in conclusion, once more to quote Leonard Bloomfield. The forecast made 45 years ago (December 30, 1929; Hockett 1970:227) in his address before a joint meeting of the Linguistic Society of America and the Modern Language Association reads:

'I believe that in the near future – in the next few generations, let us say – linguistics will be one of the main sectors of scientific advance.'

Do not all of us here share this belief?

REFERENCES

Baudouin de Courtenay, Jan 1895. *Versuch einer Theorie phonetischer Alternationen.*
Bloch, Bernard 1941. Review of Jespersen, O., *Efficiency in linguistic change*, in: *Language* 17:350–53.
Bloomfield, Leonard 1939. 'Linguistic Aspects of Science', *International Encyclopedia of Unified Science* 1:4. University of Chicago Press.
— [The remaining work is quoted by reference to Hockett 1970.]
Collitz, Hermann 1925. 'Scope and aim of linguistic science', *Language* 1:14–16.
Fries, Charles C. 1954. 'Meaning and linguistic analysis', *Language* 30:57–68.
Haugen, Einar 1974. 'Half a century of the Linguistic Society', *Language* 50:619–21.
Hockett, Charles F. 1970. *A Leonard Bloomfield anthology.* Bloomington and London, Indiana University Press.
Jakobson, Roman 1971. 'The world response to Whitney's *Principles of linguistic science*', in Michael Silverstein (ed.), *Whitney on language*. Cambridge (Mass.) and London, M.I.T. Press.
— (ed.) 1975. *N. S. Trubetzkoy's letters and notes.* The Hague and Paris, Mouton.
Joos, Martin (ed.) 1957, etc. *Readings in linguistics* [I]. Washington, American Council of Learned Societies.
Sapir, Edward 1924, 'The grammarian and his language', *American Mercury* 1:149–55.
Sweet, Henry 1899. *The practical study of languages.* New York, Dent.
Weiss, Albert Paul 1917. 'The relation between structural and behavior psychology'. *Psychological Review* 24:301–317.
— 1925, etc. *A theoretical basis of human behavior*, Columbus, Adams.
Whitney, William Dwight 1867. *Language and the study of language. Twelve lectures on the principles of linguistic science.* New York, Scribner.
Whorf, Benjamin L. 1956. *Language, thought and reality.* Cambridge, Mass., M.I.T. Press.

INDEX OF NAMES

S: A. JAMESON